The Complete Slow Cooker Cookbook for Beginners

600 Delicious Recipes That Prep Fast and Cook Slow

By Teresa Jones

Legal & Disclaimer

The information contained in this book and its contents is not designed to replace or take the place of any form of medical or professional advice; and is not meant to replace the need for independent medical, financial, legal or other professional advice or services, as may be required. The content and information in this book has been provided for educational and entertainment purposes only.

The content and information contained in this book has been compiled from sources deemed reliable, and it is accurate to the best of the Author's knowledge, information and belief. However, the Author cannot guarantee its accuracy and validity and cannot be held liable for any errors and/or omissions. Further, changes are periodically made to this book as and when needed. Where appropriate and/or necessary, you must consult a professional (including but not limited to your doctor, attorney, financial advisor or such other professional advisor) before using any of the suggested remedies, techniques, or information in this book.

Table of Content

Introduction 1
Chapter 1 Understanding the Slow Cooker..2

What is Slow Cooker?........................... 2
Before Getting Start.............................. 3
Slow Cooker Settings 4

Slow Cooking Timetable 4
Clean Your Slow Cooker........................ 5
Tips to Utilize Your Slow Cooker Better ... 5

Chapter 2 Breakfast Recipes 7

Apple Cinnamon Granola 7
Cinnamon Apple Oatmeal 7
Artichoke Pepper Frittata 7
Spiced Baby Carrots 7
Boiled Bacon Eggs 8
Apricots Bread Pudding 8
Chicken Burrito Bowl 8
Nutmeg Banana Oatmeal 9
Chicken- Pork Meatballs 9
Apple Frittata....................................... 9
Strawberry Yogurt Oatmeal 9
Morning Banana Bread 10
Chocolate Vanilla Toast 10
Stuffed Baguette 10
Cranberry Almond Quinoa 10
Cheesy Cauliflower Hash 11
Creamy Bacon Millet 11
Berry-Berry Jam 11
Quinoa Oats Bake 11
Saucy Beef Meatloaf 12
Raspberry Vanilla Oatmeal 12
Peachy Cinnamon Butter 12
Zucchini Carrot Oatmeal 12
Ham Stuffed Peppers 13
Oats Craisins Granola 13
Sweet Pepper Boats............................ 13
Nutmeg Squash Oatmeal 13
Zesty Pumpkin Cubes.......................... 14

Creamy Asparagus Chicken 14
Spinach Tomato Frittata 14
Vanilla Yogurt 14
Eggplant Pate 15
Cheesy Egg Bake 15
Swiss Ham Quiche 15
Greek Mushrooms Casserole 16
Mushroom Chicken Casserole 16
Chicken Cabbage Medley 16
Ham Stuffed Pockets 16
Scrambled Spinach Eggs 17
Quinoa Bars 17
Mexican Egg Bake 17
Vanilla Maple Oats 17
Green Muffins 18
Tropical Cherry Granola 18
Cinnamon Pumpkin Oatmeal 18
Broccoli Omelette 18
Biscuit Roll Bread 19
Biscuit Roll Bread 19
Hash Browns Casserole 19
Mayo Sausage Rolls 20
Quinoa Cauliflower Medley................... 20
Bacon Cider Muffins 20
Saucy Sriracha Red Beans 21
Herbed Pork Meatballs 21
Nutty Sweet Potatoes 21
Mix Vegetable Casserole 22

Chapter 3 Vegetable Recipes 22

Tri-Bean Chili 22
Pinto Beans with Rice 22
Cinnamon Banana Sandwiches 23
Couscous Halloumi Salad 23
Marjoram Carrot Soup 23
Creamy Corn Chili 23
Honey Carrot Gravy 24
Onion Chives Muffins 24
French Vegetable Stew 24
Creamy Garlic Potatoes 24
Fennel Lentils..................................... 25

Chorizo Cashew Salad 25
Warming Butternut Squash Soup 25
Lentil Rice Salad 25
Potato Parmesan Pie 26
Allspice Beans Stew 26
Eggplant Mini Wraps 26
Oregano Cheese Pie 27
Minestrone Zucchini Soup 27
Quinoa Avocado Salad 27
Mediterranean Veggies........................ 27
White Beans Luncheon 28

Lemon Spinach Orzo 28
Quinoa Avocado Salad 28
Pumpkin Bean Chili 28
Broccoli Egg Pie........................ 29
Green Peas Risotto 29
Bulgur Mushroom Chili 29
Quinoa Black Bean Chili 30
Rice Stuffed Apple Cups 30

Rice Stuffed Eggplants 30
Sweet Potato Tarragon Soup 30
Wild Rice Peppers 31
Zucchini Spinach Lasagne 31
Spaghetti Cheese Casserole 31
Vegetable Bean Stew 32
Rice Cauliflower Casserole 32

Chapter 4 Poultry Recipes 33

African Chicken Meal 33
Chicken with Green Onion Sauce 33
Adobo Chicken Thighs 33
Chicken Broccoli Casserole 33
Apple Chicken Bombs.................. 34
Creamy Chicken 34
Bourbon Honey Chicken 34
ButteryChicken Wings 34
Chicken Chickpeas 35
Chicken Liver Stew 35
Chicken with Mushroom Sauce 35
Chicken Pumpkin Stew 35
Saucy Chicken 36
Chicken with Lentils 36
Chicken Ricotta Meatloaf 36
Chicken with Tomatillos 37
Chicken Potato Casserole 37
Chicken Tomato Salad 37
Chicken Vegetable Pot Pie 38
Citrus Glazed Chicken 38
Chocolaty Chicken Mash 38
Chicken Mushrooms Stroganoff 39
Cola Marinated Chicken 39
Spinach and Artichoke Chicken 39
Chicken Curry 39
Romano Chicken Thighs 40
Chicken Dumplings Medley 40
Lime Dipped Chicken Drumsticks 40
Sauce Goose 40
Coca Cola Dipped Chicken 41
Creamy Bacon Chicken 41
Cuban Chicken 41
Chicken Mole 41
Duck with Potatoes 42
Saucy Chicken Drumsticks 42
Ginger Turkey 42
Goose with Mushroom Cream........ 42
Fennel Chicken 43
Duck Chili 43
Turkey Cranberry Stew................ 43

Hawaiian Pineapple Chicken 44
Lemon Sauce Dipped Chicken 44
Horseradish Mixed Chicken 44
Pomegranate Turkey 44
Continental Beef Chicken 45
Sesame Chicken Wings 45
Latin Chicken 45
Moscow Bacon Chicken 45
Mushrooms Stuffed with Chicken 46
Puerto Rican Chicken 46
Orange Duck Fillets 46
Chicken Cacciatore 46
Parmesan Chicken Fillet 47
Chicken Pepper Chili 47
Pepperoni Chicken 47
Chicken Stuffed with Beans 47
Red Sauce Chicken Soup 48
Saffron Chicken Thighs 48
Cheesy Chicken Breasts 48
Thai Peanut Chicken 48
Chicken Taco Soup 49
Peppercorn Chicken Thighs 49
Poultry Stew 49
Hot Chicken Wings 49
Maple Ginger Chicken 50
Cashew Thai Chicken 50
Sweet Potato Jalapeno Stew 50
Tomato Chicken 50
Turkey Pepper Chili 51
Chicken Potato Sandwich 51
Chicken Sausage Stew 51
Saucy Chicken Thighs 51
Caesar Chicken Wraps 52
Thyme Chicken 52
Mexican Black Beans Salad 52
Pulled Maple Chicken 52
Herbed Chicken Salsa 53
Vegetable Almond Pilaf 53
Curried Chicken Strips 53
Spaghetti Chicken Salad 53

Chapter 5 Red Meat Recipes 54

Saucy Beef Cheeks 54
Cauliflower Beef Soup 54
Beef Onions Mix 54
Jamaican Pork Shoulder 54
Brisket Turnips Medley 55
Beef Roast with Cauliflower 55
Dill Beef Roast 55
Chinese Mushroom Pork 55
Potato Beef Gratin 56
Salsa Bean Pie 56
Parmesan Rosemary Potato 56
Greek Olive Lamb 56
Enchilada Pork Luncheon 57
Mushroom Pork Chop Stew 57
Cheesy Pork Wraps 57
Saucy French Lamb 57
Pork Sweet Potato Stew...................... 58
Lamb Leg with Sweet Potatoes 58
Garlic Lamb Chilli 58
Indian Harissa Pork 58
Lamb Cashews Tagine 59
Herbed Lamb Shanks 59
Lamb Cheese Casserole 59
Lamb Leg Mushrooms Satay 59
Herbed Cinnamon Beef 60

Lamb Semolina Meatballs 60
Lamb Shoulder with Artichokes 60
Pork Sirloin Salsa 60
Lamb Potato Stew 61
Pork Chops Pineapple Satay 61
Herbed Lamb Fillet 61
Lamb Carrot Medley........................... 61
Zesty Pesto Pork 62
Seasoned Beef Stew 62
Wine Dipped Lamb Leg 62
Pork with Apples 62
Tomatillo Lamb 63
Thai Spiced Pork 63
Mexican Lamb Fillet 63
Roast with Pepperoncini...................... 63
Cider Dipped Pork Roast 64
Short Ribs with Tapioca Sauce............... 64
Moroccan Apricot Lamb 64
Smoke Infused Lamb 64
Soy Dipped Pork Ribs 65
Sausage with Onion Jam 65
Sweet Mongolian Beef 65
Maple Rosemary Lamb 65
Coconut Meatballs Gravy 66

Chapter 6 Fish & Seafood Recipes 66

Carp Millet Soup 66
Japanese Pea Shrimp 66
Cod with Shrimp Sauce 67
Chili Tamarind Mackerel 67
Chinese Miso Mackerel 67
Dill Shrimp Medley............................. 67
Butter Dipped Crab Legs 68
Semolina Fish Balls 68
Cider Dipped Clams 68
Spiced Cod with Peas......................... 68
Tuna Mushroom Noodles...................... 69
Indian Fish Curry............................... 69
Tuna Noodles Casserole 69
Italian Parsley Clams 69
Dill Crab Cutlets 70
White Fish with Olives Sauce................ 70
Shrimp Chicken Jambalaya 70
Maple Mustard Salmon 70
Mackerel Stuffed Tacos 71
Rice Stuffed Squid 71
Turmeric Coconut Squid 71
Mussels and Sausage Satay 71
Flounder Cheese Casserole 72
Balsamic-Glazed Salmon 72
Halibut with Peach Sauce..................... 72

Harissa Dipped Cod 73
Herbed Octopus Mix 73
Japanese Cod Fillet 73
Lobster Cheese Soup 74
Thai Salmon Cakes 74
Seabass Mushrooms Ragout 74
Citrus Glazed Flounder 75
Octopus with Mixed Vegetable.............. 75
Lamb Bacon Stew 75
Crispy Mackerel 76
Clams- Mussels Boil 76
Shrimp Mushroom Curry 76
Mussels Tomato Soup 76
Sweet Orange Fish 77
Orange Marmalade Salmon 77
Vinaigrette Dipped Salmon 77
Salmon with Saffron Rice 77
Salmon with Lemon Relish.................... 78
Cream White Fish 78
Cod Bacon Chowder 78
Chipotle Salmon Fillets........................ 78
Salmon Tofu Soup 79
Seafood Bean Chili 79
Salmon Chickpea Fingers 79
Shri Lanka Fish Cutlet 80

Cod with Asparagus 80
Shrimp Potato Boil 80
Salmon with Green Sauce 80
Lamb Vegetable Curry 81
Spicy Harissa Perch 81
Fish Potato Cakes 81
Mushrooms Snapper 82
Rice Stuffed Trout 82
Herbed Shrimps 82

Italian Trout Croquettes 83
Tuna with Chimichurri Sauce 83
Chicken Stuffed Squid 83
Tuna with Potatoes 84
Seafood Medley............................. 84
Shrimp Clam Stew 84
Crab with Oyster Sauce 85
Lamb Potato Stew 85
Trout Capers Piccata 85

Chapter 7 Side Dish Recipes 86

Asian Sesame Asparagus.................... 86
Blueberry Spinach Salad 86
Baked Potato 86
Slow-Cooked White Onions 86
Broccoli Filling.............................. 87
Garlicky Black Beans 87
Balsamic-Glazed Beets 87
Beets Salad 87
Buttery Artichokes 88
Orange Squash 88
Carrot Beet Salad 88
Cornbread Cream Pudding 88
Cauliflower Carrot Gratin 89
Mac Cream Cups 89
Rainbow Carrots 89
Herbed Eggplant Cubes 89
Creamy Butter Parsnips 90
Cheesy Rice 90
Muffin Corn Pudding 90
Cinnamon Applesauce 90
Carrot Shallots Medley 91
Honey Glazed Vegetables 91
Butter Glazed Yams 91
Pumpkin Nutmeg Rice 91
Beans and Red Peppers 92
Butter Green Beans 92
Herbed Balsamic Beets 92
Squash and Peppers Mix 92
Lemony Honey Beets 92
Jalapeno Meal 93
Garlic Mushrooms 93
Cream Cheese Macaroni 93
Nut Berry Salad 93

Turmeric Potato Strips 94
Green Beans with Mushrooms 94
Saucy Macaroni 94
Zucchini Onion Pate 94
Creamy Red Cabbage 95
Refried Black Beans 95
Rice with Artichokes 95
Farro Rice Pilaf 95
Beans Risotto............................... 96
Veggies Rice Pilaf 96
Cider Dipped Farro 96
Mexican Avocado Rice 96
Hasselback Potatoes 97
Scalloped Cheese Potatoes 97
Eggplants with Mayo Sauce 97
Corn Cucumber Salad 97
Tamale Side Dish 98
Ramen Noodles 98
Tangy Red Potatoes 98
Dill Mixed Fennel 98
Millet with Dill 99
Sweet Red Onions 99
Summer Squash Medley 99
Lemony Pumpkin Wedges 99
Thyme Mixed Beets 99
Tomato Okra Mix 100
Eggplant Salad.............................100
Turmeric Buckwheat 100
Chicken with Sweet Potato..................100
Pink Salt Rice 100
Berry Wild Rice 101
Zucchini Crackers Casserole 101

Chapter 8 Snack Recipes 101

Apple Sausage Snack 101
Carrot Broccoli Fritters 101
Bean Pesto Dip 102
Thyme Pepper Shrimp 102
Beef Tomato Meatballs 102
Cheeseburger Cream Dip 102
Bean Salsa Salad 103

Caramel Milk Dip 103
Cashew Hummus Dip 103
Butter Stuffed Chicken Balls 103
Cordon Bleu Dip 104
Zucchini Sticks 104
Cheesy Chili Pepper Dip 104
Apple Wedges with Peanuts 104

Dill Butter Muffins	105	Jalapeno Onion Dip	111
Egg Bacon Muffins	105	Peanut Butter Chicken	111
Eggplant Zucchini Dip	105	Black Eyes Peas Dip	111
Eggplant Capers Salsa	105	Chickpea Hummus	111
Fajita Chicken Dip	106	Herbed Pecans Snack	112
Fava Bean Onion Dip	106	Cheesy Pork Rolls	112
Pork Stuffed Tamales	106	Cheesy Potato Dip	112
Pork Tostadas	107	Potato Onion Salsa	112
Slow-Cooked Lemon Peel	107	Bacon Fingerling Potatoes	113
Garlicky Bacon Slices	107	Peanut Bombs	113
Garlic Parmesan Dip	107	Sausage Cream Dip	113
Maple Glazed Turkey Strips	108	Pesto Pitta Pockets	113
Spinach Mussels Salad	108	Creamy Mushroom Bites	114
Tomato Mussels Salad	108	Basic Pepper Salsa	114
Ginger Chili Peppers	108	Chicken Taco Nachos	114
Jalapeno Chorizo Poppers	109	Mixed Nuts	115
Blue Cheese Parsley Dip	109	Spicy Mussels	115
Marsala Cheese Mushrooms	109	Crumbly Chickpeas Snack	115
Cheese Onion Dip	109	Apple Chutney	115
Cheese Stuffed Meat Balls	110	Spinach Cream Dip	116
Jalapeno Salsa Snack	110	Potato Cups	116
Mozzarella Basil Tomatoes	110	Mixed Vegetable Spread	116
Cheesy Mushroom Dip	110		

Chapter 9 Dessert Recipes...117

Avocado Peppermint Pudding	117	Coffee Cinnamon Roll	122
Mixed-Berry Marmalade	117	Lemony Orange Marmalade	122
Spongy Banana Bread	117	Cornmeal Apricot Pudding	123
Banana Almond Foster	117	Lemon Cream Dessert	123
Butternut Squash Pudding	118	Cardamom Lemon Pie	123
Creamy Caramel Dessert	118	Wine Dipped Pears	123
Vanilla Cheesecake	118	Cheesecake with Lime Filling	124
Choco Liquor Crème	118	Berry-Berry Mascarpone Cream	124
Citron Vanilla Bars	119	Maple Chocolate Fondue	124
Candied Sweet Lemon	119	Spiced Peach Crisp	124
Nutty Caramel Apples	119	Mango Cream Dessert	125
Cocoa Vanilla Cake	119	Raspberry Nutmeg Cake	125
Green Tea Avocado Pudding	119	Pears with Grape Sauce	125
Creamy Dark Chocolate Dessert	120	Poppy Cream Pie	125
Cocoa Peanut Candies	120	Raisin-Flax meal Bars	126
Apricot Rice Pudding	120	Rice Vanilla Pudding	126
Coconut Vanilla Pudding	120	Espresso Ricotta Cream	126
Vanilla Blueberry Cream	120	Lemony Figs	126
Cinnamon Cream Dessert	121	Creamy Lemon Mix	127
Tangerine Cream Pie	121	Tapioca Pearls Pudding	127
Latte Vanilla Cake	121	Banana-Melon Pudding	127
Cinnamon Apple Butter	121	Cinnamon Hot Chocolate	127
Cinnamon Pear Toasts	122	Vanilla Crème Cups	127
Pear Apple Jam	122		

Appendix 1: Measurement Conversion Chart...................................... **128**
Appendix 2: Recipes Index... **129**

Introduction

According to research conducted by Professor Carlos Monteiro of Sao Paulo University, the British diet is the unhealthiest in Europe. The study suggests that those living in the United Kingdom have a higher risk of strokes, heart attacks, and obesity. Ultra-processed junk food such as low-quality microwave meals, chicken nuggets, and crisps make up more than half of the foods eaten in the average household. Nineteen European countries took part in the study, and it was found that the British are five times more likely to eat these meals than people in Portugal, and four times more likely than those in Italy, Greece, and France. Ireland and Germany were the next biggest consumers of an unhealthy diet, which accounted for 46 percent of their average diet. The remainder of Europe ate higher rates of healthy organic foods and less junk food. Tim Lang, Professor of food policy at City University states that "There is a national crisis in the United Kingdom with diet-related ill health." The problem with ultra-processed foods is that they are high in salt, sugars, and unsaturated fats, all of which increase the risk of heart attack and stroke.

So, what is the solution to this problem? One of the reasons why the Brits consume such an unhealthy diet is because these foods are extremely cheap to buy, and people simply don't have the time to stand in the kitchen cooking homemade dinners. The good news is that there is a way to combat this conundrum with a slow cooker.

Chapter 1 Understanding the Slow Cooker

What is Slow Cooker?

A slow cooker is also referred to as a crockpot. It is an extremely useful appliance that not only produces delicious meals but will save you time and money. The slow cooker initially became popular in the 1970s just as women began to enter the workforce. A slow cooker meant that dinner would be prepared by the time she returned home from work. A slow cooker is an electrical cooking countertop appliance, and it does exactly what its name states, it facilitates unattended slow cooking for several hours.

If you want to improve your health by cooking nutritious, homely meals without burning a hole in your pocket, then a slow cooker is exactly what you need. With a slow cooker, your only job is to spend 15 minutes preparing the ingredients, and while the food cooks, you can get on with the rest of your day. It is ideal for anyone who has a busy schedule, for those who work shifts, for students who have lectures during the day, for the stay at home mum, you can put the dinner on after the morning school run and then get your errands out of the way, by the time it's time to collect the kids from school, the dinner is ready. The slow cooker is ideal for people who are retired. You can put the supper on, go out and enjoy your day and return to a nice home-cooked meal.

Because the food is cooked at a slow pace on a low temperature, you don't need to worry about the bottom burning, food spilling over, or it boiling dry. Slow-cooked food is a lot more flavourful than foods cooked in other ways. People got really excited when the microwave oven first came out; yes, it allows you to prepare food in minutes, but radiation experts state that they can increase the risk of cancer. This is not the case with a slow cooker. They are environmentally friendly because they don't use the same amount of electricity as an oven. They are cheap to run as they only use the same amount of energy as an electric light bulb. If you find that the good quality meat is too expensive, not to worry, your slow cooker will make the cheapest meat taste like you are eating a gourmet dinner! They have the ability to transform the toughest meat into succulent, juicy, melt in the mouth, fall off the bone meat!

Slow cookers are also great for steaming puddings. There is no need to add additional water because it doesn't evaporate, so you don't have to worry about the pudding drying out. Additional water can be used as a water bath or bain marie to cook terrines, pates, or baked custards. You can also pour fruit juice or alcoholic mixes into the port to make hot toddies or warming hot party punchies.

You can use the slow cooker to make cheese or chocolate fondues, simple chutneys, or lemon curd. You can also boil up a chicken carcass or meat bones to make a hearty homemade stock.

Before Getting Start

Get the Right Size

Slow cookers come in a variety of sizes. The size you choose will depend on your requirements, such as whether you are a single person, or you have a family. However, you also want to bear in mind that if you are a single person or a couple with no kids who hold dinner parties often, you might want to consider getting a bigger size.

- **2 people: 2 ½ pints – a mini oval slow cooker**

- **4 people: 6 pints – a medium round slow cooker**

- **6 people: 7 pints a large oval slow cooker**

There is not much of a price difference between the mini and large slow cookers, but you should also keep in mind that when cooking fish, meats, and vegetable dishes, you will need to fill the slow cooker halfway. Oval is the most versatile shape for cooking things like a whole chicken. It also provides plenty of room if you want to make soups and pudding. It is also a good idea to choose a slow cooker that has an indicator light. This will let you know whether the slow cooker is turned on or not.

Read the Handbook

Although slow cookers all provide the same function, different manufacturers will have different instructions; therefore, make sure you read the manual before getting started to familiarize yourself with your slow cooker.

Filling the Pot

It is essential that you add liquid to your slow cooker before making a meal. Ideally, it should be filled halfway, for soups, the liquid should be no more than 1 inch from the top. Joints of meat shouldn't take up any more than two-thirds of the space; if you are using a pudding basin, make sure there is 1.5 cm space around the circumference of the slow cooker.

Slow Cooker Settings

There is a 'high,' 'low,' 'warm,' 'medium,' or 'auto,' setting on all slow cookers. The high and low settings will reach just below 100 degrees C, boiling point while cooking. But on a 'high' setting, it will get there quicker. It can be useful to use a combination of settings while cooking, some manufacturers recommend this; however, read your manual for further instructions.

Getting the Setting Right For Different Foods

In general, these are the settings you should use for certain foods; again, check your handbook for specific instructions:

Low Setting	High Setting
• Fish dishes	• Half shoulder of lamb
• Rice dishes	• Gammon joint
• Egg custard dishes	• Pheasant
• Soups	• Guinea fowl
• Chicken joints or chops	• Whole chicken
• Vegetable casseroles or diced meat	• Pates or terrines
	• Sweet or savoury steamed puddings
	• Sweet dishes that include a raising agent

Slow Cooking Timetable

Poultry	
Type of Poultry	**Cooking Time**
Boneless, Skinless Chicken Breast	1-2 hours on low
Bone-in Split Chicken Breasts	2-3 hours on low
Chicken Thighs	4-5 hours on low
Whole Chicken	4-5 hours on low
Turkey breast	5-6 hours on low

Roasts		
Type of Roast	Cookin Time on Low	Cooking Time on High
Top Sirloin Beef Roast	1-2 hours	/
Boneless Beef Chuck-eye Roast	9-10 hours	6-7 hours
Beef Brisket	9-10 hours	6-7 hours
Pork Tenderloin	1-2 hours	/
Boneless Pork Loin	2-3 hours	/
Boneless Pork Butt Roast	9-10 hours	6-7 hours
Ham	5-6 hours	/

Clean Your Slow Cooker

Your slow cooker might have specific cleaning instructions; therefore, check with your manual beforehand. However, whatever model you have, it is advised that you clean it as soon as it has been used. You can make the cleaning process easier by spraying it with a non-stick cooking spray before using it to prevent staining. It is also advised that you don't overfill the dish to avoid spillages that will leave residue on the pot. However, if you do get some stubborn stains on your slow cooker, here are a few tips for easier cleaning:

- Fill the cooker dish with water so that it covers the stain and leave it to cook for two hours

- Before washing, unplug the unit and never soak the base in water

- Dampen a soft cloth with dishwashing detergent and wipe clean

- Use a mixture of vinegar and baking powder, or fresh lemon juice applied to a sponge for more stubborn stains

- Do not use harsh detergents or abrasive cleaners

Tips to Utilize Your Slow Cooker Better

A slow cooker is one of the most efficient and convenient cooking utensils you can own. But you can make life even easier for yourself by following these simple tips and tricks when using your slow cooker:

- Trim off excess fat and brown the meat in a frying pan before adding it to the slow cooker.

- Cut the chicken skin off the chicken thighs before browning

- Do not lift the lid off the slow cooker to check the food while it is cooking. This will reduce the temperature, increase the cooking time, and affect the moisture of the food.

- Unless the recipe requires that you place the cooker dish in the base after heating it, do not do so. Place the cooker dish in the base before you heat it.

- Do not reheat foods in a slow cooker. Their only purpose is to cook foods and not for reheating. If you want to reheat food from the day before, you can do this in a saucepan on the stove.

- Slow cookers don't evaporate; therefore, make sure you use recipes that are specifically for slow cookers (like the ones in this book).

- To add additional flavour to a dish, sprinkle fresh herbs over the top of a dish or add a dash of lemon juice.

- When cooking rice dishes, if you can get your hands on easy cook rice, it cooks better in a slow cooker. Also, wash off as much of the starch as possible, you will have a better finished dish.

- Add pasta at the last 30 minutes of cooking, or it will get extremely soggy if cooked for any longer than this.

- If you are adding fresh herbs, add them at the last 30 minutes of cooking, or they will lose their intense flavour.

- Root vegetables take a lot longer to cook than meat; therefore, you can either chop them up into smaller chunks, or sauté them before adding them to the dish. Make sure that all vegetables are on the base (which is the hottest area of the slow cooker), and fully immersed in the liquid.

- If the stew or sauce you are cooking is too thin, mix 1 tablespoon of cornflour with 2 tablespoons of the stew or sauce and add it to the slow cooker.

- Do not cook frozen foods in a slow cooker; make sure that you defrost them first, this applies even more so with meat. This is extremely important because the slow cooker is designed to safely cook foods at a low temperature, but if the required heat is not maintained, the risk of food poisoning is increased by the spread of bacteria. If you are adding quick-cook frozen vegetables such as prawns, sweetcorn and peas, add them in the last 30 minutes of cooking.

- Milk, creams, crème fraiche, and Greek yogurt can separate when cooked for long periods of time in a slow cooker; therefore, it is advised that you add them right at the end just before serving.

Okay, so now it's time to get cooking! Whether you are new to the slow cooking experience or you are an expert looking for some inspiration, there is something in this book for everyone……. Bon appetite!

Chapter 2 Breakfast Recipes

Apple Cinnamon Granola

Prep time: 12 minutes; Cook Time: 4 hrs; Serves: 6

Ingredients:

2 green apples, peeled, cored and sliced
½ cup granola
½ cup bran flakes
¼ cup apple juice
1/8 cup maple syrup
1 tsp cinnamon powder
2 tbsp soft butter
½ tsp nutmeg, ground

Instructions:

1. Toss the apples with granola, bran flakes, maple syrup, apple juice, butter, cinnamon, nutmeg, and butter in a large bowl.
2. Spread this apple crumble into the base of your Slow Cooker.
3. Put the cooker's lid on and set the cooking time to 4 hours on Low settings.
4. Serve and devour.

Nutrition Facts Per Serving:

Calories 363, Total Fat 5g, Fiber 6g, Total Carbs 20g, Protein 6g

Cinnamon Apple Oatmeal

Prep time: 15 minutes; Cook Time: 10 hrs; Serves: 4

Ingredients:

2 tbsp butter, soft
¾ cup brown sugar
4 apples, cored, peeled and chopped
2 cups old-fashioned
oats
1 and ½ tbsp cinnamon powder
4 cups of water

Instructions:

1. Brush the base of your Slow Cooker with butter.
2. Now start adding apples, sugar, oats, water, and cinnamon.
3. Put the cooker's lid on and set the cooking time to 8 hours on Low settings.
4. Dish out into the serving bowls.
5. Garnish with as desired.
6. Enjoy.

Nutrition Facts Per Serving:

Calories 282, Total Fat 4g, Fiber 9g, Total Carbs 20g, Protein 5g

Artichoke Pepper Frittata

Prep time: 15 minutes; Cook Time: 3 hrs; Serves: 4

Ingredients:

14 oz. canned artichokes hearts, drained and chopped
12 oz. roasted red peppers, chopped
8 eggs, whisked
¼ cup green onions, chopped
4 oz. feta cheese, crumbled
Cooking spray

Instructions:

1. Coat the base of your Slow Cooker with cooking spray.
2. Add green onions, roasted peppers, and artichokes to the slow cooker.
3. Pour whisked eggs over the veggies and drizzle cheese on top.
4. Put the cooker's lid on and set the cooking time to 3 hours on Low settings.
5. Slice and serve.

Nutrition Facts Per Serving:

Calories 232, Total Fat 7g, Fiber 9g, Total Carbs 17g, Protein 6g

Spiced Baby Carrots

Prep time: 15 minutes; Cook Time: 8 hrs; Serves: 6

Ingredients:

2 tsp fresh dill, chopped
1 lb. baby carrot
1 tsp honey
1 tsp paprika
1 tsp ground ginger
3 tbsp butter
½ tsp salt
2 eggs

Instructions:

1. Beat eggs with chopped dill, honey, paprika, salt, and ginger in a bowl.
2. Spread the baby carrots in the base of your Slow Cooker.
3. Pour the egg- dill mixture over the carrots.
4. Put the cooker's lid on and set the cooking time to 8 hours on Low settings.
5. Serve warm.

Nutrition Facts Per Serving:

Calories 128, Total Fat 9.2g, Fiber 3g, Total Carbs 8.36g, Protein 4g

Boiled Bacon Eggs

Prep time: 15 minutes; Cook Time: 2 hrs; Serves: 6

Ingredients:

7 oz. bacon, sliced	1 tbsp minced garlic
1 tsp salt	1 tsp ground black
6 eggs, hard-boiled, peeled	pepper
½ cup cream	4 oz. Parmesan cheese, shredded
3 tbsp mayonnaise	1 tsp dried dill

Instructions:

1. Place a non-skillet over medium heat and add bacon slices.
2. Drizzle salt and black pepper on top, then cook for 1 minute per side.
3. Transfer the bacon slices to a plate and keep them aside.
4. Whisk mayonnaise with minced garlic, dried dill, and cream in a bowl.
5. Spread this creamy mixture into the base of your Slow Cooker.
6. Take the peeled eggs and wrap then with cooked bacon slices.
7. Place the wrapped eggs in the creamy mixture.
8. Drizzle shredded cheese over the wrapped eggs.
9. Put the cooker's lid on and set the cooking time to 2 hours on High settings.
10. Serve and devour.

Nutrition Facts Per Serving:
Calories 381, Total Fat 31g, Fiber 1g, Total Carbs 8.07g, Protein 19g

Apricots Bread Pudding

Prep time: 21 minutes; Cook Time: 5 hrs; Serves: 9

Ingredients:

10 oz. French bread	½ tsp ground nutmeg
6 tbsp dried apricots	
10 oz. milk	½ tsp ground cardamom
3 eggs, beaten	
4 tbsp butter	¼ cup whipped cream
½ tsp salt	
1 tsp vanilla sugar	4 tbsp brown sugar

Instructions:

1. Melt butter by heating in a saucepan then add milk.
2. Cook until warm, then stir in vanilla sugar, salt, ground cardamom, ground nutmeg, and brown sugar.

3. Continue mixing the milk mixture until sugar is fully dissolved.
4. Spread French bread and dried apricots in the slow cooker.
5. Beat eggs in a bowl and add to the milk mixture.
6. Stir in cream and mix well until fully incorporated.
7. Pour this milk-cream mixture over the bread and apricots in the Slow cooker.
8. Put the cooker's lid on and set the cooking time to 5 hours on Low settings.
9. Serve.

Nutrition Facts Per Serving:
Calories 229, Total Fat 11.5g, Fiber 1g, Total Carbs 24.3g, Protein 8g

Chicken Burrito Bowl

Prep time: 18 minutes; Cook Time: 7 hrs; Serves: 6

Ingredients:

10 oz. chicken breast, sliced	canned
	¼ cup green peas
1 tbsp chili flakes	1 cup chicken stock
1 tsp salt	½ avocado, pitted and chopped
1 tsp onion powder	
1 tsp minced garlic	1 tsp ground black pepper
½ cup white beans,	

Instructions:

1. Place the chicken breast in the Slow Cooker.
2. Drizzle salt, onion powder, chili flakes, black pepper, and minced garlic on top.
3. Pour the chicken stock on top of the chicken.
4. Put the cooker's lid on and set the cooking time to 2 hours on High settings.
5. Now add white beans and green peas to the chicken.
6. Close the lid again and cook for 5 hours on Low setting.
7. Shred the slow-cooked chicken and return to the bean's mixture.
8. Mix well and add chopped avocado.
9. Serve the burrito with avocado on top.

Nutrition Facts Per Serving:
Calories 192, Total Fat 7.7g, Fiber 5g, Total Carbs 15.66g, Protein 16g

Nutmeg Banana Oatmeal

Prep time: 15 minutes; Cook Time: 7 hrs; Serves: 6

Ingredients:

Cooking spray
2 bananas, sliced
1 cup steel-cut oats
28 oz. canned coconut milk
½ cup of water
1 tbsp butter
2 tbsp brown sugar
¼ tsp nutmeg, ground
½ tsp cinnamon powder
½ tsp vanilla extract
1 tbsp flaxseed, ground

Instructions:

1. Coat the base of your Slow cooker with cooking spray.
2. Spread oats, banana slices, water, coconut milk, sugar, butter, cinnamon, flaxseed, and vanilla in this cooker.
3. Put the cooker's lid on and set the cooking time to 7 hours on Low settings.
4. Serve fresh.
5. Enjoy.

Nutrition Facts Per Serving:

Calories 251, Total Fat 6g, Fiber 8g, Total Carbs 16g, Protein 6g

Chicken- Pork Meatballs

Prep time: 15 minutes; Cook Time: 7 hrs; Serves: 8

Ingredients:

1 cup bread crumbs
2 tbsp sour cream
9 oz. ground chicken
7 oz. ground pork
1 tsp onion powder
1 onion, chopped
1 tsp ketchup
¼ tsp olive oil

Instructions:

1. Thoroughly mix ground chicken, onion powder, sour cream, ground pork, ketchup, and onion in a large bowl.
2. Add breadcrumbs to bind this mixture well.
3. Make small meatballs out of this mixture and roll them in extra breadcrumbs.
4. Brush the base of your slow cooker with olive oil.
5. Gently place the chicken-pork meatballs in the slow cooker.
6. Put the cooker's lid on and set the cooking time to 7 hours on Low settings.
7. Serve warm.

Nutrition Facts Per Serving:

Calories 116, Total Fat 5g, Fiber 0g, Total Carbs 4.08g, Protein 14g

Apple Frittata

Prep time: 15 minutes; Cook Time: 3 hrs, Serves: 8

Ingredients:

7 oz. mozzarella, sliced
10 eggs
1 cup milk
3 tbsp flour
1 tsp salt
1 tsp chili flakes
½ cup cherry tomatoes, chopped
1 red sweet pepper
1 yellow sweet pepper
1 apple
1 tsp butter

Instructions:

1. Add eggs into a bowl one by one, then beat using a hand mixer.
2. Gradually pour in milk, salt, butter, chili flakes, and flour into the eggs.
3. Whisk well and add the chopped apple and sweet peppers to the egg mixture.
4. Pour this egg and veggie mixture into the base of your Slow Cooker.
5. Top the frittata mixture with sliced mozzarella.
6. Put the cooker's lid on and set the cooking time to 3 hours on Low settings.
7. Slice the cooked frittata pie and serve warm.

Nutrition Facts Per Serving:

Calories 252, Total Fat 13.7g, Fiber 2g, Total Carbs 11.25g, Protein 21g

Strawberry Yogurt Oatmeal

Prep time: 15 minutes, Cook Time: 8 hrs; Serves: 8

Ingredients:

6 cups of water
2 cups of milk
2 cups steel-cut oats
1 cup Greek yogurt
1 tsp cinnamon
powder
2 cups strawberries, halved
1 tsp vanilla extract

Instructions:

1. Add oats, milk, cinnamon, yogurt, water, vanilla, and strawberries to the Slow Cooker.
2. Put the cooker's lid on and set the cooking time to 8 hours on Low settings.
3. Serve.

Nutrition Facts Per Serving:

Calories 200, Total Fat 4g, Fiber 6g, Total Carbs 8g, Protein 4g

Morning Banana Bread

Prep time: 12 minutes; Cook Time: 4 hrs; Serves: 4

Ingredients:

2 eggs	1 tsp baking powder
1 cup of sugar	3 bananas, mashed
2 cups flour	½ tsp baking soda
½ cup butter	

Instructions:

1. Crack eggs in a bowl and beat until well mixed.
2. Stir in eggs, sugar, baking powder, baking soda, bananas, and flour.
3. Continue mixing the eggs-flour mixture until it forms a smooth batter.
4. Pour the egg-flour mixture in a loaf pan.
5. Place this loaf pan in the slow cooker.
6. Put the cooker's lid on and set the cooking time to 4 hours on Low settings.
7. Slice the bread.
8. Serve.

Nutrition Facts Per Serving:

Calories 261, Total Fat 9g, Fiber 6g, Total Carbs 20g, Protein 16g

Chocolate Vanilla Toast

Prep time: 12 minutes, Cook Time: 4 hrs; Serves: 4

Ingredients:

Cooking spray	milk
1 loaf of bread, cubed	1 tsp vanilla extract
¾ cup brown sugar	¾ cup of chocolate chips
3 eggs	1 tsp cinnamon powder
1 and ½ cups of	

Instructions:

1. Cover the base of your Slow cooker with cooking spray.
2. Spread the bread pieces in the cooker.
3. Beat eggs with vanilla, milk, sugar, chocolate chips, and cinnamon in a bowl.
4. Pour this egg-chocolate mixture over the bread pieces.
5. Put the cooker's lid on and set the cooking time to 4 hours on Low settings.
6. Serve.

Nutrition Facts Per Serving:

Calories 261, Total Fat 6g, Fiber 5g, Total Carbs 19g, Protein 6g

Stuffed Baguette

Prep time: 15 minutes; Cook Time: 5 hrs; Serves: 4

Ingredients:

6 oz. baguette	4 oz. ham, cooked and shredded
7 oz. breakfast sausages, chopped	6 oz. Parmesan, shredded
3 tbsp whipped cream	3 tbsp ketchup
1 tsp minced garlic	2 oz. green olives
1 tsp onion powder	

Instructions:

1. Slice the baguette in half and remove the flesh from the center of these halves.
2. Toss chopped sausages with cheese shreds, onion powder, minced garlic, cream, shredded ham and ketchup in a large bowl.
3. Divide this cheese-sausage mixture into the baguette halves.
4. Place these stuffed baguette halves in the Slow cooker.
5. Put the cooker's lid on and set the cooking time to 5 hours on Low settings.
6. Slice the stuffed baguettes and serve.

Nutrition Facts Per Serving:

Calories 483, Total Fat 17.2g, Fiber 2g, Total Carbs 47.06g, Protein 35g

Cranberry Almond Quinoa

Prep time: 15 minutes; Cook Time: 2 hrs; Serves: 4

Ingredients:

3 cups of coconut water	sliced
1 tsp vanilla extract	1/8 cup coconut flakes
1 cup quinoa	¼ cup cranberries, dried
3 tsp honey	
1/8 cup almonds,	

Instructions:

1. Add coconut water, honey, vanilla, quinoa, almonds, cranberries, and coconut flakes to the Slow Cooker.
2. Put the cooker's lid on and set the cooking time to 2 hours on High settings.
3. Dish out and serve.

Nutrition Facts Per Serving:

Calories 261, Total Fat 7g, Fiber 8g, Total Carbs 18g, Protein 4g

Cheesy Cauliflower Hash

Prep time: 17 minutes; Cook Time: 8 hrs; Serves: 5

Ingredients:

7 eggs
¼ cup milk
1 tsp salt
1 tsp ground black pepper
½ tsp ground mustard
10 oz. cauliflower,

shredded
¼ tsp chili flakes
5 oz. breakfast sausages, chopped
½ onion, chopped
5 oz. Cheddar cheese, shredded

Instructions:

1. First, beat the eggs with milk, mustard, black pepper, salt, onion, and chili flakes in a bowl.
2. Spread the cauliflower shreds in the Slow Cooker.
3. Pour the egg-milk mixture over the cauliflower shreds.
4. Drizzle cheese and chopped sausages on top.
5. Put the cooker's lid on and set the cooking time to 8 hours on Low settings.
6. Slice and serve.

Nutrition Facts Per Serving:

Calories 329, Total Fat 21.8g, Fiber 2g, Total Carbs 10.31g, Protein 23g

Creamy Bacon Millet

Prep time: 14 minutes; Cook Time: 4 hrs 10 minutes, Serves: 6

Ingredients:

3 cup millet
6 cup chicken stock
1 tsp salt

4 tbsp heavy cream
5 oz. bacon, chopped

Instructions:

1. Add millet and chicken stock to the Slow cooker.
2. Stir in chopped bacon and salt.
3. Put the cooker's lid on and set the cooking time to 4 hours on High settings.
4. Stir in cream and again cover the lid of the Slow Cooker.
5. Cook for 10 minutes on High setting.
6. Serve.

Nutrition Facts Per Serving:

Calories 572, Total Fat 17.8g, Fiber 9g, Total Carbs 83.09g, Protein 20g

Berry-Berry Jam

Prep time: 22 minutes; Cook Time: 4 hrs; Serves: 6

Ingredients:

1 cup white sugar
1 cup strawberries
1 tbsp gelatin
3 tbsp water

1 tbsp lemon zest
1 tsp lemon juice
½ cup blueberries

Instructions:

1. Take a blender jug and add berries, sugar, lemon juice, and lemon zest to puree.
2. Blend this blueberry-strawberry mixture for 3 minutes until smooth.
3. Pour this berry mixture into the base of your Slow Cooker.
4. Put the cooker's lid on and set the cooking time to 1 hour on High settings.
5. Mix gelatin with 3 tbsp water in a bowl and pour it into the berry mixture.
6. Again, put the cooker's lid on and set the cooking time to 3 hours on High settings.
7. Allow the jam to cool down.
8. Serve.

Nutrition Facts Per Serving:

Calories 163, Total Fat 8.3g, Fiber 2g, Total Carbs 20.48g, Protein 3g

Quinoa Oats Bake

Prep time: 15 minutes; Cook Time: 7 hrs; Serves: 6

Ingredients:

½ cup quinoa
1 and ½ cups steel cut oats
4 and ½ cups of almond milk

2 tbsp maple syrup
4 tbsp brown sugar
1 and ½ tsp vanilla extract
Cooking spray

Instructions:

1. Coat the base of your Slow cooker with cooking spray.
2. Stir in oats, quinoa, maple syrup, vanilla extract, sugar, and almond milk.
3. Put the cooker's lid on and set the cooking time to 7 hours on Low settings.
4. Serve.

Nutrition Facts Per Serving:

Calories 251, Total Fat 8g, Fiber 8g, Total Carbs 20g, Protein 5g

Saucy Beef Meatloaf

Prep time: 18 minutes; Cook Time: 7 hrs; Serves: 8

Ingredients:

12 oz. ground beef
1 tsp salt
1 tsp ground coriander
1 tbsp ground mustard
¼ tsp ground chili
pepper
6 oz. white bread, chopped
½ cup milk
1 tsp ground black pepper
3 tbsp tomato sauce

Instructions:

1. Soak the white bread cubes in the milk and keep them aside for 3 minutes.
2. Whisk ground beef with chili pepper, mustard, black pepper, salt, and ground coriander in a bowl.
3. Now add the bread-milk mixture into the beef and mix well.
4. Cover the base of your Slow Cooker with aluminum foil.
5. Spread the beef-bread mixture in the foil.
6. Top the meatloaf with tomato sauce.
7. Put the cooker's lid on and set the cooking time to 7 hours on Low settings.
8. Slice and serve.

Nutrition Facts Per Serving:

Calories 214, Total Fat 14g, Fiber 3g, Total Carbs 12.09g, Protein 9g

Raspberry Vanilla Oatmeal

Prep time: 15 minutes; Cook Time: 8 hrs; Serves: 4

Ingredients:

2 cups of water
1 tbsp coconut oil
1 cup steel-cut oats
1 tbsp sugar
1 cup milk
½ tsp vanilla extract
1 cup raspberries
4 tbsp walnuts, chopped

Instructions:

1. Add oil, oats, water, milk, vanilla, raspberries, and sugar to the Slow cooker.
2. Put the cooker's lid on and set the cooking time to 8 hours on Low settings.
3. Give the oatmeal a gentle stir then divide it into the serving bowls.
4. Garnish with walnuts.
5. Serve.

Nutrition Facts Per Serving:

Calories 200, Total Fat 10g, Fiber 4g, Total Carbs 20g, Protein 4g

Peachy Cinnamon Butter

Prep time: 15 minutes; Cook Time: 8 hrs; Serves: 8

Ingredients:

15 oz. peach, pitted, peeled and cubed
2 cup of sugar
¼ tsp salt
1 tbsp ground
cinnamon
1 tsp fresh ginger, peeled and grated
5 tbsp lemon juice

Instructions:

1. Take a blender jug and add peach cubes into the jug.
2. Blender until peaches are pureed.
3. Pour this peach puree into the Slow cooker.
4. Stir in salt, sugar, grated ginger, and cinnamon.
5. Put the cooker's lid on and set the cooking time to 8 hours on Low settings.
6. Stir in lemon juice and mix well.
7. Add the peach butter to glass jars.
8. Allow the jars to cool and serve with bread.

Nutrition Facts Per Serving:

Calories 141, Total Fat 0.1g, Fiber 1g, Total Carbs 37.03g, Protein 0g

Zucchini Carrot Oatmeal

Prep time: 15 minutes; Cook Time: 8 hrs; Serves: 4

Ingredients:

½ cup steel cut oats
1 carrot, grated
1 and ½ cups of coconut milk
¼ zucchini, grated
A pinch of cloves, ground
A pinch of nutmeg, ground
½ tsp cinnamon powder
2 tbsp brown sugar
¼ cup pecans, chopped

Instructions:

1. Toss oats with milk, carrot, cloves, zucchini, cinnamon, nutmeg, and sugar in the Slow Cooker.
2. Put the cooker's lid on and set the cooking time to 8 hours on Low settings.
3. Divide the oatmeal in the serving bowls.
4. Garnish with pecans.
5. Serve.

Nutrition Facts Per Serving:

Calories 251, Total Fat 6g, Fiber 8g, Total Carbs 19g, Protein 6g

Ham Stuffed Peppers

Prep time: 12 minutes; Cook Time: 4 hrs; Serves: 3

Ingredients:

3 bell peppers, halved and deseeded
Salt and black pepper to the taste
4 eggs
½ cup milk

2 tbsp green onions, chopped
½ cup ham, chopped
¼ cup spinach, chopped
¾ cup cheddar cheese, shredded

Instructions:

1. Beat eggs with green onion, salt, black pepper, spinach, milk, half of the cheese and ham in a medium bowl.
2. Cover the base of your Slow cooker with aluminum foil.
3. Divide the egg-spinach mixture into the bell pepper halves.
4. Place these stuffed pepper halves in the Slow cooker.
5. Drizzle the cheese over the bell peppers.
6. Put the cooker's lid on and set the cooking time to 4 hours on Low settings.
7. Serve warm.
8. Devour.

Nutrition Facts Per Serving:

Calories 162, Total Fat 4g, Fiber 1g, Total Carbs 6g, Protein 11g

Oats Craisins Granola

Prep time: 15 minutes; Cook Time: 2 hrs; Serves: 8

Ingredients:

5 cups old-fashioned rolled oats
1/3 cup coconut oil
2/3 cup honey
½ cup almonds, chopped

½ cup peanut butter
1 tbsp vanilla
2 tsp cinnamon powder
1 cup craisins
Cooking spray

Instructions:

1. Toss oats with honey, oil, craisins, cinnamon, vanilla, peanut butter, and almonds in the Slow cooker.
2. Put the cooker's lid on and set the cooking time to 2 hours on High settings.
3. Serve.

Nutrition Facts Per Serving:

Calories 200, Total Fat 3g, Fiber 6g, Total Carbs 9g, Protein 4g

Sweet Pepper Boats

Prep time: 15 minutes; Cook Time: 3 hrs; Serves: 4

Ingredients:

2 red sweet pepper, cut in half
7 oz. ground chicken
5 oz. Parmesan, cubed
1 tbsp sour cream
1 tbsp flour

1 egg
2 tsp almond milk
1 tsp salt
½ tsp ground black pepper
¼ tsp butter

Instructions:

1. Take the ground chicken in a large bowl.
2. Stir in sour cream, flour, almond milk, butter, whisked eggs, and black pepper.
3. Mix well and divide this chicken mixture in the sweet peppers.
4. Top each stuffed pepper with cheese cube.
5. Put the cooker's lid on and set the cooking time to 3 hours on High settings.
6. Serve warm.

Nutrition Facts Per Serving:

Calories 261, Total Fat 8.9g, Fiber 1g, Total Carbs 19.15g, Protein 26g

Nutmeg Squash Oatmeal

Prep time: 15 minutes; Cook Time: 8 hrs; Serves: 6

Ingredients:

½ cup almonds, soaked for 12 hours in water and drained
½ cup walnuts, chopped
2 apples, peeled, cored and cubed
1 butternut squash,

peeled and cubed
½ tsp nutmeg, ground
1 tsp cinnamon powder
1 tbsp sugar
1 cup milk

Instructions:

1. Toss almond with apples, walnuts, nutmeg, sugar, squash, and cinnamon in the base of your Slow Cooker.
2. Pour in milk and give it a gentle stir.
3. Put the cooker's lid on and set the cooking time to 8 hours on Low settings.
4. Serve.

Nutrition Facts Per Serving:

Calories 178, Total Fat 7g, Fiber 7g, Total Carbs 9g, Protein 4g

Zesty Pumpkin Cubes

Prep time: 15 minutes; Cook Time: 10 hrs; Serves: 4

Ingredients:

2 tbsp lemon juice	1 tbsp lemon zest
3 tbsp honey	2 tbsp water
1 tbsp ground cinnamon	1 lb. pumpkin, peeled and cubed
1 tbsp brown sugar	

Instructions:

1. Toss the pumpkin cubes with lemon juice, water, honey, cinnamon, sugar, lemon zest in a large bowl.
2. Spread the pumpkin with sugar mixture in the Slow cooker.
3. Put the cooker's lid on and set the cooking time to 10 hours on Low settings.
4. Toss well and serve.

Nutrition Facts Per Serving:

Calories 81, Total Fat 0.2g, Fiber 2g, Total Carbs 21.84g, Protein 1g

Creamy Asparagus Chicken

Prep time: 23 minutes; Cook Time: 8 hrs; Serves: 7

Ingredients:

1 cup cream	1 tsp oregano
2 lb. chicken breast, skinned, boneless, sliced	1 tsp ground white pepper
1 tsp chili powder	1 tsp sriracha
3 tbsp flour	6 oz. asparagus
	1 tsp sage

Instructions:

1. Whisk chili powder, oregano, sage, white pepper, and flour in a shallow tray.
2. Add the chicken slices to this spice mixture and coat them well.
3. Now add cream, chopped veggies, and Sriracha to the Slow cooker.
4. Place the coated chicken slices in the cooker.
5. Put the cooker's lid on and set the cooking time to 8 hours on Low settings.
6. Serve warm.

Nutrition Facts Per Serving:

Calories 311, Total Fat 18.8g, Fiber 1g, Total Carbs 5.71g, Protein 29g

Spinach Tomato Frittata

Prep time: 15 minutes; Cook Time: 2 hrs, Serves: 6

Ingredients:

1 tbsp olive oil	3 eggs
1 yellow onion, chopped	2 tbsp milk
1 cup mozzarella cheese, shredded	Salt and black pepper to the taste
3 egg whites	1 cup baby spinach
	1 tomato, chopped

Instructions:

1. Grease your Slow cooker with the oil and spread onion, spinach, and tomatoes on the bottom.
2. In a bowl, mix the eggs with egg whites, milk, salt, and pepper, whisk well and pour over the veggies from the pot.
3. Sprinkle mozzarella all over, cover the slow cooker, cook on Low for 2 hrs; slice, divide between plates, and serve for breakfast.

Nutrition Facts Per Serving:

Calories 200, Total Fat 8g, Fiber 2g, Total Carbs 5g, Protein 12g

Vanilla Yogurt

Prep time: 15 minutes; Cook Time: 10 hrs; Serves: 8

Ingredients:

3 tsp gelatin	1 and ½ tbsp vanilla extract
½ gallon milk	½ cup maple syrup
7 oz. plain yogurt	

Instructions:

1. Add milk to the Slow cooker to heat it up.
2. Put the cooker's lid on and set the cooking time to 3 hours on Low settings.
3. Take 1 cup of this hot milk in a bowl and stir in gelatin.
4. Now take another cup of milk in another bowl and add yogurt.
5. Mix well, then pour into the slow cooker.
6. Add the gelatin-milk mixture, maple syrup, and vanilla.
7. Put the cooker's lid on and set the cooking time to 7 hours on Low settings.
8. Allow it to cool then serve.

Nutrition Facts Per Serving:

Calories 200, Total Fat 4g, Fiber 5g, Total Carbs 10g, Protein 5g

Eggplant Pate

Prep time: 27 minutes; Cook Time: 6 hrs; Serves: 15

Ingredients:

5 medium eggplants, peeled and chopped
2 sweet green pepper, chopped
1 cup bread crumbs
1 tsp salt
1 tbsp sugar
½ cup tomato paste
2 yellow onion, chopped
1 tbsp minced garlic
¼ chili pepper, chopped
1 tsp olive oil
1 tsp kosher salt
1 tbsp mayonnaise

Instructions:

1. Place the eggplants in a colander and drizzle salt on top.
2. Leave them for 10 minutes at room temperature.
3. Whisk tomatoes paste with sugar, salt, mayonnaise, and garlic in a bowl.
4. Grease the base of your Slow cooker with olive oil.
5. Spread chopped onion and eggplant in the cooker.
6. Pour the tomato sauce over the veggies.
7. Top the sauce with green peppers and chili pepper.
8. Put the cooker's lid on and set the cooking time to 6 hours on Low settings.
9. Blend the cooked eggplant mixture with an immersion blender until smooth.
10. Top the eggplant pate with breadcrumbs.
11. Serve.

Nutrition Facts Per Serving:
Calories 83, Total Fat 0.8g, Fiber 7g, Total Carbs 18.15g, Protein 3g

Cheesy Egg Bake

Prep time: 15 minutes; Cook Time: 8 hrs; Serves: 8

Ingredients:

20 oz. tater tots
2 yellow onions, chopped
6 oz. bacon, chopped
2 cups cheddar cheese, shredded
12 eggs
¼ cup parmesan, grated
1 cup milk
Salt and black pepper to the taste
4 tbsp white flour
Cooking spray

Instructions:

1. Coat the base of your Slow cooker with cooking spray.
2. Spread tater tots, bacon, onions, parmesan, and cheddar in the cooker.
3. Beat eggs with milk, flour, salt, and black pepper in a bowl.
4. Pour this mixture over the tater tots' layer.
5. Put the cooker's lid on and set the cooking time to 8 hours on Low settings.
6. Serve fresh.

Nutrition Facts Per Serving:
Calories 290, Total Fat 9g, Fiber 1g, Total Carbs 9g, Protein 22g

Swiss Ham Quiche

Prep time: 15 minutes, Cook Time: 3 hrs; Serves: 6

Ingredients:

1 pie crust
1 cup ham, cooked and chopped
2 cups Swiss cheese, shredded
6 eggs
1 cup whipping cream
4 green onions, chopped
Salt and black pepper to the taste
A pinch of nutmeg, ground
Cooking spray

Instructions:

1. Grease the base of your Slow Cooker with cooking spray.
2. Spread the pie crust in the slow cooker.
3. Put the cooker's lid on and set the cooking time to 1 hour 30 minutes on High settings.
4. Meanwhile, beat eggs with cream, nutmeg, black pepper, and salt in a bowl.
5. Pour the egg mixture in the pie crust and top it with cheese, green onions, and ham.
6. Put the cooker's lid on and set the cooking time to 1 hour 30 minutes on High settings.
7. Slice and serve.

Nutrition Facts Per Serving:
Calories 300, Total Fat 4g, Fiber 7g, Total Carbs 15g, Protein 5g

Greek Mushrooms Casserole

Prep time: 14 minutes, Cook Time: 4 hrs; Serves: 4

Ingredients:

12 eggs, whisked	mushrooms, sliced
Salt and black pepper to the taste	½ cup sun-dried tomatoes
½ cup milk	1 tsp garlic, minced
1 red onion, chopped	2 cups spinach
1 cup baby bell	½ cup feta cheese, crumbled

Instructions:

1. Beat eggs with milk, salt, and black pepper in a suitable bowl.
2. Toss mushrooms, spinach, onion, garlic, and tomatoes in your Slow cooker.
3. Pour the egg mixture on top and drizzle the cheese over it.
4. Put the cooker's lid on and set the cooking time to 4 hours on Low settings.
5. Slice and serve.

Nutrition Facts Per Serving:

Calories 325, Total Fat 7g, Fiber 7g, Total Carbs 27g, Protein 18g

Mushroom Chicken Casserole

Prep time: 18 minutes; Cook Time: 8 hrs; Serves: 5

Ingredients:

8 oz. mushrooms, sliced	7 oz. chicken fillet, sliced
1 cup cream	1 tsp butter
1 carrot, peeled and grated	1 tsp fresh rosemary
6 oz. Cheddar cheese, shredded	1 tsp salt
	½ tsp coriander

Instructions:

1. Add the mushroom slices, grated carrot in the Slow cooker.
2. Season the chicken strips with coriander and rosemary.
3. Place these chicken slices in the cooker and top it with cream, butter, salt, and cheese.
4. Put the cooker's lid on and set the cooking time to 8 hours on Low settings.
5. Serve.

Nutrition Facts Per Serving:

Calories 405, Total Fat 19.2g, Fiber 6g, Total Carbs 49.93g, Protein 15g

Chicken Cabbage Medley

Prep time: 17 minutes; Cook Time: 4.5 hrs; Serves: 5

Ingredients:

6 oz. ground chicken	½ tsp salt
10 oz. cabbage, chopped	1 tsp ground black pepper
1 white onion, sliced	4 tbsp chicken stock
½ cup tomato juice	2 garlic cloves
1 tsp sugar	

Instructions:

1. Whisk tomato juice with black pepper, salt, sugar, and chicken stock in a bowl.
2. Spread the onion slices, chicken, and cabbage in the Slow Cooker.
3. Pour the tomato-stock mixture over the veggies and top with garlic cloves.
4. Put the cooker's lid on and set the cooking time to 4 hours 30 minutes on High settings.
5. Serve.

Nutrition Facts Per Serving:

Calories 91, Total Fat 3.1g, Fiber 2g, Total Carbs 9.25g, Protein 8g

Ham Stuffed Pockets

Prep time: 14 minutes; Cook Time: 1.5 minutes, Serves: 6

Ingredients:

6 pita bread, sliced	7 oz. ham, sliced
7 oz. mozzarella, sliced	1 big tomato, sliced
1 tsp minced garlic	1 tbsp mayo
	1 tbsp heavy cream

Instructions:

1. First, heat your Slow cooker for 30 minutes on High setting.
2. Meanwhile, whisk the mayonnaise with garlic and cream.
3. Layer inside each half of the pita bread with mayo-garlic mixture.
4. Now add a slice of tomato, ham, and mozzarella to the bread.
5. Wrap the bread pieces with a foil sheet.
6. Place the packed pita bread in the Slow Cooker.
7. Put the cooker's lid on and set the cooking time to 1 hour 30 minutes on Low settings.
8. Remove the bread from the foil.
9. Serve.

Nutrition Facts Per Serving:

Calories 273, Total Fat 3.3g, Fiber 2g, Total Carbs 38.01g, Protein 22g

Scrambled Spinach Eggs

Prep time: 25 minutes; Cook Time: 2 Hrs; Serves: 9

Ingredients:

8 eggs	3 tbsp butter
½ cup spinach	1 tsp minced garlic
½ cup cherry	5 oz. Cheddar
tomatoes	cheese
1 tsp dried oregano	½ cup milk
1 tsp salt	

Instructions:

1. First, beat the eggs with cheddar cheese, milk, oregano, garlic, salt, cherry tomatoes, and spinach in a large bowl.
2. Coat the base of your Slow Cooker with butter.
3. Pour the egg-tomato mixture into the Slow Cooker.
4. Put the cooker's lid on and set the cooking time to 2 hours on High settings.
5. Serve.

Nutrition Facts Per Serving:

Calories 187, Total Fat 14.3g, Fiber 0g, Total Carbs 3.55g, Protein 11g

Quinoa Bars

Prep time: 14 minutes; Cook Time: 4 hrs; Serves: 8

Ingredients:

2 tbsp maple syrup	½ cup raisins
2 tbsp almond	1/3 cup quinoa
butter, melted	1/3 cup almonds,
Cooking spray	toasted and chopped
½ tsp cinnamon	1/3 cup dried
powder	apples, chopped
1 cup almond milk	2 tbsp chia seeds
2 eggs	

Instructions:

1. Mix quinoa with almond butter, cinnamon, milk, maple syrup, eggs, apples, chia seeds, almonds, and raisins in a suitable bowl.
2. Coat the base of your Slow Cooker with cooking spray and parchment paper.
3. Now evenly spread the quinoa-oats mixture over the parchment paper.
4. Put the cooker's lid on and set the cooking time to 4 hours on Low settings.
5. Slice and serve.

Nutrition Facts Per Serving:

Calories 300, Total Fat 7g, Fiber 8g, Total Carbs 22g, Protein 5g

Mexican Egg Bake

Prep time: 14 minutes; Cook Time: 2 hours and 15 minutes, Serves: 8

Ingredients:

Cooking spray	minced
10 eggs	A pinch of salt and
12 oz. Monterey	black pepper
Jack, shredded	10 oz. taco sauce
1 cup half and half	4 oz. canned green
½ tsp chili powder	chilies, chopped
1 garlic clove,	8 corn tortillas

Instructions:

1. Beat eggs with 8 oz. cheese, half and half, black pepper, salt, green chilies, chili powder, and garlic in a bowl.
2. Coat the base of your Slow cooker with cooking spray.
3. Pour the egg-cheese mixture into the cooker.
4. Put the cooker's lid on and set the cooking time to 2 hours on Low settings.
5. Now top the egg with remaining cheese and taco sauce.
6. Cover again and cook for 15 minutes on the low setting.
7. Serve warm with a tortilla.

Nutrition Facts Per Serving:

Calories 312, Total Fat 4g, Fiber 8g, Total Carbs 12g, Protein 5g

Vanilla Maple Oats

Prep time: 15 minutes; Cook Time: 8 hrs; Serves: 4

Ingredients:

1 cup steel-cut oats	powder
2 tsp vanilla extract	2 cups of water
2 cups vanilla	2 tsp flaxseed
almond milk	Cooking spray
2 tbsp maple syrup	2 tbsp blackberries
2 tsp cinnamon	

Instructions:

1. Coat the base of your Slow cooker with cooking spray.
2. Stir in oats, almond milk, vanilla extract, cinnamon, maple syrup, flaxseeds, and water.
3. Put the cooker's lid on and set the cooking time to 8 hours on Low settings.
4. Stir well and serve with blackberries on top.
5. Devour.

Nutrition Facts Per Serving:

Calories 200, Total Fat 3g, Fiber 6g, Total Carbs 9g, Protein 3g

Green Muffins

Prep time: 20 minutes; Cook Time: 2 ½ hrs; Serves: 8

Ingredients:

1 cup spinach, washed	½ tsp baking soda
5 tbsp butter	1 tbsp lemon juice
1 cup flour	1 tbsp sugar
1 tsp salt	3 eggs

Instructions:

1. Add the spinach leaves to a blender jug and blend until smooth.
2. Whisk the eggs in a bowl and add the spinach mixture.
3. Stir in baking soda, salt, sugar, flour, and lemon juice.
4. Mix well to form a smooth spinach batter.
5. Divide the dough into a muffin tray lined with muffin cups.
6. Place this muffin tray in the Slow Cooker.
7. Put the cooker's lid on and set the cooking time to 2 hours 30 minutes on High settings.
8. Serve.

Nutrition Facts Per Serving:

Calories 172, Total Fat 6.1g, Fiber 1g, Total Carbs 9.23g, Protein 20g

Tropical Cherry Granola

Prep time: 13 minutes; Cook Time: 1 hr and 30 minutes, Serves: 6

Ingredients:

1 cup almonds, sliced	½ cup of coconut oil
4 cups old-fashioned oats	½ cup dried coconut
½ cup pecans, chopped	½ cup raisins
½ tsp ginger, ground	½ cup dried cherries
	½ cup pineapple, dried

Instructions:

1. Toss oil with pecans, ginger, almonds, and all other ingredients in the Slow cooker.
2. Put the cooker's lid on and set the cooking time to 1 hour 30 minutes on High settings.
3. Mix well and serve.

Nutrition Facts Per Serving:

Calories 172, Total Fat 5g, Fiber 8g, Total Carbs 10g, Protein 4g

Cinnamon Pumpkin Oatmeal

Prep time: 15 minutes, Cook Time: 9 hrs; Serves: 4

Ingredients:

Cooking spray	A pinch of cloves, ground
1 cup steel-cut oats	A pinch of ginger, grated
½ cup milk	A pinch of allspice, ground
4 cups of water	A pinch of nutmeg, ground
2 tbsp brown sugar	
½ cup pumpkin puree	
½ tsp cinnamon powder	

Instructions:

1. Layer the base of Slow Cooker with cooking spray.
2. Stir in milk, sugar, water, oats, cinnamon, cloves, sugar, pumpkin puree, ginger, nutmeg, and allspice.
3. Put the cooker's lid on and set the cooking time to 9 hours on Low settings.
4. Serve.

Nutrition Facts Per Serving:

Calories 342, Total Fat 5g, Fiber 8g, Total Carbs 20g, Protein 5g

Broccoli Omelette

Prep time: 15 minutes; Cook Time: 2 hrs; Serves: 4

Ingredients:

½ cup milk	chopped
6 eggs	1 cup broccoli florets
Salt and black pepper to the taste	1 yellow onion, chopped
A pinch of chili powder	1 garlic clove, minced
A pinch of garlic powder	1 tbsp cheddar cheese, shredded
1 red bell pepper,	Cooking spray

Instructions:

1. Start by cracking eggs in a large bowl and beat them well.
2. Stir in all the veggies, cheese, and spices then mix well.
3. Pour the eggs-veggie mixture into the Slow cooker.
4. Put the cooker's lid on and set the cooking time to 2 hours on High settings.
5. Slice and serve warm.

Nutrition Facts Per Serving:

Calories 142, Total Fat 7g, Fiber 1g, Total Carbs 8g, Protein 10g

Biscuit Roll Bread

Prep time: 20 minutes; Cook Time: 2 hrs; Serves: 6

Ingredients:

12 oz. biscuit rolls, diced
1 tbsp ground cinnamon
3 oz. white sugar
1 tsp vanilla extract
4 tbsp butter, melted
1 egg white
4 tbsp brown sugar

Instructions:

1. Whisk sugar with melted butter, cinnamon in a bowl.
2. Split the biscuit roll cubes into 2 parts and place on half of all the cubes in the Slow cooker.
3. Top this layer with the cinnamon butter mixture evenly.
4. Place the remaining parts of the biscuit roll cubes on top.
5. Put the cooker's lid on and set the cooking time to 2 hours on Low settings.
6. Now beat egg white with brown sugar until it is fluffy.
7. Top the cooked bread with the egg white icing.
8. Serve.

Nutrition Facts Per Serving:

Calories 313, Total Fat 16.8g, Fiber 3g, Total Carbs 34.14g, Protein 7g

Biscuit Roll Bread

Prep time: 20 minutes; Cook Time: 2 hrs; Serves: 6

Ingredients:

12 oz. biscuit rolls, diced
1 tbsp ground cinnamon
3 oz. white sugar
1 tsp vanilla extract
4 tbsp butter, melted
1 egg white
4 tbsp brown sugar

Instructions:

1. Whisk sugar with melted butter, cinnamon in a bowl.
2. Split the biscuit roll cubes into 2 parts and place on half of all the cubes in the Slow cooker.
3. Top this layer with the cinnamon butter mixture evenly.
4. Place the remaining parts of the biscuit roll cubes on top.
5. Put the cooker's lid on and set the cooking time to 2 hours on Low settings.
6. Now beat egg white with brown sugar until it is fluffy.
7. Top the cooked bread with the egg white icing.
8. Serve.

Nutrition Facts Per Serving:

Calories 313, Total Fat 16.8g, Fiber 3g, Total Carbs 34.14g, Protein 7g

Hash Browns Casserole

Prep time: 14 minutes; Cook Time: 4 hrs; Serves: 12

Ingredients:

30 oz. hash browns
1 lb. sausage, browned and sliced
8 oz. mozzarella cheese, shredded
8 oz. cheddar cheese, shredded
6 green onions, chopped
½ cup milk
12 eggs
Cooking spray
Salt and black pepper to the taste

Instructions:

1. Coat the base of your Slow cooker with cooking spray.
2. Spread half of the hash browns, mozzarella, sausage, green onions, and cheddar to the cooker.
3. Beat eggs with milk, black pepper, and salt in a bowl.
4. Pour half of this egg-milk mixture over the layer of hash browns.
5. Top it with the remaining half of the hash browns, sausages, cheddar, green onions, and mozzarella.
6. Pour in the remaining egg-milk mixture.
7. Put the cooker's lid on and set the cooking time to 4 hours on High settings.
8. Slice and serve warm.

Nutrition Facts Per Serving:

Calories 300, Total Fat 3g, Fiber 7g, Total Carbs 10g, Protein 12g

Mayo Sausage Rolls

Prep time: 23 minutes; Cook Time: 3 hrs; Serves: 11

Ingredients:

1 lb. puff pastry	10 oz. breakfast
2 tbsp flour	sausages
1 tbsp mustard	1 tsp paprika
1 egg, whisked	1 tbsp mayo

Instructions:

1. Spread the puff pastry with a rolling pin and drizzle flour over it.
2. Slice the puff pastry into long thick strips.
3. Spread mustard, mayonnaise, and paprika on top of each pastry strip.
4. Place one sausage piece at one end of each strip.
5. Roll the puff pastry strip and brush the rolls with whisked egg.
6. Cover the base of your Slow Cooker with a parchment sheet.
7. Place the puff pastry rolls in the cooker.
8. Put the cooker's lid on and set the cooking time to 3 hours on High settings.
9. Serve fresh.

Nutrition Facts Per Serving:
Calories 311, Total Fat 21.8g, Fiber 1g, Total Carbs 20.49g, Protein 8g

Quinoa Cauliflower Medley

Prep time: 20 minutes; Cook Time: 9 hrs; Serves: 7

Ingredients:

8 oz. potato, peeled and cubed	1 cup tomatoes, chopped
7 oz. cauliflower, cut in florets	13 oz. almond milk
	3 cup chicken stock
1 cup onion, chopped	8 tbsp quinoa
	1/3 tbsp miso
7 oz. chickpea, canned	1 tsp minced garlic
	2 tsp curry paste

Instructions:

1. Spread the chopped potatoes, tomatoes, and onion in the Slow cooker.
2. Whisk curry paste with chicken stock and miso in a separate bowl.
3. Pour this mixture over the layer of the veggies.
4. Now top this mixture with chickpeas, cauliflower florets, quinoa, garlic, and almond milk.

5. Put the cooker's lid on and set the cooking time to 9 hours on Low settings.
6. Serve.

Nutrition Facts Per Serving:
Calories 262, Total Fat 4.6g, Fiber 7g, Total Carbs 44.31g, Protein 12g

Bacon Cider Muffins

Prep time: 15 minutes; Cook Time: 4.5 hrs; Serves: 9

Ingredients:

1 cup flour	vinegar
6 tbsp butter	1 tsp baking powder
3 eggs	5 oz. bacon,
1 tsp salt	chopped
½ tbsp apple cider	

Instructions:

1. Whisk butter with apple cider vinegar, flour, baking powder, and salt in a bowl.
2. Take a non-skillet and toss in bacon.
3. Stir cook until crispy and crunchy then transfer it to the butter mixture.
4. Beat eggs with the bacon-mixture and liquid in the bigger bowl to form a batter
5. Layer the muffin tins with paper cups.
6. Divide the eggs batter into the muffin cups.
7. Pour 1 cup water into the base of your Slow Cooker and place the muffin tray in it.
8. Put the cooker's lid on and set the cooking time to 4 hours 30 minutes on High settings.
9. Serve.

Nutrition Facts Per Serving:
Calories 211, Total Fat 15.7g, Fiber 1g, Total Carbs 12.13g, Protein 6g

Saucy Sriracha Red Beans

Prep time: 21 minutes; Cook Time: 6 hrs;
Serves: 5
Ingredients:

1 cup red beans, soaked and drained	1 chili pepper, sliced
3 chicken stock	1 tsp sriracha
3 tbsp tomato paste	1 tbsp butter
1 onion, sliced	1 tsp turmeric
1 tsp salt	1 cup green peas

Instructions:

1. Spread the red beans in the Slow cooker.
2. Add turmeric, salt, and chicken stock on its top.
3. Put the cooker's lid on and set the cooking time to 4 hours on High settings.
4. Toss the sliced onion with Sriracha, butter, chili pepper, and sriracha in a separate bowl.
5. Spread this onion-pepper mixture over the cooked beans in the Slow Cooker.
6. Cover the beans again and slow cook for another 1 hour on Low setting.
7. Serve after a gentle stir.

Nutrition Facts Per Serving:
Calories 190, Total Fat 3.1g, Fiber 8g, Total Carbs 31.6g, Protein 11g

Herbed Pork Meatballs

Prep time: 14 minutes; Cook Time: 4 hrs;
Serves: 9
Ingredients:

2 lb. ground pork	½ cup tomato juice
1 tbsp dried parsley	3 tbsp flour
1 tsp dried dill	1 tbsp minced garlic
1 tsp paprika	1 tsp onion powder
1 tsp salt	1 tsp sugar
1 egg	1 tsp chives
1 tbsp semolina	1 oz. bay leaves

Instructions:

1. Beat egg in a bowl then stir in ground pork, parsley, dill, salt, paprika, garlic, semolina, and onion powder in a large bowl.
2. Make medium-sized meatballs out of this mixture.
3. Cover the base of your Slow cooker with a parchment sheet.
4. Place the meatballs in the cooker.
5. Now mix tomato juice, flour, bay leaf, sugar and chives in a separate bowl.
6. Pour this mixture over the meatballs.
7. Put the cooker's lid on and set the cooking time to 4 hours on Low settings.
8. Serve the meatballs with their sauce.

Nutrition Facts Per Serving:
Calories 344, Total Fat 22.4g, Fiber 1g, Total Carbs 6.87g, Protein 28g

Nutty Sweet Potatoes

Prep time: 13 minutes, Cook Time: 6 hrs;
Serves: 8
Ingredients:

2 tbsp peanut butter	1 cup onion, chopped
¼ cup peanuts	½ cup chicken stock
1 lb. sweet potato, peeled and cut in strips.	1 tsp salt
1 garlic clove, peeled and sliced	1 tsp paprika
2 tbsp lemon juice	1 tsp ground black pepper

Instructions:

1. Toss the sweet potato with lemon juice, paprika, salt, black pepper, and peanut butter in a large bowl.
2. Place the sweet potatoes in the Slow cooker.
3. Add onions and garlic clove on top of the potatoes.
4. Put the cooker's lid on and set the cooking time to 6 hours on Low settings.
5. Serve with crushed peanuts on top.
6. Devour.

Nutrition Facts Per Serving:
Calories 376, Total Fat 22.4g, Fiber 6g, Total Carbs 39.36g, Protein 5g

Mix Vegetable Casserole

Prep time: 16 minutes; Cook Time: 4 hrs; Serves: 8

Ingredients:

4 egg whites
8 eggs
Salt and black pepper to the taste
2 tsp ground mustard
¾ cup milk
30 oz. hash browns
4 bacon strips, cooked and chopped
1 broccoli head, chopped
2 bell peppers, chopped
Cooking spray
6 oz. cheddar cheese, shredded
1 small onion, chopped

Instructions:

1. Beat egg with black pepper, salt, milk, and mustard in a bowl.
2. Coat the base of your Slow cooker with cooking spray.
3. Place broccoli, onion, hash browns, and bell peppers in the cooker.
4. Pour the eggs on top and drizzle bacon and cheddar over it.
5. Put the cooker's lid on and set the cooking time to 4 hours on Low settings.
6. Serve.

Nutrition Facts Per Serving:

Calories 300, Total Fat 4g, Fiber 8g, Total Carbs 18g, Protein 8g

Chapter 3
Vegetable Recipes

Tri-Bean Chili

Prep time: 15 minutes; Cook Time: 8 hrs; Serves: 6

Ingredients:

15 oz. canned kidney beans, drained
30 oz. canned chili beans in sauce
15 oz. canned black beans, drained
2 green bell peppers, chopped
30 oz. canned tomatoes, crushed
2 tbsp chili powder
2 yellow onions, chopped
2 garlic cloves, minced
1 tsp oregano, dried
1 tbsp cumin, ground
Salt and black pepper to the taste

Instructions:

1. Add kidney beans, black beans, chili beans, and all the spices and veggies to the Slow cooker.
2. Put the cooker's lid on and set the cooking time to 8 hours on Low settings.
3. Serve warm.

Nutrition Facts Per Serving:

Calories 314, Total Fat 6g, Fiber 5g, Total Carbs 14g, Protein 4g

Pinto Beans with Rice

Prep time: 15 minutes; Cook Time: 3 hrs; Serves: 6

Ingredients:

1 lb. pinto beans, dried
1/3 cup hot sauce
Salt and black pepper to the taste
1 tbsp garlic, minced
1 tsp garlic powder
½ tsp cumin, ground
1 tbsp chili powder
3 bay leaves
½ tsp oregano, dried
1 cup white rice, cooked

Instructions:

1. Add pinto beans along with the rest of the ingredients to your Slow cooker.
2. Put the cooker's lid on and set the cooking time to 3 hours on High settings.
3. Serve warm on top of rice.

Nutrition Facts Per Serving:

Calories 381, Total Fat 7g, Fiber 12g, Total Carbs 35g, Protein 10g

Cinnamon Banana Sandwiches

Prep time: 15 minutes; Cook Time: 2 hrs; Serves: 4

Ingredients:

2 bananas, peeled and sliced
8 oz. French toast slices, frozen
1 tbsp peanut butter
¼ tsp ground cinnamon
5 oz. Cheddar cheese, sliced
¼ tsp turmeric

Instructions:

1. Layer half of the French toast slices with peanut butter.
2. Whisk cinnamon with turmeric and drizzle over the peanut butter layer.
3. Place the banana slice and cheese slices over the toasts.
4. Now place the remaining French toast slices on top.
5. Place these banana sandwiches in the Slow cooker.
6. Put the cooker's lid on and set the cooking time to 2 hours on High settings.
7. Serve.

Nutrition Facts Per Serving:

Calories 248, Total Fat 7.5g, Fiber 2g, Total Carbs 36.74g, Protein 10g

Couscous Halloumi Salad

Prep time: 16 minutes; Cook Time: 4 hrs; Serves: 5

Ingredients:

1 cup couscous
1 green sweet pepper, chopped
2 garlic cloves
1 cup beef broth
1 tsp chives
½ cup cherry tomatoes halved
1 zucchini, diced
7 oz. halloumi cheese, chop
1 tsp olive oil
1 tsp paprika
¼ tsp ground cardamom
1 tsp salt

Instructions:

1. Add couscous, cardamom, salt, and paprika to the Slow Cooker.
2. Stir in garlic, zucchini, and beef broth to the couscous.
3. Put the cooker's lid on and set the cooking time to 4 hours on High settings.
4. Stir in the remaining ingredients and toss it gently.
5. Serve.

Nutrition Facts Per Serving:

Calories 170, Total Fat 9.6g, Fiber 1g, Total Carbs 12.59g, Protein 9g

Marjoram Carrot Soup

Prep time: 18 minutes; Cook Time: 12 hrs; Serves: 9

Ingredients:

1 lb. carrot
1 tsp ground cardamom
¼ tsp nutmeg
1 tsp salt
3 tbsp fresh parsley
1 tsp honey
1 tsp marjoram
5 cups chicken stock
½ cup yellow onion, chopped
1 tsp butter

Instructions:

1. Add butter and all the veggies to a suitable pan.
2. Sauté these vegetables on low heat for 5 minutes then transfer to the Slow cooker.
3. Stir in cardamom, salt, chicken stock, marjoram, and nutmeg.
4. Put the cooker's lid on and set the cooking time to 12 hours on Low settings.
5. Puree the cooked veggie mixture using an immersion blender until smooth.
6. Garnish with honey and parsley.
7. Devour.

Nutrition Facts Per Serving:

Calories 80, Total Fat 2.7g, Fiber 2g, Total Carbs 10.19g, Protein 4g

Creamy Corn Chili

Prep time: 14 minutes; Cook Time: 6 hrs; Serves: 6

Ingredients:

2 jalapeno chilies, chopped
1 cup yellow onion, chopped
1 tbsp olive oil
4 poblano chilies, chopped
4 Anaheim chilies,
chopped
3 cups corn
6 cups veggie stock
½ bunch cilantro, chopped
Salt and black pepper to the taste

Instructions:

1. Add jalapenos, oil, onion, poblano, corn, stock, and Anaheim chilies to the Slow cooker.
2. Put the cooker's lid on and set the cooking time to 6 hours on Low settings.
3. Puree the cooked mixture with the help of an immersion blender.
4. Stir in black pepper, salt and cilantro.
5. Serve warm.

Nutrition Facts Per Serving:

Calories 209, Total Fat 5g, Fiber 5g, Total Carbs 33g, Protein 5g

Honey Carrot Gravy

Prep time: 20 minutes; Cook Time: 2 ½ hrs; Serves: 4

Ingredients:

3 tbsp mustard	1 tsp cinnamon
2 tbsp honey	½ tsp salt
1 lb. carrot, peeled and sliced	2 tsp butter
	2 tbsp water
1 tsp white sugar	

Instructions:

1. Toss the sliced carrots with cinnamon, water, salt, and sugar in a bowl.
2. Spread the seasoned carrots in the Slow cooker.
3. Put the cooker's lid on and set the cooking time to 2 hours on High settings.
4. Meanwhile, beat butter with honey and mustard in a separate bowl.
5. Pour this butter-honey mixture over the cooked carrots.
6. Cover again and slow cook them for another 30 minutes on the low setting.
7. Serve.

Nutrition Facts Per Serving:
Calories 99, Total Fat 2.7g, Fiber 4g, Total Carbs 19.27g, Protein 1g

Onion Chives Muffins

Prep time: 15 minutes; Cook Time: 8 hrs; Serves: 7

Ingredients:

1 egg	1 tsp cilantro
5 tbsp butter, melted	½ tsp sage
1 cup flour	1 tsp apple cider vinegar
½ cup milk	
1 tsp baking soda	1 tbsp chives
1 cup onion, chopped	1 tsp olive oil

Instructions:

1. Whisk egg with melted butter, onion, milk, and all other ingredients to make a smooth dough.
2. Grease a muffin tray with olive oil and divide the batter into its cups.
3. Pour 2 cups water into the Slow cooker and set the muffin tray in it.
4. Put the cooker's lid on and set the cooking time to 8 hours on Low settings.
5. Serve.

Nutrition Facts Per Serving:
Calories 180, Total Fat 11g, Fiber 1g, Total Carbs 16.28g, Protein 4g

French Vegetable Stew

Prep time: 15 minutes; Cook Time: 9 hrs; Serves: 6

Ingredients:

2 yellow onions, chopped	medium wedges
1 eggplant, sliced	1 tsp oregano, dried
4 zucchinis, sliced	1 tsp sugar
2 garlic cloves, minced	1 tsp basil, dried
2 green bell peppers, cut into medium strips	Salt and black pepper to the taste
6 oz. canned tomato paste	2 tbsp parsley, chopped
2 tomatoes, cut into	¼ cup olive oil
	A pinch of red pepper flakes, crushed

Instructions:

1. Add onions, zucchinis, eggplant, garlic, tomato paste, bell peppers, sugar, basil, salt, black pepper, and oregano to the Slow Cooker.
2. Put the cooker's lid on and set the cooking time to 9 hours on Low settings.
3. Stir in parsley and pepper flakes.
4. Serve warm.

Nutrition Facts Per Serving:
Calories 269, Total Fat 7g, Fiber 6g, Total Carbs 17g, Protein 4g

Creamy Garlic Potatoes

Prep time: 11 minutes; Cook Time: 7 hrs; Serves: 6

Ingredients:

2 lb. potatoes	½ tsp salt
1 cup heavy cream	1 tbsp fresh dill
1 tbsp minced garlic	1 tsp butter
1 tsp garlic powder	

Instructions:

1. Liberally rub the potatoes with butter and place them in the Slow Cooker.
2. Whisk cream with garlic powder, minced garlic fill, and salt in a bowl.
3. Add cream mixture to the potatoes.
4. Put the cooker's lid on and set the cooking time to 7 hours on Low settings.
5. Serve warm.

Nutrition Facts Per Serving:
Calories 198, Total Fat 8.3g, Fiber 4g, Total Carbs 28g, Protein 4g

Fennel Lentils

Prep time: 15 minutes; Cook Time: 5 hrs; Serves: 11

Ingredients:

1 tsp cumin	4 oz. onion, chopped
1 oz. mustard seeds	½ tsp fresh ginger, grated
10 oz. lentils	
1 tsp fennel seeds	1 oz. bay leaf
7 cups of water	1 tsp turmeric
6 oz. tomato, canned	1 tsp salt
	2 cups of rice

Instructions:

1. Add tomatoes, onion, lentils, and all other ingredients to the Slow cooker.
2. Put the cooker's lid on and set the cooking time to 5 hours on Low settings.
3. Serve warm.

Nutrition Facts Per Serving:

Calories 124, Total Fat 5.9g, Fiber 6g, Total Carbs 20.68g, Protein 6g

Chorizo Cashew Salad

Prep time: 16 minutes; Cook Time: 4 hours 30 minutes, Serves: 6

Ingredients:

8 oz. chorizo, chopped	2 garlic cloves
1 tsp olive oil	3 tomatoes, chopped
1 tsp cayenne pepper	1 cup lettuce, torn
1 tsp chili flakes	1 cup fresh dill
1 tsp ground black pepper	1 tsp oregano
1 tsp onion powder	3 tbsp crushed cashews

Instructions:

1. Add chorizo sausage to the Slow cooker.
2. Put the cooker's lid on and set the cooking time to 4 hours on High settings.
3. Mix chili flakes, cayenne pepper, black pepper, and onion powder in a bowl.
4. Now add tomatoes to the Slow cooker and cover again.
5. Slow cooker for another 30 minutes on High setting.
6. Stir in oregano and dill then mix well.
7. Add sliced garlic and torn lettuce to the mixture.
8. Garnish with cashews.
9. Serve.

Nutrition Facts Per Serving:

Calories 249, Total Fat 19.8g, Fiber 2g, Total Carbs 7.69g, Protein 11g

Warming Butternut Squash Soup

Prep time: 15 minutes; Cook Time: 8 hrs; Serves: 9

Ingredients:

2 lb. butternut squash, peeled and cubed	¼ tsp ground nutmeg
4 tsp minced garlic	1 tsp ground black pepper
½ cup onion, chopped	8 cups chicken stock
1 tsp salt	1 tbsp fresh parsley

Instructions:

1. Spread the butternut squash in your Slow cooker.
2. Add stock, garlic, and onion to the squash.
3. Put the cooker's lid on and set the cooking time to 8 hours on Low settings.
4. Add salt, black pepper, and nutmeg to the squash.
5. Puree the cooked squash mixture using an immersion blender until smooth.
6. Garnish with chopped parsley.
7. Enjoy.

Nutrition Facts Per Serving:

Calories 129, Total Fat 2.7g, Fiber 2g, Total Carbs 20.85g, Protein 7g

Lentil Rice Salad

Prep time: 15 minutes; Cook Time: 7 hrs; Serves: 5

Ingredients:

¼ chili pepper, chopped	1 tsp chili flakes
1 red onion, chopped	¼ tsp ground ginger
½ cup lentils	½ tsp ground thyme
¼ cup of rice	1 tsp salt
¼ tsp minced garlic	2 cups chicken stock
	3 tbsp sour cream
	1 cup lettuce, torn

Instructions:

1. Add lentils with all other ingredients to the Slow Cooker except the lettuce and sour cream.
2. Put the cooker's lid on and set the cooking time to 7 hours on High settings.
3. Stir in torn lettuce leaves and mix gently.
4. Garnish with sour cream.
5. Serve warm.

Nutrition Facts Per Serving:

Calories 84, Total Fat 3.3g, Fiber 2g, Total Carbs 11.29g, Protein 5g

Potato Parmesan Pie

Prep time: 25 minutes; Cook Time: 6 hrs; Serves: 8

Ingredients:

2 sweet potatoes, peeled and sliced	1 tsp curry powder
2 red potatoes, peeled and sliced	2 red onions, sliced
6 oz. Parmesan, shredded	1 cup flour
	1 tsp baking soda
	½ tsp apple cider vinegar
1 cup sweet corn	1 cup Greek Yogurt
1 tsp salt	3 tomatoes, sliced
1 tsp paprika	¼ tsp butter

Instructions:

1. Toss the vegetables with curry, salt, paprika, and curry powder for seasoning.
2. Coat the base of your Slow cooker with butter.
3. At first, make a layer of red potatoes in the cooker.
4. Now add layers of sweet potatoes and onion.
5. Add corns and tomatoes on top.
6. Whisk yogurt with baking soda, flour, and apple cider vinegar in a bowl.
7. Add the yogurt-flour mixture on top of the layers of veggies.
8. Lastly, drizzle the shredded cheese over it.
9. Put the cooker's lid on and set the cooking time to 6 hours on High settings.
10. Slice and serve.

Nutrition Facts Per Serving:

Calories 272, Total Fat 1.9g, Fiber 4g, Total Carbs 51.34g, Protein 14g

Allspice Beans Stew

Preparation time: 10 minutes; Cook Time: 6 hours and 20 minutes, Serves: 6

Ingredients:

1 yellow onion, chopped	½ tsp oregano, dried
1 tbsp olive oil	30 oz. canned black beans, drained
1 red bell pepper, chopped	½ tsp sugar
1 jalapeno, chopped	1 cup chicken stock
2 garlic cloves, minced	Salt and black pepper
1 tsp ginger, grated	3 cups brown rice, cooked
½ tsp cumin	2 mangoes, peeled and chopped
½ tsp allspice, ground	

Instructions:

1. Take a non-stick skillet and heat oil in it.
2. Stir in onion and sauté for 4 minutes.
3. Toss in jalapeno, ginger, and garlic, then stir cook for 3 minutes.
4. Transfer the onion-jalapeno mixture to the Slow cooker.
5. Add allspice, bell pepper, cumin, black beans, oregano, salt, black pepper, stock, and sugar.
6. Put the cooker's lid on and set the cooking time to 6 hours on Low settings.
7. Now add mangoes and rice then again cover the lid.
8. Slow cook for another 10 minutes.
9. Serve.

Nutrition Facts Per Serving:

Calories 490, Total Fat 6g, Fiber 20g, Total Carbs 80g, Protein 17g

Eggplant Mini Wraps

Prep time: 17 minutes; Cook Time: 5 hrs; Serves: 6

Ingredients:

10 oz. eggplant, sliced into rounds	chopped
	½ tsp ground black pepper
5 oz. halloumi cheese	1 tsp salt
1 tsp minced garlic	1 tsp paprika
3 oz. bacon,	1 tomato

Instructions:

1. Season the eggplant sliced with salt, paprika, and black pepper.
2. Add these slices to the Slow cooker and spread in a single layer.
3. Put the cooker's lid on and set the cooking time to 1 hour on High settings.
4. Allow the eggplant to cool then top them with tomato and cheese slices.
5. And top them with bacon and garlic.
6. Roll each slice and insert the toothpick to seal them.
7. Place these wrap in the Slow cooker carefully.
8. Put the cooker's lid on and set the cooking time to 4 hours on High settings.
9. Serve fresh.

Nutrition Facts Per Serving:

Calories 131, Total Fat 9.4g, Fiber 2g, Total Carbs 7.25g, Protein 6g

Oregano Cheese Pie

Prep time: 18 minutes; Cook Time: 3.5 hrs; Serves: 6

Ingredients:

1 tsp baking soda	cheese, shredded
1 tbsp lemon juice	5 oz. Parmesan
1 cup flour	cheese, shredded
1 cup milk	2 eggs
1 tsp salt	½ tsp oregano
5 oz. Cheddar	1/3 tsp olive oil

Instructions:

1. Sift flour with salt, oregano, baking soda and shredded cheese in a bowl.
2. Beat eggs with lemon juice and milk in a separate bowl.
3. Gradually stir in flour mixture and mix using a hand mixer until it forms a smooth dough.
4. Layer the base of Slow cooker with olive oil and spread the dough in the cooker.
5. Put the cooker's lid on and set the cooking time to 3 hours 30 minutes on High settings.
6. Serve.

Nutrition Facts Per Serving:

Calories 288, Total Fat 13.7g, Fiber 1g, Total Carbs 24.23g, Protein 16g

Minestrone Zucchini Soup

Prep time: 12 minutes; Cook Time: 4 hrs; Serves: 8

Ingredients:

2 zucchinis, chopped	garbanzo beans
3 carrots, chopped	1 lb. lentils, cooked
1 yellow onion, chopped	4 cups veggie stock
1 cup green beans, halved	28 oz. canned tomatoes, chopped
3 celery stalks, chopped	1 tsp curry powder
4 garlic cloves, minced	½ tsp garam masala
10 oz. canned	½ tsp cumin, ground
	Salt and black pepper to the taste

Instructions:

1. Add carrots, zucchinis, and all other ingredients to the Slow cooker.
2. Put the cooker's lid on and set the cooking time to 4 hours on High settings.
3. Serve warm.

Nutrition Facts Per Serving:

Calories 273, Total Fat 12g, Fiber 7g, Total Carbs 34g, Protein 10g

Quinoa Avocado Salad

Prep time: 15 minutes; Cook Time: 7 hrs; Serves: 6

Ingredients:

½ lemon, juiced	1 tsp canola oil
1 avocado, pitted, peeled and diced	½ cup fresh dill
1 red onion, diced	1 cup green peas, frozen
1 cup white quinoa	1 tsp garlic powder
1 cup of water	

Instructions:

1. Add quinoa, green peas and water to the Slow Cooker.
2. Put the cooker's lid on and set the cooking time to 7 hours on Low settings.
3. Transfer the cooked quinoa and peas to a salad bowl.
4. Stir in the remaining ingredients for the salad and toss well.
5. Serve fresh.

Nutrition Facts Per Serving:

Calories 195, Total Fat 7.7g, Fiber 6g, Total Carbs 26.77g, Protein 6g

Mediterranean Veggies

Prep time: 15 minutes; Cook Time: 7 hrs; Serves: 8

Ingredients:

1 zucchini, peeled and diced	2 tbsp olive oil
2 eggplants, peeled and diced	1 tsp ground black pepper
2 red onion, diced	1 tsp paprika
4 potatoes, peeled and diced	1 tsp salt
4 oz. asparagus, chopped	1 tbsp Mediterranean seasoning
	1 tsp minced garlic

Instructions:

1. Mix Mediterranean seasoning with olive oil, paprika, salt, garlic, and black pepper in a large bowl.
2. Toss in all the veggies to this mixture and mix well.
3. Spread all the seasoned veggies in the Slow cooker.
4. Put the cooker's lid on and set the cooking time to 7 hours on Low settings.
5. Serve warm.

Nutrition Facts Per Serving:

Calories 227, Total Fat 3.9g, Fiber 9g, Total Carbs 44.88g, Protein 6g

White Beans Luncheon

Prep time: 17 minutes; Cook Time: 4 hrs; Serves: 10

Ingredients:

2 lbs. white beans	dried
3 celery stalks, chopped	1 tsp oregano, dried
2 carrots, chopped	1 tsp thyme, dried
1 bay leaf	10 cups water
1 yellow onion, chopped	Salt and black pepper to the taste
3 garlic cloves, minced	28 oz. canned tomatoes, chopped
1 tsp rosemary,	6 cups chard, chopped

Instructions:

1. Add beans, carrots, and all other ingredients to a Slow Cooker.
2. Put the cooker's lid on and set the cooking time to 4 hours on High settings.
3. Serve warm.

Nutrition Facts Per Serving:

Calories 341, Total Fat 8, Fiber 12, Total Carbs 20, Protein 6

Lemon Spinach Orzo

Prep time: 20 minutes; Cook Time: 2 hrs 30 minutes, Serves: 5

Ingredients:

4 oz. shallot, chopped	1 tsp salt
7 oz. orzo	1 lemon
2 cup chicken stock	¼ cup cream
1 tsp paprika	2 yellow sweet pepper, chopped
1 tsp ground black pepper	1 cup baby spinach, chopped

Instructions:

1. Add shallot, chicken stock, and paprika to the Slow Cooker.
2. Drizzle salt, and black pepper in the cooker.
3. Put the cooker's lid on and set the cooking time to 30 minutes on High settings.
4. Now add spinach, sweet pepper, lemon zest and lemon juice, cream, and orzo to the shallot.
5. Put the cooker's lid on and set the cooking time to 2 hours on Low settings.
6. Serve warm.

Nutrition Facts Per Serving:

Calories 152, Total Fat 4g, Fiber 3g, Total Carbs 24.79g, Protein 7g

Quinoa Avocado Salad

Prep time: 15 minutes; Cook Time: 7 hrs; Serves: 6

Ingredients:

½ lemon, juiced	1 tsp canola oil
1 avocado, pitted, peeled and diced	½ cup fresh dill
1 red onion, diced	1 cup green peas, frozen
1 cup white quinoa	1 tsp garlic powder
1 cup of water	

Instructions:

1. Add quinoa, green peas and water to the Slow Cooker.
2. Put the cooker's lid on and set the cooking time to 7 hours on Low settings.
3. Transfer the cooked quinoa and peas to a salad bowl.
4. Stir in the remaining ingredients for the salad and toss well.
5. Serve fresh.

Nutrition Facts Per Serving:

Calories 195, Total Fat 7.7g, Fiber 6g, Total Carbs 26.77g, Protein 6g

Pumpkin Bean Chili

Prep time: 15 minutes; Cook Time: 5 hrs; Serves: 6

Ingredients:

1 cup pumpkin puree	1 jalapeno pepper, chopped
30 oz. canned kidney beans, drained	1 tbsp chili powder
	1 tbsp cocoa powder
30 oz. canned roasted tomatoes, chopped	½ tsp cinnamon powder
2 cups of water	2 tsp cumin, ground
1 cup red lentils, dried	A pinch of cloves, ground
	Salt and black pepper to the taste
1 cup yellow onion, chopped	2 tomatoes, chopped

Instructions:

1. Add pumpkin puree along with other ingredients except for tomatoes, to the Slow Cooker.
2. Put the cooker's lid on and set the cooking time to 5 hours on High settings.
3. Serve with tomatoes on top.
4. Enjoy.

Nutrition Facts Per Serving:

Calories 266, Total Fat 6g, Fiber 4g, Total Carbs 12g, Protein 4g

Broccoli Egg Pie

Prep time: 22 minutes; Cook Time: 4 hrs 25 minutes, Serves: 7

Ingredients:

7 oz. pie crust
¼ cup broccoli, chopped
1/3 cup sweet peas
¼ cup heavy cream
2 tbsp flour
3 eggs
4 oz. Romano cheese, shredded
1 tsp cilantro
1 tsp salt
¼ cup spinach, chopped
1 tomato, chopped

Instructions:

1. Cover the base of your Slow cooker with a parchment sheet.
2. Spread the pie crust in the cooker and press it with your fingertips.
3. Mix chopped broccoli, sweet peas, flour, cream, salt, and cilantro in a bowl.
4. Beat eggs and add them to the cream mixture.
5. Stir in tomatoes and spinach to this mixture.
6. Spread this broccoli filling in the crust evenly
7. Put the cooker's lid on and set the cooking time to 4 hours on High settings.
8. Drizzle cheese over the quiche and cover it again.
9. Put the cooker's lid on and set the cooking time to 25 minutes on High settings.
10. Serve warm.

Nutrition Facts Per Serving:
Calories 287, Total Fat 18.8g, Fiber 1g, Total Carbs 17.1g, Protein 11g

Green Peas Risotto

Prep time: 20 minutes; Cook Time: 3 hrs 30 minutes, Serves: 6

Ingredients:

7 oz. Parmigiano-Reggiano
2 cup chicken broth
1 tsp olive oil
1 onion, chopped
½ cup green peas
1 garlic clove, peeled and sliced
2 cups long-grain rice
¼ cup dry wine
1 tsp salt
1 tsp ground black pepper
1 carrot, chopped
1 cup beef broth

Instructions:

1. Layer a nonstick skillet with olive oil and place it over medium heat.
2. Stir in carrot and onion, then sauté for 3 minutes.
3. Transfer these veggies to the slow cooker.
4. Add rice to the remaining oil to the skillet.
5. Stir cook for 1 minute then transfers the rice to the cooker.
6. Add garlic, dry wine, green peas, black pepper, beef broth, and chicken broth.
7. Put the cooker's lid on and set the cooking time to 3 hours on Low settings.
8. Add Parmigiano-Reggiano to the risotto.
9. Put the cooker's lid on and set the cooking time to 30 minutes on Low settings.
10. Serve warm.

Nutrition Facts Per Serving:
Calories 268, Total Fat 3g, Fiber 4g, Total Carbs 53.34g, Protein 7g

Bulgur Mushroom Chili

Prep time: 15 minutes; Cook Time: 8 hrs; Serves: 4

Ingredients:

2 cups white mushrooms, sliced
¾ cup bulgur, soaked in 1 cup hot water for 15 minutes and drained
2 cups yellow onion, chopped
½ cup red bell pepper, chopped
1 cup veggie stock
2 garlic cloves, minced
1 cup strong brewed
coffee
14 oz. canned kidney beans, drained
14 oz. canned pinto beans, drained
2 tbsp sugar
2 tbsp chili powder
1 tbsp cocoa powder
1 tsp oregano, dried
2 tsp cumin, ground
1 bay leaf
Salt and black pepper to the taste

Instructions:

1. Add bulgur with all other ingredients to the base of your Slow cooker.
2. Put the cooker's lid on and set the cooking time to 12 hours on Low settings.
3. Remove the bay leaf from the chili and discard it.
4. Serve warm.

Nutrition Facts Per Serving:
Calories 351, Total Fat 4g, Fiber 6g, Total Carbs 20g, Protein 4g

Quinoa Black Bean Chili

Prep time: 15 minutes; Cook Time: 3 hrs; Serves: 4

Ingredients:

15 oz. canned black beans, drained	2 garlic cloves, minced
2 and ¼ cups veggie stock	½ chili pepper, chopped
½ cup quinoa	½ cup of corn
14 oz. canned tomatoes, chopped	2 tsp chili powder
¼ cup red bell pepper, chopped	1 small yellow onion, chopped
1 carrot, sliced	Salt and black pepper to the taste
¼ cup green bell pepper, chopped	1 tsp oregano, dried
	1 tsp cumin, ground

Instructions:

1. Add black beans and other ingredients to the Slow Cooker.
2. Put the cooker's lid on and set the cooking time to 3 hours on High settings.
3. Serve warm.

Nutrition Facts Per Serving:

Calories 291, Total Fat 7g, Fiber 4g, Total Carbs 28g, Protein 8g

Rice Stuffed Apple Cups

Prep time: 16 minutes; Cook Time: 6 hrs; Serves: 4

Ingredients:

4 red apples	7 tbsp water
1 cup white rice	1 tsp salt
3 tbsp raisins	1 tsp curry powder
1 onion, diced	4 tsp sour cream

Instructions:

1. Remove the seeds and half of the flesh from the center of the apples to make apple cups.
2. Toss onion with white rice, curry powder, salt, and raisin in a separate bowl.
3. Divide this rice-raisins mixture into the apple cups.
4. Pour water into the Slow cooker and place the stuffed cups in it.
5. Top the apples with sour cream.
6. Put the cooker's lid on and set the cooking time to 6 hours on Low settings.
7. Serve.

Nutrition Facts Per Serving:

Calories 317, Total Fat 1.3g, Fiber 7g, Total Carbs 71.09g, Protein 4g

Rice Stuffed Eggplants

Prep time: 20 minutes; Cook Time: 8 hrs; Serves: 4

Ingredients:

4 medium eggplants	1 tsp paprika
1 cup rice, half-cooked	½ cup fresh cilantro
½ cup chicken stock	3 tbsp tomato sauce
1 tsp salt	1 tsp olive oil

Instructions:

1. Slice the eggplants in half and scoop 2/3 of the flesh from the center to make boats.
2. Mix rice with tomato sauce, paprika, salt, and cilantro in a bowl.
3. Now divide this rice mixture into the eggplant boats.
4. Pour stock and oil into the Slow Cooker and place the eggplants in it.
5. Put the cooker's lid on and set the cooking time to 8 hours on Low settings.
6. Serve warm.

Nutrition Facts Per Serving:

Calories 277, Total Fat 9.1g, Fiber 24g, Total Carbs 51.92g, Protein 11g

Sweet Potato Tarragon Soup

Prep time: 15 minutes; Cook Time: 5 hrs and 20 minutes, Serves: 6

Ingredients:

5 cups veggie stock	1 tsp tarragon, dried
3 sweet potatoes, peeled and chopped	2 garlic cloves, minced
2 celery stalks, chopped	2 cups baby spinach
1 cup yellow onion, chopped	8 tbsp almonds, sliced
1 cup milk	Salt and black pepper to the taste

Instructions:

1. Add potatoes, tarragon, and all other ingredients except spinach and almonds, to the Slow Cooker.
2. Put the cooker's lid on and set the cooking time to 5 hours on High settings.
3. Blend the cooked potatoes mixture until smooth and creamy.
4. Stir in almond and spinach to the cooker.
5. Mix well and serve warm.

Nutrition Facts Per Serving:

Calories 301, Total Fat 5g, Fiber 4g, Total Carbs 12g, Protein 5g

Wild Rice Peppers

Prep time: 22 minutes; Cook Time: 7.5 hrs; Serves: 5

Ingredients:

1 tomato, chopped	1 tsp turmeric
1 cup wild rice, cooked	1 tsp curry powder
4 oz. ground chicken	1 cup chicken stock
2 oz. mushroom, sliced	2 tsp tomato paste
½ onion, sliced	1 oz. black olives
1 tsp salt	5 red sweet pepper, cut the top off and seeds removed

Instructions:

1. Toss rice with salt, turmeric, olives, tomato, onion, chicken, mushrooms, curry powder in a bowl.
2. Pour tomato paste and chicken stock into the Slow cooker.
3. Stuff the sweet peppers with chicken mixture.
4. Place the stuffed peppers in the cooker.
5. Put the cooker's lid on and set the cooking time to 7 hours 30 minutes on Low settings.
6. Serve warm with tomato gravy.

Nutrition Facts Per Serving:
Calories 232, Total Fat 3.7g, Fiber 5g, Total Carbs 41.11g, Protein 12g

Zucchini Spinach Lasagne

Prep time: 26 minutes; Cook Time: 5 hrs; Serves: 7

Ingredients:

1 lb. green zucchini, sliced	shredded
7 tbsp tomato sauce	1 onion, chopped
½ cup fresh parsley, chopped	4 tbsp ricotta cheese
1 tbsp fresh dill, chopped	5 oz. mozzarella, shredded
1 tbsp minced garlic	2 eggs
7 oz. Parmesan,	½ cup baby spinach
	1 tsp olive oil

Instructions:

1. Grease the base of your Slow cooker with olive oil.
2. Spread 3 zucchini slices at the bottom of the cooker.
3. Whisk tomato sauce with garlic, onion, dill, ricotta cheese, parsley, and spinach.
4. Stir in shredded parmesan, mozzarella, and eggs, then mix well.
5. Add a layer of this tomato-cheese mixture over the zucchini layer.
6. Again, place the zucchini slices over this tomato mixture layer.
7. Continue adding alternating layers of zucchini and tomato sauce
8. Put the cooker's lid on and set the cooking time to 5 hours on High settings.
9. Slice and serve warm.

Nutrition Facts Per Serving:
Calories 233, Total Fat 6.4, Fiber 3g, Total Carbs 20.74g, Protein 23g

Spaghetti Cheese Casserole

Prep time: 21 minutes; Cook Time: 7 hrs; Serves: 8

Ingredients:

1 lb. cottage cheese	3 tbsp white sugar
7 oz. spaghetti, cooked	1 tsp vanilla extract
5 eggs	1 tsp marjoram
1 cup heavy cream	1 tsp lemon zest
5 tbsp semolina	1 tsp butter

Instructions:

1. Start by blending cottage cheese in a blender jug for 1 minute.
2. Add eggs to the cottage cheese and blend again for 3 minutes.
3. Stir in semolina, cream, sugar, marjoram, vanilla extract, butter and lemon zest.
4. Blend again for 1 minute and keep the cheese-cream mixture aside.
5. Spread the chopped spaghetti layer in the Slow cooker.
6. Top the spaghetti with 3 tbsp with the cheese-cream mixture.
7. Add another layer of spaghetti over the mixture.
8. Continue adding alternate layers in this manner until all ingredients are used.
9. Put the cooker's lid on and set the cooking time to 7 hours on Low settings.
10. Slice and serve.

Nutrition Facts Per Serving:
Calories 242, Total Fat 13.8g, Fiber 1g, Total Carbs 17.44g, Protein 12g

Vegetable Bean Stew

Prep time: 20 minutes; Cook Time: 7 hrs; Serves: 8

Ingredients:

½ cup barley
1 cup black beans
¼ cup red beans
2 carrots, peeled and julienned
1 cup onion, chopped
1 cup tomato juice
2 potatoes, peeled

and diced
1 tsp salt
1 tsp ground black pepper
4 cups of water
4 oz. tofu
1 tsp garlic powder
1 cup fresh cilantro

Instructions:

1. Add black beans, red beans, and barley to the Slow cooker.
2. Stir in tomato juice, onion, garlic powder, black pepper, salt, and water.
3. Put the cooker's lid on and set the cooking time to 4 hours on High settings.
4. Add carrots, cilantro, and potatoes to the cooker.
5. Put the cooker's lid on and set the cooking time to 3 hours on Low settings.
6. Serve warm.

Nutrition Facts Per Serving:

Calories 207, Total Fat 3.5g, Fiber 8g, Total Carbs 37.67g, Protein 8g

Rice Cauliflower Casserole

Prep time: 16 minutes; Cook Time: 8 hrs 10 minutes, Serves: 6

Ingredients:

1 cup white rice
5 oz. broccoli, chopped
4 oz. cauliflower, chopped
1 cup Greek Yogurt
1 cup chicken stock
6 oz. Cheddar

cheese, shredded
1 tsp onion powder
2 yellow onions, chopped
1 tsp paprika
1 tbsp salt
2 cups of water
1 tsp butter

Instructions:

1. Add cauliflower, broccoli, water, chicken stock, salt, paprika, rice, and onion powder to the Slow cooker.
2. Top the broccoli-cauliflower mixture with onion slices.
3. Put the cooker's lid on and set the cooking time to 8 hours on Low settings.
4. Add butter and cheese on top of the casserole.
5. Put the cooker's lid on and set the cooking time to 10 minutes on High settings.
6. Serve warm.

Nutrition Facts Per Serving:

Calories 229, Total Fat 4.2g, Fiber 3g, Total Carbs 36.27g, Protein 12g

Chapter 4 Poultry Recipes

African Chicken Meal

Prep time: 14 minutes Cook Time: 8 hrs Serves: 6
Ingredients:

13 oz. chicken breast
1 tsp peanut oil
1 tsp ground black pepper
1 tsp oregano
1 chili pepper
1 carrot
1 tbsp tomato sauce
1 cup tomatoes, canned
1 tbsp kosher salt
¼ tsp ground cardamom
½ tsp ground anise

Instructions:

1. Rub the chicken breast with peanut oil then and sear for 1 minute per side in the skillet.
2. Transfer the chicken to the Slow cooker.
3. Add tomato sauce, salt, and all other ingredients to the cooker.
4. Put the cooker's lid on and set the cooking time to 8 hours on Low settings.
5. Serve.

Nutrition Facts Per Serving:
Calories: 131, Total Fat: 6.6g, Fiber: 1g, Total Carbs: 4.14g, Protein: 14g

Chicken with Green Onion Sauce

Prep time: 14 minutes Cook Time: 4 hrs Serves: 4
Ingredients:

2 tbsp butter, melted
4 green onions, chopped
4 chicken breast halves, skinless and
boneless
Salt and black pepper to the taste
8 oz. sour cream

Instructions:

1. Add melted butter, chicken, and all other ingredients to the Slow cooker.
2. Put the cooker's lid on and set the cooking time to 4 hours on High settings.
3. Serve warm.

Nutrition Facts Per Serving:
Calories: 200, Total Fat: 7g, Fiber: 2g, Total Carbs: 11g, Protein: 20g

Adobo Chicken Thighs

Prep time: 17 minutes Cook Time: 8 hours Serves: 6
Ingredients:

5 garlic cloves, peeled and minced
6 white onions, peeled and diced
1 tbsp fresh ginger
1 oz. bay leaf
6 medium chicken
thighs
5 tbsp soy sauce
1 tbsp apple cider vinegar
1 tsp white pepper
½ tsp sugar

Instructions:

1. Arrange the medium-sized chicken thighs in the Slow cooker.
2. Mix onion with all other ingredients in a bowl.
3. Pour this onion mixture over the chicken thighs.
4. Put the cooker's lid on and set the cooking time to 8 hours on Low settings.
5. Serve warm.

Nutrition Facts Per Serving:
Calories: 216, Total Fat: 5.6g, Fiber: 4g, Total Carbs: 18.91g, Protein: 23g

Chicken Broccoli Casserole

Prep time: 14 minutes Cook Time: 4 hrs Serves: 4
Ingredients:

3 cups cheddar cheese, grated
10 oz. broccoli florets
3 chicken breasts, skinless, boneless, cooked and cubed
1 cup mayonnaise
1 tbsp olive oil
1/3 cup chicken stock
Salt and black pepper to the taste
Juice of 1 lemon

Instructions:

1. Grease the base of your Slow cooker with olive oil.
2. Add chicken pieces, broccoli florets, and half of the cheese to the cooker.
3. Mix salt, lemon juice, black pepper, and mayo in a bowl.
4. Spread this lemon mixture over the chicken pieces and add the remaining cheese on top.
5. Put the cooker's lid on and set the cooking time to 4 hours on High settings.
6. Serve.

Nutrition Facts Per Serving:
Calories: 320, Total Fat: 5g, Fiber: 4g, Total Carbs: 16g, Protein: 25g

Apple Chicken Bombs

Prep time: 18 minutes Cook Time: 4 hrs Serves: 7
Ingredients:

2 green apples, peeled and grated	1 tsp onion powder
	1 tsp chili flakes
12 oz. ground chicken	½ tsp salt
1 tsp minced garlic	1 tsp garlic powder
1 tsp turmeric	1 tsp butter
1 egg	½ cup panko bread crumbs
1 tbsp flour	

Instructions:
1. Mix garlic, flour, turmeric, chili flakes, onion powder, garlic powder, and salt in a bowl.
2. Whisk in egg, ground chicken, and apple, then mix well.
3. Make small meatballs out of this mixture and coat them with breadcrumbs.
4. Grease the insert of the Slow cooker with butter.
5. Add the coated meatballs to the greased cooker.
6. Put the cooker's lid on and set the cooking time to 3 hours on High settings.
7. Flip the chicken balls and cook for another 1 hour on High setting.
8. Serve.

Nutrition Facts Per Serving:
Calories: 136, Total Fat: 6.1g, Fiber: 2g, Total Carbs: 10.64g, Protein: 10g

Creamy Chicken

Prep time: 14 minutes Cook Time: 4 hrs Serves: 4
Ingredients:

4 chicken thighs	1 tsp onion powder
Salt and black pepper to the taste	¼ cup sour cream
	2 tbsp sweet paprika

Instructions:
1. Add chicken, paprika, salt, black pepper, onion powder, and sour cream to the Slow cooker.
2. Put the cooker's lid on and set the cooking time to 4 hours on High settings.
3. Serve warm.

Nutrition Facts Per Serving:
Calories: 384, Total Fat: 31g, Fiber: 2g, Total Carbs: 11g, Protein: 33g

Bourbon Honey Chicken

Prep time: 11 minutes Cook Time: 5 hours Serves: 6
Ingredients:

4 oz. cup bourbon	1 tsp minced garlic
3 tbsp soy sauce	3 lb. chicken breast, skinless, boneless
1 tbsp honey	
1 tsp ketchup	7 oz. water
3 oz. yellow onion, chopped	1 tsp salt

Instructions:
1. Add water, garlic, salt, ketchup, honey, and soy sauce in a bowl then mix well.
2. Arrange the chicken breast in the Slow cooker and top it with honey mixture, bourbon, and onion.
3. Put the cooker's lid on and set the cooking time to 5 hours on High settings.
4. Mix well and serve.

Nutrition Facts Per Serving:
Calories: 461, Total Fat: 24g, Fiber: 0g, Total Carbs: 6.37g, Protein: 48g

ButteryChicken Wings

Prep time: 23 minutes Cook Time: 5 hours Serves: 6
Ingredients:

14 oz. chicken wings	melted
1 tsp onion powder	1 tbsp flour
1 tsp chili flakes	¼ cup milk
1 tsp garlic powder	1 tsp salt
1 tsp cilantro	1 tbsp heavy cream
1 tsp olive oil	1 egg, beaten
1/3 cup butter,	

Instructions:
1. Add chicken wings, butter, onion powder, salt, garlic powder, cilantro, olive oil, and chili flakes to the Slow cooker.
2. Mix well to coat the chicken wings with the spices.
3. Put the cooker's lid on and set the cooking time to 2 hours on High settings.
4. Beat egg with olive oil, milk, flour, and cream in a mixer.
5. Pour this cream mixture over the cooked chicken.
6. Put the cooker's lid on and set the cooking time to 3 hours on Low settings.
7. Serve warm.

Nutrition Facts Per Serving:
Calories: 225, Total Fat: 16.2g, Fiber: 0g, Total Carbs: 2.64g, Protein: 17g

Chicken Chickpeas

Prep time: 14 minutes Cook Time: 4 hrs
Serves: 4
Ingredients:

1 yellow onion, chopped	pepper
2 tbsp butter	15 oz. canned tomatoes, crushed
4 garlic cloves, minced	¼ cup lemon juice
1 tbsp ginger, grated	1 lb. spinach, chopped
1 and ½ tsp paprika	3 lbs. chicken drumsticks and thighs
1 tbsp cumin, ground	½ cup cilantro, chopped
1 and ½ tsp coriander, ground	½ cup chicken stock
1 tsp turmeric, ground	15 oz. canned chickpeas, drained
Salt and black pepper to the taste	½ cup heavy cream
A pinch of cayenne	

Instructions:
1. Grease the base of the Slow cooker with butter.
2. Stir in chicken, chickpeas, and all other ingredients to the Slow cooker.
3. Put the cooker's lid on and set the cooking time to 4 hours on High settings.
4. Serve warm.

Nutrition Facts Per Serving:
Calories: 300, Total Fat: 4g, Fiber: 6g, Total Carbs: 30g, Protein: 17g

Chicken Liver Stew

Prep Time: 8 minutes Cook Time: 2 hours
Serves: 8
Ingredients:

1 tsp olive oil	1 bay leaf
¾ lb. chicken livers	1 tbsp capers
1 yellow onion, chopped	1 tbsp butter
¼ cup tomato sauce	A pinch of salt and black pepper

Instructions:
1. Add chicken lives, capers, and all other ingredients to the Slow cooker.
2. Put the cooker's lid on and set the cooking time to 1.5 hours on High settings.
3. Serve.

Nutrition Facts Per Serving:
Calories: 152, Total Fat: 4g, Fiber: 2g, Total Carbs: 5g, Protein: 7g

Chicken with Mushroom Sauce

Prep time: 14 minutes Cook Time: 4 hrs
Serves: 4
Ingredients:

8 chicken thighs	minced
Salt and black pepper to the taste	10 oz. cremini mushrooms halved
1 yellow onion, chopped	2 cups white chardonnay wine
1 tbsp olive oil	1 cup whipping cream
4 bacon strips, cooked and chopped	Handful parsley, chopped
4 garlic cloves,	

Instructions:
1. Add oil, chicken pieces, black pepper, and salt to a pan.
2. Stir cook the chicken until it turns golden brown.
3. Transfer the chicken to the Slow cooker and the remaining ingredients.
4. Put the cooker's lid on and set the cooking time to 4 hours on High settings.
5. Serve warm.

Nutrition Facts Per Serving:
Calories: 340, Total Fat: 10g, Fiber: 7g, Total Carbs: 14g, Protein: 24g

Chicken Pumpkin Stew

Prep time: 23 minutes Cook Time: 10 hours Serves: 8
Ingredients:

1 lb. pumpkin, diced	1 tbsp minced garlic
1 lb. chicken fillet, chopped	1 tsp ground black pepper
2 carrot, chopped	3 apples, chopped
1 yellow onion, chopped	1 cup of water
1 cup chicken stock	1 tbsp sugar
½ cup tomato sauce	½ tsp cinnamon

Instructions:
1. Toss pumpkin cubes with sugar and cinnamon in the Slow cooker.
2. Stir in chicken, garlic, tomato sauce, onion, carrot, water, and black pepper.
3. Put the cooker's lid on and set the cooking time to 10 hours on Low settings.
4. Serve warm.

Nutrition Facts Per Serving:
Calories: 560, Total Fat: 36.5g, Fiber: 8g, Total Carbs: 40.01g, Protein: 25g

Saucy Chicken

Prep Time: 14 minutes Cook Time: 5 hours Serves: 4
Ingredients:

1 chicken, cut into medium pieces
Salt and black pepper to the taste
1 tbsp olive oil
½ tsp sweet paprika
¼ cup white wine
½ tsp marjoram,
dried
¼ cup chicken stock
2 tbsp white vinegar
¼ cup apricot preserves
1 and ½ tsp ginger, grated
2 tbsp honey

Instructions:
1. Add chicken, marjoram, and all other ingredients to the Slow cooker.
2. Put the cooker's lid on and set the cooking time to 5 hours on Low settings.
3. Serve warm.

Nutrition Facts Per Serving:
Calories: 230, Total Fat: 3g, Fiber: 5g, Total Carbs: 12g, Protein: 22g

Chicken with Lentils

Prep time: 14 minutes Cook Time: 4 hrs Serves: 4
Ingredients:

8 oz. bacon, cooked and chopped
2 tbsp olive oil
1 cup yellow onion, chopped
8 oz. lentils, dried
2 carrots, chopped
12 parsley springs, chopped
Salt and black pepper to the taste
2 bay leaves
2 ½ lbs. of chicken pieces
1-quart chicken stock
2 tsp sherry vinegar

Instructions:
1. Add oil, onions, bacon, lentils, carrots, parsley, stock, bay leaves, chicken pieces, salt, and black pepper to the Slow cooker.
2. Put the cooker's lid on and set the cooking time to 4 hours on High settings.
3. Transfer the slow-cooked chicken to a cutting board and remove the meat from the bones.
4. Shred the meat and return to the Slow cooker
5. Mix well and vinegar.
6. Serve warm.

Nutrition Facts Per Serving:
Calories: 321, Total Fat: 3g, Fiber: 12g, Total Carbs: 29g, Protein: 16g

Chicken Ricotta Meatloaf

Prep Time: 14 minutes Cook Time: 4 hrs 20 minutes Serves: 8
Ingredients:

1 cup marinara sauce
2-lb. chicken meat, ground
2 tbsp parsley, chopped
4 garlic cloves,
minced
2 tsp onion powder
2 tsp Italian seasoning
Salt and black pepper to the taste
Cooking spray

For the filling:

½ cup ricotta cheese
1 cup parmesan, grated
1 cup mozzarella, shredded
2 tsp chives,
chopped
2 tbsp parsley, chopped
1 garlic clove, minced

Instructions:
1. Add chicken, half of the marinara sauce, Italian seasoning, black pepper, salt, garlic cloves, onion powder, and 2 tbsp parsley to the Slow cooker.
2. Whisk ricotta, half of the parmesan, chives, half of the mozzarella, 1 garlic clove, black pepper, salt, and 2 tbsp parsley in a bowl, then mix well.
3. Grease the base of Slow cooker with cooking spray and place half of the chicken to the cooker.
4. Top it with cheese filling, and remaining meat mixture.
5. Put the cooker's lid on and set the cooking time to 4 hours on High settings.
6. Add the remaining marinara sauce, parmesan, and mozzarella to the cooker.
7. Put the cooker's lid on and set the cooking time to 20 minutes on High settings.
8. Serve.

Nutrition Facts Per Serving:
Calories: 273, Total Fat: 14g, Fiber: 1g, Total Carbs: 14g, Protein: 28g

Chicken with Tomatillos

Preparation time: 10 minutes Cook Time: 4 hrs Serves: 6
Ingredients:

1 lb. chicken thighs, skinless and boneless
2 tbsp olive oil
1 yellow onion, chopped
1 garlic clove, minced
4 oz. canned green chilies, chopped
Handful cilantro, chopped
Salt and black pepper to the taste
15 oz. canned tomatillos, chopped
5 oz. canned garbanzo beans, drained
15 oz. rice, cooked
5 oz. tomatoes, chopped
15 oz. cheddar cheese, grated
4 oz. black olives, pitted and chopped

Instructions:

1. Toss onion, chicken, garlic, chilies, salt, black pepper, tomatillos, and cilantro to the Slow cooker.
2. Put the cooker's lid on and set the cooking time to 3 hours on High settings.
3. Shred the chicken and return to the cooker.
4. Stir in beans, cheese, rice, olives, and tomatoes.
5. Put the cooker's lid on and set the cooking time to 1 hour on High settings.
6. Serve.

Nutrition Facts Per Serving:
Calories: 300, Total Fat: 11g, Fiber: 3g, Total Carbs: 14g, Protein: 30g

Chicken Potato Casserole

Prep time: 23 minutes Cook Time: 10 hours Serves: 6
Ingredients:

10 oz. ground chicken
4 large potatoes, peeled and sliced
2 egg, beaten
1 large onion, diced
1 tsp ground black pepper
1 cup heavy cream
8 oz. Parmesan, shredded
1 tsp paprika
1 tsp cilantro
½ tsp nutmeg
1 tsp butter
1 carrot, grated

Instructions:

1. Grease the base of the Slow cooker with butter.
2. Spread the ground chicken in the cooker and top it with potatoes and onion.
3. Whisk egg with cream, cilantro, nutmeg, paprika, and black pepper in a bowl.
4. Pour this cream-egg mixture over the veggies and top it with grated carrot and ½ of the shredded cheese.
5. Put the cooker's lid on and set the cooking time to 10 hours on Low settings.
6. Garnish with remaining cheese.
7. Serve.

Nutrition Facts Per Serving:
Calories: 534, Total Fat: 17.4g, Fiber: 6g, Total Carbs: 63.33g, Protein: 32g

Chicken Tomato Salad

Prep time: 55 minutes Cook Time: 3 hours Serves: 2
Ingredients:

1 chicken breast, skinless and boneless
1 cup chicken stock
2 cups of water
Salt and black pepper to the taste
1 tbsp mustard
3 garlic cloves, minced
1 tbsp balsamic vinegar
1 tbsp honey
3 tbsp olive oil
Mixed salad greens
Handful cherry tomatoes halved

Instructions:

1. Mix water with a pinch of salt in a bowl and chicken.
2. Soak the chicken and refrigerate for 45 minutes.
3. Drain the chicken and transfer to a slow cooker.
4. Along with stock, black pepper, and salt.
5. Put the cooker's lid on and set the cooking time to 3 hours on High settings.
6. Transfer the slow-cooked chicken to a cutting board then cut into strips.
7. Mix garlic, salt, black pepper, honey, mustard, olive oil, and vinegar in a bowl.
8. Toss in salad greens, tomatoes, and chicken strips.
9. Mix well and serve.

Nutrition Facts Per Serving:
Calories: 200, Total Fat: 4g, Fiber: 6g, Total Carbs: 15g, Protein: 12g

Chicken Vegetable Pot Pie

Prep Time: 23 minutes Cook Time: 8 hours Serves: 8

Ingredients:

8 oz. biscuit dough	1 carrot, chopped
1 cup sweet corn, frozen	1 tsp onion powder
1 cup green peas	1 tbsp ground paprika
11 oz. chicken fillets, chopped	1 tsp cilantro
1 cup white onion, chopped	½ tsp oregano
8 oz. chicken creamy soup, canned	1 tsp turmeric
	1 tbsp salt
	1 tsp butter
	1 cup of water

Instructions:

1. Mix the chicken pieces with onion powder, oregano, cilantro, turmeric, and paprika in a Slow cooker.
2. Stir in green peas, salt, carrot, onion, and sweet corn.
3. Pour in chicken soup, water, and butter.
4. Put the cooker's lid on and set the cooking time to 5 hours on High settings.
5. Spread the biscuit dough and place it over the cooked chicken.
6. Put the cooker's lid on and set the cooking time to hours on High settings.
7. Slice and serve.

Nutrition Facts Per Serving:
Calories: 283, Total Fat: 10.9g, Fiber: 4g, Total Carbs: 38.42g, Protein: 10g

Citrus Glazed Chicken

Prep Time: 14 minutes Cook Time: 4 hrs Serves: 4

Ingredients:

2 lbs. chicken thighs, skinless, boneless and cut into pieces	¼ cup of orange juice
Salt and black pepper to the taste	2 tsp sugar
3 tbsp olive oil	1 tbsp orange zest
¼ cup flour	¼ tsp sesame seeds
For the sauce:	2 tbsp scallions, chopped
2 tbsp fish sauce	½ tsp coriander, ground
1 and ½ tsp orange extract	1 cup of water
1 tbsp ginger, grated	¼ tsp red pepper flakes
	2 tbsp soy sauce

Instructions:

1. Whisk flour with black pepper, salt, and chicken pieces in a bowl to coat well.
2. Add chicken to a pan greased with oil and sear it over medium heat until golden brown.
3. Transfer the chicken to the Slow cooker.
4. Blend orange juice, fish sauce, soy sauce, ginger, water, coriander, orange extract, and stevia in a blender jug.
5. Pour this fish sauce mixture over the chicken and top it with orange zest, scallions, sesame seeds, and pepper flakes.
6. Put the cooker's lid on and set the cooking time to 4 hours on High settings.
7. Serve warm.

Nutrition Facts Per Serving:
Calories: 423, Total Fat: 20g, Fiber: 5g, Total Carbs: 12g, Protein: 45g

Chocolaty Chicken Mash

Prep time: 17 minutes Cook Time: 3 hours 10 minutes Serves: 7

Ingredients:

4 oz. milk chocolate	1 tsp hot chili sauce
½ cup heavy cream	1 cup of water
14 oz. ground chicken	1 tbsp sesame oil
1 tsp salt	1 tsp cumin seeds
1 tbsp tomato sauce	¼ cup baby carrot, chopped

Instructions:

1. Mix the ground chicken with tomato sauce, salt, water, cumin seeds, sesame oil, and hot chili sauce in a bowl.
2. Spread the chicken in the Slow cooker and top with baby carrots.
3. Put the cooker's lid on and set the cooking time to 3 hours on High settings.
4. Stir the chicken after 1 hour of cooking.
5. Melt the milk chocolate in a bowl by heating in the microwave.
6. Stir in cream and mix well, then add this mixture to the Slow cooker.
7. Mix it with ground chicken.
8. Put the cooker's lid on and set the cooking time to 10 minutes on High settings.
9. Serve.

Nutrition Facts Per Serving:
Calories: 219, Total Fat: 14.6g, Fiber: 1g, Total Carbs: 10.56g, Protein: 11g

Chicken Mushrooms Stroganoff

Prep time: 16 minutes Cook Time: 4 hrs
Serves: 4
Ingredients:

2 garlic cloves, minced
8 oz. mushrooms, roughly chopped
¼ tsp celery seeds
1 yellow onion, chopped
1 cup chicken stock
1 cup of coconut milk
1 lb. chicken

breasts, cut into pieces
1 and ½ tsp thyme, dried
2 tbsp parsley, chopped
Salt and black pepper to the tasted
Already cooked pasta for serving

Instructions:

1. Add chicken, salt, onion, black pepper, garlic, coconut milk, stock, thyme, half of the parsley, celery seeds, and mushrooms to the Slow cooker.
2. Put the cooker's lid on and set the cooking time to 4 hours on High settings.
3. Stir in pasta and parsley.
4. Serve.

Nutrition Facts Per Serving:
Calories: 364, Total Fat: 22g, Fiber: 2g, Total Carbs: 14g, Protein: 24g

Cola Marinated Chicken

Prep time: 27 minutes Cook Time: 5 hours Serves: 6
Ingredients:

2 cup coca-cola
1 tbsp minced garlic
1 tsp salt
1 onion, wedged
16 oz. chicken, diced
1 tsp ground black

pepper
1 tsp olive oil
½ cup fresh dill, chopped
2 tsp oregano

Instructions:

1. Add coca-cola to a bowl and soak chicken for 15 minutes, then drain it.
2. Mix salt with garlic, olive oil, oregano, and black pepper in a small bowl.
3. Strain the chicken and reserve half of the coco-cola.
4. Transfer the chicken, coca-cola, and all other ingredients to the Slow cooker.
5. Put the cooker's lid on and set the cooking time to 5 hours on High settings.
6. Serve warm.

Nutrition Facts Per Serving:
Calories: 154, Total Fat: 7g, Fiber: 1g, Total Carbs: 9.56g, Protein: 14g

Spinach and Artichoke Chicken

Prep time: 14 minutes Cook Time: 4 hrs
Serves: 4
Ingredients:

4 oz. cream cheese
4 chicken breasts, boneless and skinless
10 oz. canned artichoke hearts, chopped
10 oz. spinach

½ cup parmesan, grated
1 tbsp dried onion
1 tbsp garlic, dried
Salt and black pepper to the taste
4 oz. mozzarella, shredded

Instructions:

1. Add chicken, artichokes, and all other ingredients to the Slow cooker.
2. Put the cooker's lid on and set the cooking time to 4 hours on High settings.
3. Serve warm.

Nutrition Facts Per Serving:
Calories: 450, Total Fat: 23g, Fiber: 1g, Total Carbs: 14g, Protein: 39g

Chicken Curry

Prep time: 17 minutes Cook Time: 9 hours Serves: 9
Ingredients:

22 oz. chicken thighs
2 tbsp curry
1 tbsp curry paste
1 cup baby carrot
2 red onions
1 tsp fresh rosemary
1 tsp ground black

pepper
1 tsp salt
3 tbsp tomato juice
1 tsp butter
1 tsp minced garlic
2 cups beef stock
1 cup of water

Instructions:

1. Arrange the chicken thighs in the Slow cooker.
2. Mix curry, curry paste, water, and carrot in a bowl.
3. Pour this curry mixture and beef stock over the chicken.
4. Add butter, tomato juice, garlic, salt, black pepper, and rosemary to the cooker.
5. Put the cooker's lid on and set the cooking time to 9 hours on Low settings.
6. Mix well and serve.

Nutrition Facts Per Serving:
Calories: 130, Total Fat: 6.4g, Fiber: 2g, Total Carbs: 4.98g, Protein: 14g

Romano Chicken Thighs

Prep time: 14 minutes Cook Time: 4 hrs Serves: 4

Ingredients:

6 chicken things, boneless and skinless and cut into medium chunks
Salt and black pepper to the taste
½ cup white flour
2 tbsp olive oil
10 oz. tomato sauce
1 tsp white wine vinegar
4 oz. mushrooms, sliced
1 tbsp sugar
1 tbsp oregano, dried
1 tsp garlic, minced
1 tsp basil, dried
1 yellow onion, chopped
1 cup Romano cheese, grated

Instructions:

1. Grease the base of the Slow cooker with oil.
2. Stir in chicken pieces and all other ingredients to the Slow cooker.
3. Put the cooker's lid on and set the cooking time to 4 hours on High settings.
4. Serve warm.

Nutrition Facts Per Serving:

Calories: 430, Total Fat: 12g, Fiber: 6g, Total Carbs: 25g, Protein: 60g

Chicken Dumplings Medley

Prep Time: 27 minutes Cook Time: 6 hours Serves: 6

Ingredients:

8 oz. chicken fillets
1 tbsp salt
1 cup flour
1 onion, chopped
1 tsp olive oil
1 pinch salt
¼ cup milk
1 egg
1 tsp ground black pepper
1 cup of water
1 carrot, sliced
1 tsp ground cinnamon
1 tbsp butter

Instructions:

1. Whisk egg with salt, flour, and milk in a bowl until smooth.
2. Shape the dough into a medium-sized log and cut it into small pieces.
3. Grease the base of the Slow cooker with butter and add chicken fillets.
4. Add cinnamon, black pepper, 1 tbsp salt, and water to the cooker.
5. Put the cooker's lid on and set the cooking time to 3 hours on High settings.
6. Add olive oil, carrot, and onion to a pan and saute for 4 minutes.
7. Transfer the veggies and dough pieces to the Slow cooker.
8. Put the cooker's lid on and set the cooking time to 3.5 hours on High settings.
9. Serve.

Nutrition Facts Per Serving:

Calories: 221, Total Fat: 8.7g, Fiber: 2g, Total Carbs: 28.83g, Protein: 7g

Lime Dipped Chicken Drumsticks

Prep time: 14 minutes Cook Time: 3.5 hours Serves: 7

Ingredients:

3 oz. garlic, peeled and minced
17 oz. chicken drumsticks
1 lime, finely
chopped
1 tsp lemon zest
1 tsp kosher salt
1 tsp coriander
1 tsp butter

Instructions:

1. Add butter, chicken and all other ingredients to the Slow cooker.
2. Put the cooker's lid on and set the cooking time to 3.5 hours on High settings.
3. Serve warm.

Nutrition Facts Per Serving:

Calories: 136, Total Fat: 7g, Fiber: 0g, Total Carbs: 4.68g, Protein: 13g

Sauce Goose

Prep Time: 14 minutes Cook Time: 5 hours Serves: 4

Ingredients:

1 goose breast half, skinless, boneless and cut into thin slices
¼ cup olive oil
1 sweet onion,
chopped
2 tsp garlic, chopped
Salt and black pepper to the taste
¼ cup sweet chili sauce

Instructions:

1. Add goose, oil and all other ingredients to the Slow cooker.
2. Put the cooker's lid on and set the cooking time to 5 hours on Low settings.
3. Serve warm.

Nutrition Facts Per Serving:

Calories: 192, Total Fat: 4g, Fiber: 8g, Total Carbs: 12g, Protein: 22g

Coca Cola Dipped Chicken

Prep time: 14 minutes Cook Time: 4 hrs Serves: 4
Ingredients:

1 yellow onion, minced
4 chicken drumsticks
1 tbsp balsamic vinegar
1 chili pepper, chopped
15 oz. coca cola
Salt and black pepper to the taste
2 tbsp olive oil

Instructions:

1. Add chicken to a pan greased with oil and sear it until golden brown from both the sides.
2. Transfer the chicken to the Slow cooker.
3. Stir in coca-cola, chili, onion, vinegar, black pepper, and salt to the cooker.
4. Put the cooker's lid on and set the cooking time to 4 hours on High settings.
5. Serve warm.

Nutrition Facts Per Serving:
Calories: 372, Total Fat: 14g, Fiber: 3g, Total Carbs: 20g, Protein: 15g

Creamy Bacon Chicken

Prep time: 17 minutes Cook Time: 12 hours Serves: 4
Ingredients:

5 oz. bacon, cooked
8 oz. chicken breast
1 garlic clove, peeled and chopped
½ carrot, peeled and chopped
1 cup heavy cream
1 egg, beaten
1 tbsp paprika
1 tsp curry
3 tbsp chives, chopped
3 oz. scallions, chopped

Instructions:

1. Carve a cut in the chicken breasts from sideways.
2. Stuff the chicken with garlic clove and carrot.
3. Place the stuffed chicken in the Slow cooker.
4. Mix egg with cream, paprika, curry, scallions, and paprika in a bowl.
5. Pour this curry mixture over the chicken and top it with chives and bacon.
6. Add the remaining ingredients to the cooker.
7. Put the cooker's lid on and set the cooking time to 12 hours on Low settings.

8. Shred the slow-cooked chicken and return to the cooker.
9. Mix well and serve.

Nutrition Facts Per Serving:
Calories: 362, Total Fat: 29.6g, Fiber: 3g, Total Carbs: 7.17g, Protein: 19g

Cuban Chicken

Prep time: 14 minutes Cook Time: 4 hrs Serves: 4
Ingredients:

4 gold potatoes, cut into medium chunks
1 yellow onion, thinly sliced
4 big tomatoes, cut into medium chunks
1 chicken, cut into 8 pieces
Salt and black pepper to the taste
2 bay leaves
Salt and black pepper to the taste

Instructions:

1. Add potatoes, chicken and all other ingredients to the Slow cooker.
2. Put the cooker's lid on and set the cooking time to 4 hours on High settings.
3. Discard the bay leaves and mix well.
4. Serve warm.

Nutrition Facts Per Serving:
Calories: 263, Total Fat: 2g, Fiber: 1g, Total Carbs: 27g, Protein: 14g

Chicken Mole

Prep time: 16 minutes Cook Time: 5 hrs Serves: 6
Ingredients:

3 oz. yellow onion, peeled and grated
4 tbsp raisins
1 tbsp garlic, sliced
1 tbsp chipotle, chopped
1 tbsp adobo sauce
7 tbsp tomatoes, crushed
½ tbsp white sugar
1 tbsp cocoa powder
1 tsp salt
1 tsp ground coriander
½ tsp turmeric
15 oz. chicken breast, boneless

Instructions:

1. Add chicken, tomatoes, and all other ingredients to the Slow cooker.
2. Put the cooker's lid on and set the cooking time to 5 hours on High settings.
3. Serve warm.

Nutrition Facts Per Serving:
Calories: 159, Total Fat: 8.4g, Fiber: 1g, Total Carbs: 5.16g, Protein: 16g

Duck with Potatoes

Prep time: 14 minutes Cook Time: 6 hrs Serves: 4

Ingredients:

1 duck, cut into small chunks	4 garlic cloves, minced
Salt and black pepper to the taste	4 tbsp sugar
1 potato, cut into cubes	4 tbsp soy sauce
	2 green onions, chopped
1-inch ginger root, sliced	4 tbsp sherry wine
	¼ cup of water

Instructions:

1. Add duck pieces, garlic and all other ingredients to the Slow cooker.
2. Put the cooker's lid on and set the cooking time to 6 hours on Low settings.
3. Serve warm.

Nutrition Facts Per Serving:

Calories: 245, Total Fat: 12g, Fiber: 1g, Total Carbs: 6g, Protein: 16g

Saucy Chicken Drumsticks

Prep time: 16 minutes Cook Time: 4 hrs Serves: 4

Ingredients:

1 bunch lemongrass, bottom removed and trimmed	drumsticks
	1 cup of coconut milk
1-inch piece ginger root, chopped	Salt and black pepper to the taste
4 garlic cloves, minced	1 tsp butter, melted
2 tbsp fish sauce	¼ cup cilantro, chopped
3 tbsp soy sauce	1 yellow onion, chopped
1 tsp Chinese five-spice	
10 chicken	1 tbsp lime juice

Instructions:

1. Blend lemongrass with five spices, fish sauce, coconut milk, soy sauce, garlic, and ginger in a blender.
2. Add chicken, butter, black pepper, salt, onion, lemongrass mixture, and lime juice.
3. Put the cooker's lid on and set the cooking time to 4 hours on High settings.
4. Garnish with cilantro.
5. Enjoy.

Nutrition Facts Per Serving:

Calories: 400, Total Fat: 12g, Fiber: 3g, Total Carbs: 6g, Protein: 20g

Ginger Turkey

Prep time: 17 minutes Cook Time: 5 hours Serves: 4

Ingredients:

3 oz. fresh ginger, peeled and grated	1 tsp thyme
	½ tsp ground celery
9 oz. turkey fillet	1 tsp salt
1 tbsp maple syrup	1 tsp sesame oil
1 tsp brown sugar	1 tsp ground ginger
¼ cup thyme leaves	¼ cup heavy cream

Instructions:

1. Blend heavy cream with the ginger ground, sesame oil, salt, ground celery, thyme, and thyme leaves in a blender.
2. Add maple syrup and brown sugar then mix well.
3. Rub the turkey with ginger and place it in the Slow cooker.
4. Pour the cream-thyme mixture over this turkey.
5. Put the cooker's lid on and set the cooking time to 5 hours on High settings.
6. Slice and serve

Nutrition Facts Per Serving:

Calories: 390, Total Fat: 33.6g, Fiber: 1g, Total Carbs: 8.96g, Protein: 13g

Goose with Mushroom Cream

Prep time: 14 minutes Cook Time: 5 hours Serves: 5

Ingredients:

1 goose breast, Total Fat: trimmed off and cut into pieces	3 and ½ cups of water
1 goose leg, skinless	2 tsp garlic, minced
1 goose thigh, skinless	1 yellow onion, chopped
Salt and black pepper to the taste	12 oz. canned mushroom cream

Instructions:

1. Add good breast, leg, thigh, and all other ingredients to the Slow cooker.
2. Put the cooker's lid on and set the cooking time to 5 hours on Low settings.
3. Serve warm.

Nutrition Facts Per Serving:

Calories: 272, Total Fat: 4g, Fiber: 7g, Total Carbs: 16g, Protein: 22g

Fennel Chicken

Prep time: 16 minutes Cook Time: 9 hours Serves: 8
Ingredients:

8 oz. fennel bulb, chopped	pepper
1 tbsp kosher salt	¼ tsp curry powder
1 large white onion, peeled and diced	17 oz. chicken drumsticks
1 cup cherry tomatoes, halved	1 oz. fennels seeds
½ cup white wine	1 tbsp smoked paprika
1 tsp ground black	1 cup of water
	1 cup chicken stock

Instructions:
1. Mix white wine with black pepper, fennel seeds, smoked paprika, and curry powder in the bowl.
2. Add chicken drumsticks, onions, and fennel bulbs to the Slow cooker.
3. Pour in white wine mixture, chicken stock, and water.
4. Put the cooker's lid on and set the cooking time to 9 hours on Low settings.
5. Serve warm.

Nutrition Facts Per Serving:
Calories: 143, Total Fat: 6.6g, Fiber: 3g, Total Carbs: 8.15g, Protein: 13g

Duck Chili

Prep Time: 14 minutes Cook Time: 7 Serves: 4
Ingredients:

1 lb. northern beans, soaked and rinsed	trimmed off
	Salt and black pepper to the taste
1 yellow onion, cut into half	2 cloves
1 garlic heat, top	1 bay leaf
	6 cups of water

For the duck:

1 lb. duck, ground	chilies and their juice
1 tbsp vegetable oil	
1 yellow onion, minced	1 tsp brown sugar
2 carrots, chopped	15 oz. canned tomatoes and their juices, chopped
Salt and black pepper to the taste	Handful cilantro, chopped
4 oz. canned green	

Instructions:
1. Add beans, onion, garlic, water, salt, and bay leaf to the Slow cooker.
2. Put the cooker's lid on and set the cooking time to 4 hours on High settings.
3. Drain the garlic beans and transfer them to the serving plate.
4. Add oil, carrots, duck, and all other ingredients to the Slow cooker.
5. Put the cooker's lid on and set the cooking time to 3 hours on High settings.
6. Serve the duck with beans.
7. Enjoy.

Nutrition Facts Per Serving:
Calories: 283, Total Fat: 15g, Fiber: 2g, Total Carbs: 16g, Protein: 22g

Turkey Cranberry Stew

Prep time: 15 minutes; Cook Time: 8 hrs; Serves: 4
Ingredients:

3 lbs. turkey breast, skinless and boneless	1 cup of sugar
	1 tsp ginger, grated
1 cup cranberries, chopped	½ tsp nutmeg, ground
2 sweet potatoes, chopped	1 tsp cinnamon powder
½ cup raisins	½ cup veggie stock
½ cup walnuts, chopped	1 tsp poultry seasoning
1 sweet onion, chopped	Salt and black pepper to the taste
2 tbsp lemon juice	3 tbsp olive oil

Instructions:
1. Take oil in a nonstick pan and place it over medium-high heat.
2. Stir in walnuts, onion, raisins, cranberries, sugar, lemon juice, cinnamon, nutmeg, ginger, black pepper, and stock.
3. Cook this mixture to a simmer on medium heat.
4. Now place the turkey and sweet potatoes in the Slow cooker.
5. Top them with poultry seasoning and cranberries mixture.
6. Put the cooker's lid on and set the cooking time to 8 hours on Low settings.
7. Slice the slow-cooked turkey and serve with sweet potato-cranberry sauce.
8. Enjoy.

Nutrition Facts Per Serving:
Calories 264, Total Fat 4g, Fiber 6g, Total Carbs 8g, Protein 15g

Hawaiian Pineapple Chicken

Prep time: 17 minutes Cook Time: 8 hours Serves: 8

Ingredients:

10 oz. pineapple, cut into chunks	1 cup bell pepper, chopped
14 oz. chicken breast, diced	1 tsp minced garlic
5 tbsp barbecue sauce	4 tbsp chicken stock
	1 tsp sugar
	1 tsp ground paprika

Instructions:

1. Add chicken, pineapples, and all other ingredients to the Slow cooker.
2. Put the cooker's lid on and set the cooking time to 8 hours on Low settings.
3. Serve warm.

Nutrition Facts Per Serving:

Calories: 132, Total Fat: 4.8g, Fiber: 1g, Total Carbs: 11.28g, Protein: 11g

Lemon Sauce Dipped Chicken

Prep Time: 27 minutes Cook Time: 7 hours Serves: 11

Ingredients:

23 oz. chicken breast, boneless, diced	1 tbsp flour
	1 tsp ground black pepper
1 lemon, juiced and zest	1 tsp minced garlic
1 tbsp cornstarch	1 tbsp mustard
1 tsp salt	3 tbsp lemon juice
1 cup heavy cream	1 red onion, chopped

Instructions:

1. Mix lemon juice with salt, garlic, and black pepper in a bowl.
2. Toss in chicken bread, and onion then mix well. Marinate this chicken for 15 minutes.
3. Transfer the marinated chicken along with lemon marinade to the Slow cooker.
4. Put the cooker's lid on and set the cooking time to 3 hours on High settings.
5. Whisk cream with flour, cornstarch, and mustard in a bowl.
6. Cook this cream mixture in a skillet for 10 minutes then transfer to the Slow cooker.
7. Put the cooker's lid on and set the cooking time to 4 hours on Low settings.
8. Serve warm.

Nutrition Facts Per Serving:

Calories: 154, Total Fat: 9.6g, Fiber: 0g, Total Carbs: 3.59g, Protein: 13g

Horseradish Mixed Chicken

Prep time: 23 minutes Cook Time: 11 hours Serves: 9

Ingredients:

3 tbsp horseradish, grated	1/3 cup beef broth
1 tbsp mustard	6 oz. carrot, grated
1 tsp salt	1 zucchini, sliced
1 tbsp mayonnaise	1 lb. chicken breast
3 tbsp sour cream	1 tsp olive oil

Instructions:

1. Add chicken, zucchini, and all other ingredients to the Slow cooker.
2. Put the cooker's lid on and set the cooking time to 11 hours on Low settings.
3. Serve warm.

Nutrition Facts Per Serving:

Calories: 203, Total Fat: 11.3g, Fiber: 2g, Total Carbs: 4.67g, Protein: 20g

Pomegranate Turkey

Prep time: 27 minutes Cook Time: 4.5 hours Serves: 4

Ingredients:

1 lb. turkey fillet, diced	1 tsp garlic powder
½ cup pomegranate juice	¼ cup onion, grated
	1 tsp butter, melted
2 oz. pomegranate juice	3 tbsp brown sugar
	1 tsp salt
1 tbsp soy sauce	1 tsp ground white pepper
1 tbsp potato starch	

Instructions:

1. Mix turkey with garlic powder, salt, onion, white pepper in a bowl and leave it for 10 minutes.
2. Transfer the turkey to the Slow cooker along with butter and pomegranate juice.
3. Put the cooker's lid on and set the cooking time to 3 hours on High settings.
4. Mix potato starch with soy sauce, 2 oz. pomegranate juice in a bowl.
5. Pour this mixture into the Slow cooker.
6. Put the cooker's lid on and set the cooking time to 1.5 hours on High settings.
7. Serve warm.

Nutrition Facts Per Serving:

Calories: 676, Total Fat: 52.5g, Fiber: 3g, Total Carbs: 26.15g, Protein: 24g

Continental Beef Chicken

Prep time: 17 minutes Cook Time: 9 hours Servings :5

Ingredients:

6 oz. dried beef	7 oz. sour cream
12 oz. chicken breast, diced	1 can onion soup
	3 tbsp flour

Instructions:

1. Spread half of the dried beef in the Slow cooker.
2. Top it with chicken breast, sour cream, onion soup, and flour.
3. Spread the remaining dried beef on top.
4. Put the cooker's lid on and set the cooking time to 9 hours on Low settings.
5. Serve warm.

Nutrition Facts Per Serving:
Calories: 285, Total Fat: 15.1g, Fiber: 1g, Total Carbs: 12.56g, Protein: 24g

Sesame Chicken Wings

Prep time: 27 minutes Cook Time: 4 hrs Serves: 4

Ingredients:

1 lb. chicken wings	¼ cup milk
½ cup fresh parsley, chopped	1 tbsp sugar
1 tsp salt	5 tbsp honey
1 tsp ground black pepper	2 tbsp sesame seeds
	¼ cup chicken stock
	1 tsp soy sauce

Instructions:

1. Rub the chicken wings with salt and black pepper.
2. Add this chicken to the Slow cooker along with chicken stock and parsley.
3. Put the cooker's lid on and set the cooking time to 4 hours on High settings.
4. Mix milk with honey, sugar, and sesame seeds in a bowl.
5. Transfer the chicken to a baking tray.
6. Pour the sesame mixture over the chicken wings.
7. Bake them for 10 minutes at 350 degrees F in a preheated oven.
8. Enjoy.

Nutrition Facts Per Serving:
Calories: 282, Total Fat: 7.5g, Fiber: 1g, Total Carbs: 27.22g, Protein: 27g

Latin Chicken

Prep time: 17 minutes Cook Time: 5 hours Serves: 6

Ingredients:

6 oz. sweet pepper, julienned	1 tsp garlic powder
1 tsp salt	½ cup salsa verde
1 tsp chili flakes	¼ cup sweet corn, frozen
21 oz. chicken thighs	2 cups of water
1 onion, cut into petals	1 peach, pitted, chopped
	1 tsp canola oil

Instructions:

1. Add chicken, salsa verde, and all other ingredients to the Slow cooker.
2. Put the cooker's lid on and set the cooking time to 5 hours on High settings.
3. Serve warm.

Nutrition Facts Per Serving:
Calories: 182, Total Fat: 9.2g, Fiber: 1g, Total Carbs: 7.35g, Protein: 18g

Moscow Bacon Chicken

Prep time: 27 minutes Cook Time: 7 hours Serves: 5

Ingredients:

6 oz. Russian dressing	1 tsp ground black pepper
17 oz. chicken thighs	4 oz. bacon, sliced
1 tbsp minced garlic	1 tsp salt
1 tsp onion powder	1 tsp oregano
	¼ cup of water

Instructions:

1. Add bacon slices to a skillet and saute until brown from both the sides.
2. Mix garlic, onion powder, salt, oregano, and black pepper in a bowl.
3. Rub the chicken with garlic mixture and transfer to the Slow cooker.
4. Add bacon and all other ingredients to the Slow cooker.
5. Put the cooker's lid on and set the cooking time to 7 hours on Low settings.
6. Serve warm.

Nutrition Facts Per Serving:
Calories: 273, Total Fat: 18.2g, Fiber: 1g, Total Carbs: 9.05g, Protein: 20g

Mushrooms Stuffed with Chicken

Prep time: 14 minutes Cook Time: 3 hours Serves: 6

Ingredients:

16 oz. button mushroom caps
4 oz. cream cheese
¼ cup carrot, chopped
1 tsp ranch seasoning mix
4 tbsp hot sauce
¾ cup blue cheese, crumbled
¼ cup red onion, chopped
½ cup chicken meat, ground
Salt and black pepper to the taste
Cooking spray

Instructions:

1. Toss mushrooms with all other ingredients in the Slow Cooker.
2. Put the cooker's lid on and set the cooking time to 3 hours on High settings.
3. Mix well and serve warm.

Nutrition Facts Per Serving:

Calories: 240, Total Fat: 4g, Fiber: 1g, Total Carbs: 12g, Protein: 7g

Puerto Rican Chicken

Prep Time: 23 minutes Cook Time: 8 hours Serves: 6

Ingredients:

8 oz. chicken breast
7 oz. chicken filler
6 oz. chicken wings
½ tsp ground cumin
1 tsp cilantro
1 tbsp fresh thyme leaves
1 tsp ground coriander
1 tbsp ground celery root
2 jalapeno
6 tbsp dry wine
3 oz. lemon wedges
3 red potatoes
1 yellow onion
1 tbsp olive oil

Instructions:

1. Add chicken wings, fillet, and breast to the Slow cooker.
2. Blend all the veggies in a blender and add it to the cooker.
3. Stir in all tomatoes and all other ingredients to the chicken.
4. Put the cooker's lid on and set the cooking time to 8 hours on Low settings.
5. Mix well and serve warm.

Nutrition Facts Per Serving:

Calories: 310, Total Fat: 9.8g, Fiber: 4g, Total Carbs: 32.42g, Protein: 24g

Orange Duck Fillets

Prep time: 23 minutes Cook Time: 8 hours Serves: 4

Ingredients:

2 oranges, peeled and sliced
1 tbsp honey
1 lb. duck fillet, sliced
1 tsp salt
½ tsp ground black pepper
½ tsp cilantro, chopped
1 tsp coriander, chopped
7 oz. celery stalk, chopped
1 tbsp chives, chopped
¼ cup of water
2 tbsp butter
1 tsp cinnamon

Instructions:

1. Add butter, duck, and all other ingredients to the Slow cooker.
2. Put the cooker's lid on and set the cooking time to 8 hours on Low settings.
3. Serve warm.

Nutrition Facts Per Serving:

Calories: 353, Total Fat: 23.2g, Fiber: 3g, Total Carbs: 15.68g, Protein: 21g

Chicken Cacciatore

Prep time: 27 minutes Cook Time: 8 hour Serves: 7

Ingredients:

1 oz. olive oil
1 cup yellow onion, chopped
1 lb. chicken thighs
1 tsp ground black pepper
5 oz. carrot, sliced
8 oz. tomato passata
7 oz. mushrooms, sliced
1 cup green beans, frozen
1 cup of water
1 tsp oregano
1 tsp cilantro

Instructions:

1. Add onion and olive oil to a pan and saute for 2 minutes.
2. Stir in chicken thighs and cook for 5 minutes.
3. Transfer the chicken and onion to the Slow cooker.
4. Stir in carrot, mushrooms, and all other ingredients.
5. Put the cooker's lid on and set the cooking time to 8 hours on Low settings.
6. Serve warm.

Nutrition Facts Per Serving:

Calories: 53, Total Fat: 4.1g, Fiber: 2g, Total Carbs: 4g, Protein: 1g

Parmesan Chicken Fillet

Prep time: 23 minutes Cook Time: 7 hours Serves: 4

Ingredients:

10 oz. chicken fillet
6 oz. Parmesan, shredded
1 tbsp lemon juice
2 tomatoes, chopped

1 tbsp butter, melted
1 white onion, sliced
½ cup bread crumbs
3 tbsp chicken stock
1 tsp ground black pepper

Instructions:

1. Add chicken, onion, and all other ingredients to the Slow cooker.
2. Put the cooker's lid on and set the cooking time to 7 hours on Low settings.
3. Serve warm.

Nutrition Facts Per Serving:

Calories: 404, Total Fat: 15.5g, Fiber: 3g, Total Carbs: 39.82g, Protein: 27g

Chicken Pepper Chili

Prep time: 15 minutes; Cook Time: 7 hrs; Serves: 4

Ingredients:

16 oz. salsa
8 chicken thighs
1 yellow onion, chopped
16 oz. canned

tomatoes, chopped
1 red bell pepper, chopped
2 tbsp chili powder

Instructions:

1. Add salsa and all other ingredients to the Slow cooker.
2. Put the cooker's lid on and set the cooking time to 7 hours on Low settings.
3. Serve warm.

Nutrition Facts Per Serving:

Calories 250, Total Fat 3g, Fiber 3g, Total Carbs 14g, Protein 8g

Pepperoni Chicken

Prep time: 14 minutes Cook Time: 6 hrs Serves: 6

Ingredients:

14 oz. pizza sauce
1 tbsp olive oil
4 medium chicken breasts, skinless and boneless
Salt and black pepper to the taste

1 tsp oregano, dried
6 oz. mozzarella, sliced
1 tsp garlic powder
2 oz. pepperoni, sliced

Instructions:

1. Add chicken, pizza sauce and all other ingredients to the Slow cooker.
2. Put the cooker's lid on and set the cooking time to 6 hours on Low settings.
3. Serve warm.

Nutrition Facts Per Serving:

Calories: 320, Total Fat: 10g, Fiber: 6g, Total Carbs: 14g, Protein: 27g

Chicken Stuffed with Beans

Prep Time: 17 minutes Cook Time: 10 hours Serves: 12

Ingredients:

21 oz. whole chicken
1 chili pepper, chopped
1 cup soybeans, canned
2 red onion, peeled and diced
1 carrot, peeled and diced
1 tsp onion powder
1 tsp cilantro, chopped

1 tsp oregano
1 tsp apple cider vinegar
1 tsp olive oil
1 tbsp dried basil
1 tsp paprika
¼ tsp ground red pepper
½ cup fresh dill
2 potatoes, peeled and diced
4 tbsp tomato sauce

Instructions:

1. Blend chili pepper, onion powder, cilantro, oregano, olive oil, red pepper, tomato sauce, dill, paprika, basil, and vinegar in a blender.
2. Stuff the whole chicken with soybeans, and vegetables.
3. Brush it with the blender spice-chili mixture liberally.
4. Place the spiced chicken in the Slow cooker and pour the remaining spice mixture over it.
5. Put the cooker's lid on and set the cooking time to 10 hours on Low settings.
6. Slice and serve.

Nutrition Facts Per Serving:

Calories: 186, Total Fat: 4.1g, Fiber: 5g, Total Carbs: 27.23g, Protein: 11g

Red Sauce Chicken Soup

Prep time: 14 minutes Cook Time: 3 hours Serves: 4

Ingredients:

3 tbsp butter, melted
4 oz. cream cheese
2 cups chicken meat, cooked and shredded
1/3 cup red sauce
4 cups chicken stock
Salt and black pepper to the taste
½ cup sour cream
¼ cup celery, chopped

Instructions:

1. Blend stock with red sauce, sour cream, black pepper, butter, cream cheese, and salt in a blender.
2. Transfer this red sauce mixture to the Slow cooker along with chicken and celery.
3. Put the cooker's lid on and set the cooking time to 3 hours on High settings.
4. Serve warm.

Nutrition Facts Per Serving:

Calories: 400, Total Fat: 23g, Fiber: 5g, Total Carbs: 15g, Protein: 30g

Saffron Chicken Thighs

Prep time: 14 minutes; Cook Time: 6 hrs; Serves: 6

Ingredients:

2 and ½ lbs. chicken thighs, skinless and boneless
1 and ½ tbsp olive oil
2 yellow onions, chopped
1 tsp cinnamon
powder
¼ tsp cloves, ground
¼ tsp allspice, ground
Salt and black pepper to the taste
A pinch of saffron

To serve:

A handful pine nuts
A handful mint, chopped

Instructions:

1. Add chicken, onions and rest of the ingredients to the Slow Cooker.
2. Put the cooker's lid on and set the cooking time to 6 hours on Low settings.
3. Garnish with pine nuts and mint.
4. Serve.

Nutrition Facts Per Serving:

Calories 223, Total Fat 3g, Fiber 2g, Total Carbs 6g, Protein 13g

Cheesy Chicken Breasts

Prep time: 14 minutes Cook Time: 4 hrs Serves: 4

Ingredients:

6 chicken breasts, skinless and boneless
Salt and black pepper to the taste
¼ cup jalapenos, chopped
5 bacon slices, chopped
8 oz. cream cheese
¼ cup yellow onion, chopped
½ cup mayonnaise
½ cup parmesan, grated
1 cup cheddar cheese, grated

Instructions:

1. Add chicken breasts, cream cheese and all other ingredients to the Slow cooker.
2. Put the cooker's lid on and set the cooking time to 4 hours on High settings.
3. Mix well and serve warm.

Nutrition Facts Per Serving:

Calories: 340, Total Fat: 12g, Fiber: 2g, Total Carbs: 15g, Protein: 20g

Thai Peanut Chicken

Prep time: 14 minutes Cook Time: 4 hrs Serves: 8

Ingredients:

2 ½ lbs. chicken thighs and drumsticks
1 tbsp soy sauce
1 tbsp apple cider vinegar
A pinch of red pepper flakes
Salt and black
pepper to the taste
½ tsp ginger, ground
1/3 cup peanut butter
1 garlic clove, minced
½ cup of warm water

Instructions:

1. Pat dry the chicken and place it in the Slow cooker.
2. Blend peanut butter with all other ingredients in a blender.
3. Pour this peanut butter sauce over the chicken in the cooker.
4. Put the cooker's lid on and set the cooking time to 4 hours on High settings.
5. Serve warm.

Nutrition Facts Per Serving:

Calories: 375, Total Fat: 12g, Fiber: 1g, Total Carbs: 10g, Protein: 42g

Chicken Taco Soup

Prep time: 24 minutes; Cook Time: 7 hrs; Serves: 5

Ingredients:

7 oz ground chicken
½ tsp sesame oil
3 cup vegetable stock
3 oz. yellow onion, peeled and diced
1 cup tomato, canned
3 tomatoes, chopped
5 oz. corn kernels

1 jalapeno pepper, sliced
½ cup white beans, drained
3 tbsp taco seasoning
¼ tsp salt
3 oz. black olives, sliced
5 corn tortillas, for serving

Instructions:

1. Add ground chicken, stock, sesame oil, onion, olives, tomatoes, corn, and jalapeno pepper in the Slow cooker.
2. Stir in salt, taco seasoning, and white beans, then give it a gentle stir.
3. Put the cooker's lid on and set the cooking time to 7 hours on Low settings.
4. Meanwhile, slice the corn tortillas into strips and bake them for 10 minutes for 365 degrees F.
5. Serve the soup with tortilla strips.
6. Devour.

Nutrition Facts Per Serving:

Calories 328, Total Fat 9.6g, Fiber 10g, Total Carbs 45.19g, Protein 18g

Peppercorn Chicken Thighs

Prep time: 14 minutes Cook Time: 4 hrs Serves: 6

Ingredients:

5 lbs. chicken thighs
Salt and black pepper to the taste
½ cup white vinegar
1 tsp black

peppercorns
4 garlic cloves, minced
3 bay leaves
½ cup of soy sauce

Instructions:

1. Add chicken, peppercorns, and all other ingredients to the Slow cooker.
2. Put the cooker's lid on and set the cooking time to 4 hours on High settings.
3. Discard the bay leaves.
4. Serve warm.

Nutrition Facts Per Serving:

Calories: 430, Total Fat: 12g, Fiber: 3g, Total Carbs: 10g, Protein: 36g

Poultry Stew

Prep time: 23 minutes Cook Time: 8 hours Serves: 6

Ingredients:

3 garlic cloves, peeled and minced
3 carrots, cut into 3 parts
1 lb. chicken fillet, diced
1 lb. duck fillet, diced

1 tbsp smoked paprika
¼ cup of soy sauce
1 tbsp honey
1 tsp nutmeg
1 tsp fresh rosemary
1 tsp black peas
2 cups of water

Instructions:

1. Add chicken, duck, and all other ingredients to the Slow cooker.
2. Put the cooker's lid on and set the cooking time to 8 hours on Low settings.
3. Serve warm.

Nutrition Facts Per Serving:

Calories: 422, Total Fat: 24.6g, Fiber: 3g, Total Carbs: 27.21g, Protein: 23g

Hot Chicken Wings

Prep time: 14 minutes Cook Time: 4 hrs Serves: 6

Ingredients:

12 chicken wings, cut into 2 pieces
1 lb. celery, cut into thin matchsticks
¼ cup honey
4 tbsp hot sauce

Salt to the taste
¼ cup tomato puree
1 cup yogurt
1 tbsp parsley, chopped

Instructions:

1. Add chicken, tomato puree, celery, honey, salt, hot sauce, and parsley to the Slow cooker.
2. Put the cooker's lid on and set the cooking time to 3 hours on High settings.
3. Stir in yogurt and mix well.
4. Put the cooker's lid on and set the cooking time to 30 minutes on High settings.
5. Serve warm.

Nutrition Facts Per Serving:

Calories: 300, Total Fat: 4g, Fiber: 4g, Total Carbs: 14g, Protein: 22g

Maple Ginger Chicken

Prep time: 14 minutes Cook Time: 15 hours Serves: 4

Ingredients:

½ cup of soy sauce
1 tsp maple syrup
1 tbsp fresh ginger, grated
1 tsp salt
1 lb. chicken breast,
diced
1 tsp ground ginger
¼ tsp ground cinnamon
2 tbsp red wine

Instructions:

1. Toss chicken with maple syrup and all other ingredients in the Slow cooker.
2. Leave it for 10 minutes to marinate.
3. Put the cooker's lid on and set the cooking time to 15 hours on Low settings.
4. Serve warm.

Nutrition Facts Per Serving:

Calories: 259, Total Fat: 13.5g, Fiber: 1g, Total Carbs: 6.71g, Protein: 26g

Cashew Thai Chicken

Prep time: 14 minutes; Cook Time: 4 hrs; Serves: 6

Ingredients:

1 ½ lb. chicken breast, boneless, skinless and cubed
1 tbsp olive oil
3 tbsp soy sauce
2 tbsp flour
Salt and black
pepper to the taste
1 tbsp ketchup
2 tbsp white vinegar
1 tsp ginger, grated
2 tbsp sugar
2 garlic cloves, minced

To serve:

½ cup cashews, chopped
1 green onion, chopped

Instructions:

1. Coat the chicken pieces with flour, salt, and black pepper.
2. Take oil in a nonstick skillet and place it over medium-high heat.
3. Sear the chicken for 5 minutes per side in the skillet.
4. Transfer the chicken to the Slow cooker along with ketchup and remaining ingredients.
5. Put the cooker's lid on and set the cooking time to 5 hours on Low settings.
6. Garnish with green onion and cashews.
7. Serve warm.

Nutrition Facts Per Serving:

Calories 200, Total Fat 3g, Fiber 2g, Total Carbs 13g, Protein 12g

Sweet Potato Jalapeno Stew

Prep time: 15 minutes; Cook Time: 8 hrs; Serves: 8

Ingredients:

1 yellow onion, chopped
½ cup red beans, dried
2 red bell peppers, chopped
2 tbsp ginger, grated
4 garlic cloves, minced
2 lbs. sweet, peeled and cubed
3 cups chicken stock
14 oz. canned tomatoes, chopped
2 jalapeno peppers, chopped
Salt and black pepper to the taste
½ tsp cumin, ground
½ tsp coriander, ground
¼ tsp cinnamon powder
To Garnish:
¼ cup peanuts, roasted and chopped
Juice of ½ lime

Instructions:

1. Add red beans along with all other ingredients to the Slow cooker.
2. Put the cooker's lid on and set the cooking time to 8 hours on Low settings.
3. Garnish with peanuts and lime juice.
4. Serve warm.

Nutrition Facts Per Serving:

Calories 259, Total Fat 8g, Fiber 7g, Total Carbs 42g, Protein 8g

Tomato Chicken

Prep time: 17 minutes Cook Time: 9 hours Serves: 4

Ingredients:

1 lb. chicken wings
1 cup canned tomatoes, diced
½ cup fresh tomatoes
1 cup fresh parsley
1 tsp salt
1 tsp ground cinnamon
1 cup onion
1 tbsp olive oil
1 tbsp red pepper

Instructions:

1. Blend tomatoes in a blender then add parsley, salt, red pepper, and onion.
2. Puree this mixture again then pour it into the Slow cooker.
3. Add chicken wings to the cooker.
4. Put the cooker's lid on and set the cooking time to 8 hours on Low settings.
5. Mix well and serve warm.

Nutrition Facts Per Serving:

Calories: 202, Total Fat: 7.7g, Fiber: 2g, Total Carbs: 6.47g, Protein: 26g

Turkey Pepper Chili

Prep time: 17 minutes; Cook Time: 4 hrs; Serves: 8

Ingredients:

1 red bell pepper, chopped	chopped
2 lbs. turkey meat, ground	4 tbsp tomato paste
28 oz. canned tomatoes, chopped	1 tbsp oregano, dried
1 red onion, chopped	3 tbsp chili powder
1 green bell pepper,	3 tbsp cumin, ground
	Salt and black pepper to the taste

Instructions:

1. Take a nonstick skillet and place it over medium-high heat.
2. Add turkey and sear it from both the sides until brown.
3. Transfer the turkey along with all other ingredients to the Slow cooker.
4. Put the cooker's lid on and set the cooking time to 4 hours on High settings.
5. Serve warm.

Nutrition Facts Per Serving:

Calories 225, Total Fat 6g, Fiber 4g, Total Carbs 15g, Protein 18g

Chicken Potato Sandwich

Prep time: 15 minutes; Cook Time: 8 hrs; Serves: 4

Ingredients:

7 oz. chicken fillet	6 tbsp chicken gravy
1 tsp cayenne pepper	4 slices French bread, toasted
5 oz. mashed potato, cooked	2 tsp mayo
	1 cup of water

Instructions:

1. Place the chicken fillet in the Slow cooker and add chicken gravy, water, and cayenne pepper on top.
2. Put the cooker's lid on and set the cooking time to 8 hours on Low settings.
3. Layer the French bread with mashed potato mixture.
4. Slice the cooked chicken into strips and return to its gravy.
5. Mix well, then serve the chicken over the mashed potato.
6. Serve warm.

Nutrition Facts Per Serving:

Calories 314, Total Fat 9.7g, Fiber 3g, Total Carbs 45.01g, Protein 12g

Chicken Sausage Stew

Prep time: 15 minutes; Cook Time: 5 hrs; Serves: 4

Ingredients:

4 chicken breasts, skinless and boneless	seasoning
	A drizzle of olive oil
6 Italian sausages, sliced	1 tsp garlic powder
5 garlic cloves, minced	29 oz. canned tomatoes, chopped
1 white onion, chopped	15 oz. tomato sauce
1 tsp Italian	1 cup of water
	½ cup balsamic vinegar

Instructions:

1. Place sausage and chicken slices in the Slow Cooker.
2. Add onion, garlic, oil and all other ingredients to the chicken.
3. Put the cooker's lid on and set the cooking time to 5 hours High settings.
4. Serve warm.

Nutrition Facts Per Serving:

Calories 267, Total Fat 4g, Fiber 3g, Total Carbs 15g, Protein 13g

Saucy Chicken Thighs

Prep time: 15 minutes; Cook Time: 5 hrs and 20 minutes, Serves: 6

Ingredients:

6 garlic cloves, minced	1 tsp ginger, minced
4 scallions, sliced	2 lbs. chicken thighs, skinless and boneless
1 cup veggie stock	
1 tbsp olive oil	2 cups cabbage, shredded
2 tsp sugar	
1 tbsp soy sauce	

Instructions:

1. Add stock along with other ingredients except cabbage to the Slow Cooker.
2. Put the cooker's lid on and set the cooking time to 5 hours on Low settings.
3. Toss in cabbage and cook for another 30 minutes on the low setting.
4. Serve warm.

Nutrition Facts Per Serving:

Calories 240, Total Fat 3g, Fiber 4g, Total Carbs 14g, Protein 10g

Caesar Chicken Wraps

Prep time: 18 minutes; Cook Time: 6 hrs; Serves: 6

Ingredients:

6 tortillas	1 oz. bay leaf
3 tbsp Caesar dressing	1 tsp salt
1 lb. chicken breast	1 tsp ground pepper
½ cup lettuce, chopped	1 tsp coriander
1 cup of water	4 oz. Feta cheese, chopped

Instructions:

1. Place chicken breast in the Slow cooker,
2. Add water, black pepper, salt, coriander, bay leaf, and salt on top.
3. Put the cooker's lid on and set the cooking time to 6 hours on Low settings.
4. Shred the slow-cooked chicken and add to the bowl.
5. Stir in feta cheese, lettuce, and Caesar dressing.
6. Mix well then divide the chicken mixture in the tortillas.
7. Wrap the stuffed tortillas and serve.

Nutrition Facts Per Serving:
Calories 376, Total Fat 18.5g, Fiber 3g, Total Carbs 29.43g, Protein 23g

Thyme Chicken

Prep time: 16 minutes Cook Time: 10 hours Serves: 6

Ingredients:

1 lemon, sliced	1 tbsp salt
2 oz. fresh thyme leaves, chopped	1 tsp cilantro
1 tbsp dried thyme	1 tbsp tomato paste
1 tsp ground black pepper	1 cup chicken stock
	1 tsp butter
	2 lbs. whole chicken

Instructions:

1. Rub the chicken with butter and sprinkle all the spices and herbs over it.
2. Pour the stock into the Slow cooker and place the spices chicken in it.
3. Drizzle the remaining spice mixture over the chicken.
4. Put the cooker's lid on and set the cooking time to 10 hours on Low settings.
5. Serve warm.

Nutrition Facts Per Serving:
Calories: 345, Total Fat: 11.9g, Fiber: 6g, Total Carbs: 35.28g, Protein: 26g

Mexican Black Beans Salad

Prep time: 26 minutes; Cook Time: 10 hrs; Serves: 10

Ingredients:

1 cup black beans	5 oz. Cheddar cheese
1 cup sweet corn, frozen	4 tbsp mayonnaise
3 tomatoes, chopped	1 tsp minced garlic
½ cup fresh dill, chopped	1 cup lettuce, chopped
1 chili pepper, chopped	5 cups chicken stock
7 oz. chicken fillet	1 cucumber, chopped

Instructions:

1. Add stock, chicken fillet, black beans, and corn to the Slow cooker.
2. Put the cooker's lid on and set the cooking time to 10 hours on Low settings.
3. Now shred the cooked chicken with the help of two forks.
4. Add chicken shred, beans and all other ingredients in a salad bowl.
5. Toss them well and serve.

Nutrition Facts Per Serving:
Calories 182, Total Fat 7.8g, Fiber 2g, Total Carbs 19.6g, Protein 9g

Pulled Maple Chicken

Prep time: 12 minutes; Cook Time: 6 hrs; Serves: 2

Ingredients:

2 tomatoes, chopped	2 garlic cloves, minced
2 red onions, chopped	1 tbsp maple syrup
2 chicken breasts, skinless and boneless	1 tsp chili powder
	1 tsp basil, dried
	3 tbsp water
	1 tsp cloves, ground

Instructions:

1. Place chicken along with all other ingredients in the Slow Cooker.
2. Put the cooker's lid on and set the cooking time to 6 hours on Low settings.
3. Shred the cooked chicken and serve with the veggies.
4. Enjoy.

Nutrition Facts Per Serving:
Calories 220, Total Fat 3g, Fiber 3g, Total Carbs 14g, Protein 6g

Herbed Chicken Salsa

Prep time: 15 minutes; Cook Time: 7 hrs; Serves: 4

Ingredients:

4 chicken breasts, skinless and boneless
½ cup veggie stock
Salt and black pepper to the taste
16 oz. salsa
1 and ½ tbsp parsley, dried
1 tsp garlic powder
½ tbsp cilantro, chopped
1 tsp onion powder
½ tbsp oregano, dried
½ tsp paprika, smoked
1 tsp chili powder
½ tsp cumin, ground

Instructions:

1. Add chicken breasts, salsa, and all other ingredients to the Slow Cooker.
2. Put the cooker's lid on and set the cooking time to 7 hours on Low settings.
3. Serve the chicken with its sauce on top.
4. Devour.

Nutrition Facts Per Serving:

Calories 270, Total Fat 4g, Fiber 2g, Total Carbs 14g, Protein 9g

Vegetable Almond Pilaf

Prep time: 21 minutes; Cook Time: 8 hrs; Serves: 5

Ingredients:

2 cups of rice
1 cup sweet corn, frozen
6 oz. chicken fillet, cut in strips
1 sweet red pepper, chopped
1 yellow sweet pepper, chopped
½ cup green peas,
frozen
1 carrot, peeled and diced
4 cups chicken stock
2 tbsp chopped almonds
1 tsp olive oil
1 tsp salt
1 tsp ground white pepper

Instructions:

1. Add carrots cubes, green peas, and sweet corn to the Slow cooker.
2. Stir in rice, olive oil, chicken stock, white peppers, and salt.
3. Place the chicken strip and sweet peppers on top of the rice.
4. Put the cooker's lid on and set the cooking time to 8 hours on Low settings.
5. Garnish with almond and serve.

Nutrition Facts Per Serving:

Calories 390, Total Fat 18.6g, Fiber 13g, Total Carbs 54.7g, Protein 18g

Curried Chicken Strips

Prep time: 14 minutes Cook Time: 4 hrs Serves: 6

Ingredients:

1 tbsp curry paste
11 oz. chicken fillet, cut into strips
1 tsp salt
2 tbsp maple syrup
1 tsp olive oil
3 tbsp sour cream
½ cup fresh dill
1 tbsp ground paprika

Instructions:

1. Add chicken strips and all other ingredients in a Slow Cooker.
2. Mix the chicken strips to coat well.
3. Put the cooker's lid on and set the cooking time to 3 hours on High settings.
4. Serve warm.

Nutrition Facts Per Serving:

Calories: 177, Total Fat: 9.1g, Fiber: 2g, Total Carbs: 18.11g, Protein: 6g

Spaghetti Chicken Salad

Prep time: 15 minutes; Cook Time: 5.5 hrs; Serves: 6

Ingredients:

1 lb. chicken breast
½ cup onion, sliced
6 oz. spaghetti
3 cups chicken stock
1 cup heavy cream
2 tbsp mayo
1 tsp minced garlic
1 tsp paprika
½ tsp salt
½ tsp ground black pepper
1 tsp sesame oil
1 tbsp flax seeds
1 tsp sesame seeds
1 cup lettuce, chopped
2 sweet red peppers, chopped

Instructions:

1. Season the chicken breast with black pepper, salt, and paprika.
2. Place the chicken breast in the Slow Cooker and top it with chicken stock and garlic.
3. Put the cooker's lid on and set the cooking time to 4 hours on High settings.
4. Remove the slow-cooked chicken and shred with the help of two forks.
5. Return the shreds to the slow cooker.
6. Add heavy cream, spaghetti, and sesame seeds to the cooker.
7. Put the cooker's lid on and set the cooking time to 1 hour 30 minutes on High settings.
8. Stir in sweet pepper, onion, lettuce, and mayonnaise.
9. Mix well and serve fresh.

Nutrition Facts Per Serving:

Calories 312, Total Fat 17.9g, Fiber 2g, Total Carbs 16.37g, Protein 22g

Chapter 5 Red Meat Recipes

Saucy Beef Cheeks

Prep time: 12 minutes; Cook Time: 4 hrs., Serves: 4

Ingredients:

4 beef cheeks, halved
2 tbsp olive oil
Salt and black pepper to the taste
1 white onion, chopped
4 garlic cloves, minced
2 cup beef stock
5 cardamom pods
1 tbsp balsamic vinegar
3 bay leaves
7 cloves
2 vanilla beans, split
1 and ½ tbsp tomato paste
1 carrot, sliced

Instructions:

1. Add beef cheeks and all remaining ingredients to the insert of your Slow cooker.
2. Put the cooker's lid on and set the cooking time to 4 hours on High settings.
3. Mix gently and serve warm.

Nutrition Facts Per Serving:

Calories: 321, Total Fat: 5g, Fiber: 7g, Total Carbs: 18g, Protein: 12g

Cauliflower Beef Soup

Prep time: 12 minutes; Cook Time: 6 hrs., Serves: 4

Ingredients:

1 lb. beef, ground
2 cups cauliflower, chopped
1 cup yellow onion, chopped
2 red bell peppers, chopped
15 oz. tomato sauce
15 oz. tomatoes, chopped
3 cups beef stock
½ tsp basil, dried
½ tsp oregano, dried
3 garlic cloves, minced
Salt and black pepper to the taste

Instructions:

1. Add cauliflower and beef along with all other ingredients to the insert of Slow cooker.
2. Put the cooker's lid on and set the cooking time to 6 hours on Low settings.
3. Serve warm.

Nutrition Facts Per Serving:

Calories: 214, Total Fat: 6g, Fiber: 6g, Total Carbs: 18g, Protein: 7g

Beef Onions Mix

Prep time: 12 minutes; Cook Time: 6 hrs. 5 minutes, Serves: 6

Ingredients:

3 lbs. beef roast, trimmed and boneless
1 tbsp Italian seasoning
Salt and black pepper to the taste
1 garlic clove, minced
1/3 cup sun-dried tomatoes, chopped
½ cup beef stock
½ cup kalamata olives pitted and halved
1 cup yellow onions chopped
1 tbsp olive oil

Instructions:

1. Add oil to a suitable pan and place it over medium-high heat.
2. Stir in beef and sauté for 5 minutes then transfer to the insert of the Slow cooker.
3. Stir in Italian seasoning, black pepper, onions, stock, and tomatoes.
4. Put the cooker's lid on and set the cooking time to 6 hours on Low settings.
5. Slice the cooked meat and return to the tomato sauce.
6. Mix well and serve warm.

Nutrition Facts Per Serving:

Calories: 300, Total Fat: 5g, Fiber: 5g, Total Carbs: 12g, Protein: 25g

Jamaican Pork Shoulder

Prep time: 12 minutes; Cook Time: 7 hrs., Serves: 12

Ingredients:

½ cup beef stock
1 tbsp olive oil
¼ cup keto Jamaican
spice mix
4 lbs. pork shoulder

Instructions:

1. Add pork, Jamaican spice mix and all other ingredients to the Slow cooker.
2. Put the cooker's lid on and set the cooking time to 7 hours on Low settings.
3. Slice the roast and serve warm.

Nutrition Facts Per Serving:

Calories: 400, Total Fat: 6g, Fiber: 7g, Total Carbs: 10g, Protein: 25g

Brisket Turnips Medley

Prep time: 12 minutes; Cook Time: 8 hrs., Serves: 6

Ingredients:

2 and ½ lbs. beef brisket
4 cups veggie stock
2 bay leaves
3 garlic cloves, chopped
4 carrots, chopped
1 cabbage head cut into 6 wedges
Salt and black pepper to the taste
3 turnips, cut into quarters

Instructions:

1. Add beef, bay leaves, stock, carrots, garlic, salt, cabbage, black pepper, and turnips to the insert of the Slow Cooker.
2. Put the cooker's lid on and set the cooking time to 8 hours on Low settings.
3. Serve warm.

Nutrition Facts Per Serving:

Calories: 321, Total Fat: 15g, Fiber: 4g, Total Carbs: 18g, Protein: 19g

Beef Roast with Cauliflower

Prep time: 12 minutes; Cook Time: 8 hrs. 30 minutes, Serves: 6

Ingredients:

4 lbs. beef chuck roast
1 cup veggie stock
1 tbsp coconut oil
1 bay leaf
10 thyme sprigs
4 garlic cloves, minced
1 carrot, roughly chopped
1 yellow onion, roughly chopped
2 celery ribs, roughly chopped
1 cauliflower head, florets separated
Salt and black pepper to the taste

Instructions:

1. Place a suitable pan over medium-high heat and add oil to it.
2. Toss in the beef and drizzle salt and black pepper over it.
3. Sear the seasoned beef for 5 minutes per side then transfer to the insert of the Slow Cooker.
4. Toss in the garlic, thyme springs, stock, bay leaf, celery, carrot, and onion.
5. Put the cooker's lid on and set the cooking time to 8 hours on Low settings.
6. Stir in cauliflower then cover again to cook for 20 minutes on High settings.
7. Serve warm.

Nutrition Facts Per Serving:

Calories: 340, Total Fat: 5g, Fiber: 3g, Total Carbs: 14g, Protein: 22g

Dill Beef Roast

Prep time: 12 minutes; Cook Time: 8 hrs., Serves: 8

Ingredients:

2 and ½ lbs. beef chuck roast
2 cups carrots, chopped
1 tbsp olive oil
2 cup yellow onion, chopped
1 cup celery, chopped
¾ cup dill pickle, chopped
½ cup dry red wine
1/3 cup German mustard
A pinch of salt and black pepper
¼ tsp cloves, ground
2 tbsp flour
2 bay leaves
2 tbsp beef stock

Instructions:

1. Add beef, carrots, and all other ingredients to the insert of your Slow Cooker.
2. Put the cooker's lid on and set the cooking time to 8 hours on Low settings.
3. Slice the cooked beef and serve it with the celery sauce.
4. Serve warm.

Nutrition Facts Per Serving:

Calories: 256, Total Fat: 7g, Fiber: 2g, Total Carbs: 10g, Protein: 31g

Chinese Mushroom Pork

Prep time: 12 minutes; Cook Time: 7 hrs., Serves: 4

Ingredients:

2 and ½ lbs. pork shoulder
4 cups chicken stock
½ cup of soy sauce
¼ cup white vinegar
2 tbsp chili sauce
Juice of 1 lime
1 tbsp ginger, grated
1 tbsp Chinese 5 spice
2 cups portabella mushrooms, sliced
Salt and black pepper to the taste
1 zucchini, sliced

Instructions:

1. Add pork, stock, and all other ingredients to the insert of Slow Cooker.
2. Put the cooker's lid on and set the cooking time to 7 hours on Low settings.
3. Shred the cooked pork with the help of two forks.
4. Return the pork shreds to the mushrooms sauce.
5. Serve warm.

Nutrition Facts Per Serving:

Calories: 342, Total Fat: 6g, Fiber: 8g, Total Carbs: 27g, Protein: 18g

Potato Beef Gratin

Prep time: 25 minutes; Cook Time: 5 hrs; Serves: 7

Ingredients:

1 lb. potato, peeled and sliced	1/3 cup tomato juice
2 white onions, sliced	1 tsp paprika
1 cup chicken stock	1 tsp salt
7 oz. ground beef	½ tsp cayenne pepper
1 tsp ground black pepper	1 tsp cilantro, chopped

Instructions:

1. Mix beef ground with black pepper in the Slow cooker.
2. Add sliced potatoes and rest of the ingredients.
3. Put the cooker's lid on and set the cooking time to 5 hours on High settings.
4. Serve warm.

Nutrition Facts Per Serving:

Calories 175, Total Fat 9.1g, Fiber 2g, Total Carbs 16.72g, Protein 7g

Salsa Bean Pie

Prep time: 15 minutes; Cook Time: 7 hrs; Serves: 6

Ingredients:

8 tortillas	5 oz. Cheddar cheese, shredded
7 oz. ground beef	
7 oz. salsa	3 tbsp tomato sauce
5 oz. red beans, canned	¼ tbsp salt

Instructions:

1. Spread 2 tortillas at the base of your Slow Cooker.
2. Mix beef with cheese, salt, and tomato sauce in a bowl.
3. Spread this beef mixture over the tortillas.
4. Now place 4 tortillas over the beef mixture.
5. Top them with red beans and spread evenly.
6. Place the remaining tortilla on top and finally add salsa.
7. Put the cooker's lid on and set the cooking time to 7 hours on Low settings.
8. Slice and serve.

Nutrition Facts Per Serving:

Calories 433, Total Fat 16g, Fiber 6g, Total Carbs 53g, Protein 19g

Parmesan Rosemary Potato

Prep time: 17 minutes; Cook Time: 4 hrs; Serves: 5

Ingredients:

1 lb. small potato, peeled	1 tsp rosemary
½ cup fresh dill, chopped	1 tsp thyme
	1 cup of water
7 oz. Parmesan, shredded	¼ tsp chili flakes
	3 tbsp cream
	1 tsp salt

Instructions:

1. Add potatoes, salt, rosemary, chili flakes, thyme, and water to the Slow cooker.
2. Put the cooker's lid on and set the cooking time to 2 hours on High settings.
3. Drizzle the remaining ingredients over the potatoes.
4. Cover again and slow cook for another 2 hours on High.
5. Serve warm.

Nutrition Facts Per Serving:

Calories 235, Total Fat 3.9g, Fiber 2g, Total Carbs 32.26g, Protein 1g

Greek Olive Lamb

Prep time: 11 minutes; Cook Time: 7 hrs. Serves: 5

Ingredients:

1 cup Greek yogurt	1 tsp powdered chili
4 oz black olives, sliced	1 tbsp balsamic vinegar
8 oz lamb, cubed	1 tsp oregano
1 tbsp ground black pepper	½ cup chicken stock
1 chili, chopped	1 tbsp lemon zest

Instructions:

1. Add lamb, yogurt, black olives to the insert of the Slow Cooker.
2. Stir in all the seasonings and stock to the lamb.
3. Put the cooker's lid on and set the cooking time to 4 hours on Low settings.
4. Shred the cooked lamb with the help of 2 forks.
5. Return the shred to the cooker and mix well.
6. Serve warm.

Nutrition Facts Per Serving:

Calories: 190, Total Fat: 10.4g, Fiber: 2g, Total Carbs: 8.3g, Protein: 16g

Enchilada Pork Luncheon

Prep time: 12 minutes; Cook Time: 4 hrs; Serves: 8

Ingredients:

1 lb. chorizo, ground
1 lb. pork, ground
3 tbsp olive oil
1 tomato, chopped
1 avocado, pitted, peeled and chopped

Salt and black pepper to the taste
1 small red onion, chopped
2 tbsp enchilada sauce

Instructions:

1. Take oil in a non-stick skillet and place it over medium-high heat,
2. Stir in pork and sauté until brown.
3. Transfer the pork along with all other ingredients to the Slow Cooker.
4. Put the cooker's lid on and set the cooking time to 4 hours on Low settings.
5. Serve warm.

Nutrition Facts Per Serving:

Calories 300, Total Fat 12g, Fiber 3g, Total Carbs 15g, Protein 17g

Mushroom Pork Chop Stew

Prep time: 18 minutes; Cook Time: 10 hrs; Serves: 7

Ingredients:

1 lb. mushrooms, sliced
7 oz. pork chop
1 tbsp salt
2 tbsp flour
½ cup tomato juice
3 tbsp sour cream

1 cup chicken stock
1 large onion
1 tsp sugar
2 carrots, peeled and julienned
1 cup green peas
1 tsp garlic, minced

Instructions:

1. Add mushrooms, carrots, onion, green pepper, and pork chop to the Slow cooker.
2. Stir in garlic, sugar stock, and sour cream.
3. Whisk flour with tomato juice and pour it into the cooker.
4. Give all the ingredients a gentle stir.
5. Put the cooker's lid on and set the cooking time to 10 hours on Low settings.
6. Serve warm.

Nutrition Facts Per Serving:

Calories 316, Total Fat 5.1g, Fiber 10g, Total Carbs 59.71g, Protein 16g

Cheesy Pork Wraps

Prep time: 20 minutes; Cook Time: 4 hrs; Serves: 5

Ingredients:

7 oz. ground pork
5 tortillas
1 tbsp tomato paste
½ cup onion, chopped
½ cup lettuce, chopped
1 tsp ground black

pepper
1 tsp salt
1 tsp sour cream
5 tbsp water
4 oz. Parmesan, shredded
2 tomatoes, sliced

Instructions:

1. Thoroughly mix pork with black pepper, sour cream, tomato paste, and salt in a bowl.
2. Spread the pork-cream mixture in the Slow cooker.
3. Put the cooker's lid on and set the cooking time to 4 hours on High settings.
4. Add tomatoes and tortillas into each tortilla.
5. Divide the cooked pork mixture in all tortilla.
6. Top the mixture with shredded cheese then wrap the tortillas.
7. Serve warm.

Nutrition Facts Per Serving:

Calories 318, Total Fat 7g, Fiber 2g, Total Carbs 3.76g, Protein 26g

Saucy French Lamb

Prep time: 12 minutes; Cook Time: 8 hrs., Serves: 4

Ingredients:

4 lamb chops
1 cup onion, chopped
2 cups canned tomatoes, chopped
1 cup leek, chopped

2 tbsp garlic, minced
1 tsp herbs de Provence
Salt and black pepper to the taste
3 cups of water

Instructions:

1. Add lamb chops, onion, and all other ingredients to the insert of the Slow Cooker.
2. Put the cooker's lid on and set the cooking time to 8 hours on Low settings.
3. Serve warm.

Nutrition Facts Per Serving:

Calories: 430, Total Fat: 12g, Fiber: 8g, Total Carbs: 20g, Protein: 18g

Pork Sweet Potato Stew

Prep time: 12 minutes; Cook Time: 4 hrs., Serves: 6

Ingredients:

1 lb. sweet potatoes, chopped
3 and ½ lbs. pork roast
8 medium carrots, chopped
Salt and black pepper to the taste
15 oz. canned tomatoes, chopped
1 yellow onion, chopped
Grated zest and juice of 1 lemon
4 garlic cloves, minced
3 bay leaves
Black pepper to the taste
½ cup kalamata olives pitted

Instructions:

1. Add potatoes, carrots, and all other ingredients except the olives to the insert of the Slow Cooker.
2. Put the cooker's lid on and set the cooking time to 4 hours on High settings.
3. Discard the bay leaves and transfer the meat to the serving plate.
4. Roughly mash the remaining veggies and add olives.
5. Transfer the veggies mix to the serving plate.
6. Serve warm.

Nutrition Facts Per Serving:

Calories: 250, Total Fat: 4g, Fiber: 3g, Total Carbs: 6g, Protein: 13g

Lamb Leg with Sweet Potatoes

Prep time: 12 minutes; Cook Time: 8 hrs., Serves: 4

Ingredients:

2 tbsp olive oil
1 lamb leg, bone-in
1 garlic head, peeled and cloves separated
5 sweet potatoes, cubed
5 rosemary springs
2 cups chicken stock
Salt and black pepper to the taste

Instructions:

1. Liberally rub the lamb leg with salt, black pepper, and oil.
2. Place the lamb leg along with other ingredients in the Slow Cooker.
3. Put the cooker's lid on and set the cooking time to 8 hours on Low settings.
4. Serve warm.

Nutrition Facts Per Serving:

Calories: 350, Total Fat: 6g, Fiber: 5g, Total Carbs: 12g, Protein: 22g

Garlic Lamb Chilli

Prep time: 12 minutes; Cook Time: 10 hrs., Serves: 7

Ingredients:

2 oz fresh rosemary, chopped
½ cup fresh cilantro, chopped
¼ cup coriander leaves, chopped
2 lbs. lamb fillet
1 tsp salt
1 tsp black peas
1 tsp chili flakes
1 cup garlic
1 tsp garlic powder
6 cups of water

Instructions:

1. Spread all the greens and lamb fillet in the insert of the Slow Cooker.
2. Stir in garlic, garlic powder, black peas, chili flakes, salt, and water.
3. Put the cooker's lid on and set the cooking time to 10 hours on Low settings.
4. Strain the excess liquid from the lamb and serve warm.

Nutrition Facts Per Serving:

Calories: 375, Total Fat: 22.4g, Fiber: 2g, Total Carbs: 8.71g, Protein: 33g

Indian Harissa Pork

Prep time: 14 minutes; Cook Time: 5 hrs. Serves: 8

Ingredients:

21 oz pork steak, tenderized
2 tbsp curry
1 tsp harissa
1 tbsp garam masala
1 tsp chili flakes
½ cup cream
1 tsp ground black pepper
1 tsp salt
1 tsp sugar
1 cup cashew, crushed
1 tsp ground nutmeg

Instructions:

1. Season the pork steaks with harissa, curry, chili flakes, and garam masala.
2. Place the pork steak in the insert of the Slow cooker.
3. Add cream, salt, sugar, nutmeg, and black pepper to the pork.
4. Put the cooker's lid on and set the cooking time to 5 hours on High settings.
5. Serve warm.

Nutrition Facts Per Serving:

Calories: 434, Total Fat: 33.4g, Fiber: 2g, Total Carbs: 12.27g, Protein: 23g

Lamb Cashews Tagine

Prep time: 12 minutes; Cook Time: 5 hrs., Serves: 7

Ingredients:

2 lbs. lamb fillet, cubed	1 tbsp sugar
½ cup dried apricots	1 tsp salt
3 tbsp cashews	1 tsp ground white pepper
1 jalapeno pepper	1 cup of water
2 cups red wine	

Instructions:

1. Add lamb cubes, cashews, and all other ingredients to the Slow cooker.
2. Put the cooker's lid on and set the cooking time to 5 hours on Low settings.
3. Mix well and serve warm.

Nutrition Facts Per Serving:

Calories: 416, Total Fat: 25.5g, Fiber: 1g, Total Carbs: 9.96g, Protein: 33g

Herbed Lamb Shanks

Prep time: 12 minutes; Cook Time: 8 hrs. 10 minutes, Serves: 4

Ingredients:

4 lamb shanks, trimmed	chopped
3 tbsp olive oil	2 tbsp tomato paste
1 onion, chopped	2 cups veggie stock
2 carrots, chopped	1 tbsp rosemary, dried
15 oz. canned tomatoes, chopped	1 tbsp thyme, dried
2 garlic cloves, minced	1 tbsp oregano, dried
2 celery stalks,	Salt and black pepper to the taste

Instructions:

1. Place a suitable pan over medium-high heat and add 2 tbsp oil.
2. Add lamb shanks to the oil and sear for 5 minutes per side.
3. Transfer the lamb shank to the Slow cooker along with onion and other ingredients.
4. Put the cooker's lid on and set the cooking time to 8 hours on Low settings.
5. Serve warm.

Nutrition Facts Per Serving:

Calories: 350, Total Fat: 5g, Fiber: 4g, Total Carbs: 12g, Protein: 20g

Lamb Cheese Casserole

Prep time: 16 minutes; Cook Time: 9 hrs., Serves: 6

Ingredients:

1 cup of rice	3 carrots, chopped
4 cups of water	1 tbsp olive oil
13 oz lamb fillet	1 tsp salt
1 tbsp ground paprika	1 tsp ground cinnamon
1 onion	1 tbsp turmeric
9 oz Cheddar cheese, shredded	5 sweet potatoes

Instructions:

1. Toss rice with turmeric and olive oil in the insert of the Slow Cooker.
2. Spread the chopped carrot over the rice, then add a layer of the onion.
3. Place lamb fillet over the veggies and add the remaining ingredients.
4. Put the cooker's lid on and set the cooking time to 9 hours on Low settings.
5. Serve warm.

Nutrition Facts Per Serving:

Calories: 436, Total Fat: 20.8g, Fiber: 10g, Total Carbs: 42.77g, Protein: 26g

Lamb Leg Mushrooms Satay

Prep time: 12 minutes; Cook Time: 8 hrs., Serves: 8

Ingredients:

1 and ½ lbs. lamb leg, bone-in	6 garlic cloves, minced
2 carrots, sliced	2 tbsp tomato paste
½ lbs. mushrooms, sliced	1 tsp olive oil
4 tomatoes, chopped	Salt and black pepper to the taste
1 small yellow onion, chopped	Handful parsley, chopped

Instructions:

1. Add lamb, carrots, and all other ingredients to the Slow Cooker.
2. Put the cooker's lid on and set the cooking time to 8 hours on Low settings.
3. Serve warm.

Nutrition Facts Per Serving:

Calories: 372, Total Fat: 12g, Fiber: 7g, Total Carbs: 18g, Protein: 22g

Herbed Cinnamon Beef

Prep time: 12 minutes; Cook Time: 5 hrs., Serves: 6

Ingredients:

4 lbs. beef brisket	1 tbsp dill, dried
2 oranges, sliced	3 bay leaves
2 garlic cloves, minced	4 cinnamon sticks, cut into halves
2 yellow onions, thinly sliced	Salt and black pepper to the taste
11 oz. celery, thinly sliced	17 oz. veggie stock

Instructions:

1. Add beef, orange slices, and all other ingredients to the insert of Slow cooker.
2. Put the cooker's lid on and set the cooking time to 5 hours on High settings.
3. Serve warm.

Nutrition Facts Per Serving:

Calories: 300, Total Fat: 5g, Fiber: 7g, Total Carbs: 12g, Protein: 4g

Lamb Semolina Meatballs

Prep time: 21 minutes; Cook Time: 5 hrs., Serves: 6

Ingredients:

1 red onion, peeled and grated	1 tsp oregano
1 tbsp semolina	1 lb. minced lamb
2 tbsp dried parsley	2 tbsp minced garlic
1 tsp chili flakes	1 tsp onion powder
1 tsp ground black pepper	1 tbsp butter
	1 egg

Instructions:

1. Mix minced lamb with onion, parsley, chili flakes, black pepper, onion powder, minced garlic, oregano, and semolina in a bowl.
2. Add egg and mix the minced meat mixture with the help of your hands.
3. Make small meatballs of this lamb mixture and keep them aside.
4. Add melted butter along with the meatballs to the insert of the Slow cooker.
5. Put the cooker's lid on and set the cooking time to 3 hours on High settings.
6. Serve warm.

Nutrition Facts Per Serving:

Calories: 256, Total Fat: 16.4g, Fiber: 1g, Total Carbs: 5.53g, Protein: 21g

Lamb Shoulder with Artichokes

Prep time: 12 minutes; Cook Time: 8 hrs. 10 minutes, Serves: 6

Ingredients:

3 lbs. lamb shoulder, boneless	Salt and black pepper to the taste
3 onions, roughly chopped	½ tsp allspice
1 tbsp olive oil	1 and ½ cups veggie stock
1 tbsp oregano, chopped	14 oz. canned artichoke hearts, chopped
6 garlic cloves, minced	¼ cup tomato paste
1 tbsp lemon zest, grated	2 tbsp parsley, chopped

Instructions:

1. Place a suitable pan over medium-high heat and add oil.
2. Add lamb to the hot oil and cook for 5 minutes per side.
3. Transfer the lamb to the insert of the slow cooker then stir in remaining ingredients except for the artichokes.
4. Put the cooker's lid on and set the cooking time to 8 hours on Low settings.
5. Stir in artichokes and cook for 15 minutes on low heat.
6. Serve warm.

Nutrition Facts Per Serving:

Calories: 370, Total Fat: 4g, Fiber: 5g, Total Carbs: 12g, Protein: 16g

Pork Sirloin Salsa

Prep time: 12 minutes; Cook Time: 8 hrs., Serves: 4

Ingredients:

2 lbs. pork sirloin roast, cut into thick slices	2 tsp garlic powder
	2 tsp cumin, ground
Salt and black pepper to the taste	1 tbsp olive oil
	16 oz. green chili tomatillo salsa

Instructions:

1. Rub the pork with salt, black pepper, garlic powder, and cumin.
2. Add pork, salsa, and oil to the insert of the Slow Cooker.
3. Put the cooker's lid on and set the cooking time to 8 hours on Low settings.
4. Serve warm.

Nutrition Facts Per Serving:

Calories: 400, Total Fat: 7g, Fiber: 6g, Total Carbs: 10g, Protein: 25g

Lamb Potato Stew

Prep time: 20 minutes; Cook Time: 5 hrs., Serves: 10

Ingredients:

1 cup corn kernels	2 tbsp flour
4 oz fresh celery root, chopped	1 eggplant, diced
1 tbsp ground ginger	1 carrot, peeled, grated
10 oz lamb cubes	1 tsp cayenne pepper
1 tsp onion powder	2 cups of water
1 tsp garlic powder	5 medium potatoes, peeled and cubed
1 tbsp tomato sauce	
½ cup tomato puree	
1 tsp olive oil	

Instructions:

1. Season lamb cubes with onion powder, cayenne pepper, and garlic powder.
2. Add potatoes, eggplant, celery root, water, tomatoes puree, and all other ingredients to the insert of Slow cooker.
3. Put the cooker's lid on and set the cooking time to 5 hours on High settings.
4. Serve warm.

Nutrition Facts Per Serving:
Calories: 265, Total Fat: 5.9g, Fiber: 7g, Total Carbs: 42.39g, Protein: 12g

Herbed Lamb Fillet

Prep time: 20 minutes; Cook Time: 5 hrs., Serves: 4

Ingredients:

1 lemon, chopped	3 tbsp olive oil
3 tbsp lemon juice	1/3 cup fresh dill, chopped
1 tbsp lemon zest	
1 tbsp minced garlic	1 tsp salt
1 tsp paprika	1 lb. lamb fillet, sliced
1 tsp dried rosemary	
1 cup chicken stock	

Instructions:

1. Mic lemon, lemon zest, and minced garlic in a small bowl.
2. Rub the lamb slices with lemon mixture liberally.
3. Place the lamb meat in the insert of the Slow cooker.
4. Top the lamb with chicken stock, dill, and rest of the ingredients.
5. Put the cooker's lid on and set the cooking time to 5 hours on High settings.
6. Serve warm.

Nutrition Facts Per Serving:
Calories: 413, Total Fat: 30.1g, Fiber: 0g, Total Carbs: 5.1g, Protein: 30g

Pork Chops Pineapple Satay

Prep time: 12 minutes; Cook Time: 6 hrs., Serves: 4

Ingredients:

2 lbs. pork chops	3 tbsp apple cider vinegar
1/3 cup sugar	
¼ cup ketchup	5 tbsp soy sauce
15 oz. pineapple, cubed	2 tsp garlic, minced
	3 tbsp flour

Instructions:

1. Whisk ketchup with sugar, soy sauce, vinegar, and tapioca in a large bowl.
2. Add pork chops to the ketchup mixture and mix well to coat.
3. Transfer the pork along with ketchup marinade to the insert of Slow Cooker.
4. Add garlic and pineapple to the chops.
5. Put the cooker's lid on and set the cooking time to 6 hours on Low settings.
6. Serve warm.

Nutrition Facts Per Serving:
Calories: 345, Total Fat: 5g, Fiber: 6g, Total Carbs: 13g, Protein: 14g

Lamb Carrot Medley

Prep time: 12 minutes; Cook Time: 7 hrs., Serves: 4

Ingredients:

4 lamb shanks	2 tbsp tomato paste
2 tbsp olive oil	1 tsp oregano, dried
1 yellow onion, finely chopped	1 tomato, roughly chopped
3 carrots, roughly chopped	4 oz. chicken stock
2 garlic cloves, minced	Salt and black pepper to the taste

Instructions:

1. Toss the lamb with carrots and all other ingredients in the insert of the Slow Cooker.
2. Put the cooker's lid on and set the cooking time to 7 hours on Low settings.
3. Serve warm.

Nutrition Facts Per Serving:
Calories: 400, Total Fat: 13g, Fiber: 4g, Total Carbs: 17g, Protein: 24g

Zesty Pesto Pork

Prep time: 20 minutes; Cook Time: 11 hr., Serves: 6

Ingredients:

5 tbsp lime zest	1 tsp chili flakes
2 lbs. pork shoulder	1 tsp ground black
3 garlic cloves,	pepper
sliced	1 tbsp salt
2 tbsp butter	3 tsp pesto
1 tsp paprika	

Instructions:

1. Whisk lime zest, with paprika, sliced garlic, butter, chili flakes, pesto, salt, and black pepper in a small bowl.
2. Rub the pork shoulder with the lime zest mixture and wrap it with aluminum foil.
3. Place the pork should in the insert of the Slow Cooker.
4. Put the cooker's lid on and set the cooking time to 11 hours on Low settings.
5. Remove the pork shoulder from the foil.
6. Slice and serve warm.

Nutrition Facts Per Serving:

Calories: 153, Total Fat: 6.1g, Fiber: 3g, Total Carbs: 22.42g, Protein: 4g

Seasoned Beef Stew

Prep time: 12 minutes; Cook Time: 8 hrs., Serves: 6

Ingredients:

4 lbs. beef roast	1 yellow onion,
2 cups beef stock	chopped
2 sweet potatoes,	1 tbsp onion powder
cubed	1 tbsp garlic powder
6 carrots, sliced	1 tbsp sweet paprika
7 celery stalks,	Salt and black
chopped	pepper to the taste

Instructions:

1. Add sweet potatoes, beef and all other ingredients to the insert of Slow Cooker.
2. Put the cooker's lid on and set the cooking time to 8 hours on Low settings.
3. Slice the cooked roast and serve with mixed vegetables.
4. Enjoy.

Nutrition Facts Per Serving:

Calories: 372, Total Fat: 6g, Fiber: 12g, Total Carbs: 19g, Protein: 11g

Wine Dipped Lamb Leg

Prep time: 19 minutes; Cook Time: 11 hr., Serves: 7

Ingredients:

2 lbs. lamb leg	1 carrot
2 cups dry red wine	1 white onion
1 cup of water	½ tsp ground
1 tsp anise	cinnamon
1 tsp black peas	1 tbsp fresh ginger,
1 tbsp fresh	grated
rosemary	1 tsp olive oil
1 tbsp cumin seeds	

Instructions:

1. Brush the insert of your Slow cooker with olive oil.
2. Place the lamb leg and add rosemary, cumin seeds, cinnamon, ginger.
3. Put the cooker's lid on and set the cooking time to 3 hours on High settings.
4. Add water, red wine, anise, black peas, white onion, and carrot.
5. Put the cooker's lid on and set the cooking time to 8 hours on Low settings.
6. Serve warm.

Nutrition Facts Per Serving:

Calories: 208, Total Fat: 7.8g, Fiber: 1g, Total Carbs: 3.41g, Protein: 27g

Pork with Apples

Prep time: 12 minutes; Cook Time: 8 hrs., Serves: 4

Ingredients:

A pinch of nutmeg,	4 apples, cored and
ground	sliced
2 lbs. pork	2 tbsp maple syrup
tenderloin	

Instructions:

1. Add apples to the insert of the Slow cooker.
2. Drizzle nutmeg over the apples then add pork along with remaining ingredients.
3. Put the cooker's lid on and set the cooking time to 8 hours on Low settings.
4. Slice the pork and return to the apple mixture.
5. Mix well and serve warm.

Nutrition Facts Per Serving:

Calories: 400, Total Fat: 4g, Fiber: 5g, Total Carbs: 12g, Protein: 20g

Tomatillo Lamb

Prep time: 20 minutes; Cook Time: 7 hrs., Serves: 8

Ingredients:

4 tbsp dried rosemary	1 onion, grated
1 cup tomatillos, chopped	18 oz lamb leg
	1 tsp salt
1 tbsp minced garlic	1 cup cream
2 oz fresh rosemary	½ tsp ground black pepper

Instructions:

1. Add tomatillos, garlic, dried and fresh rosemary, black pepper, salt, and onion to a blender jug.
2. Blend the tomatillos mixture until smooth.
3. Add lamb leg to the insert of the Slow cooker and pour the tomatillo mixture on top.
4. Put the cooker's lid on and set the cooking time to 7 hours on Low settings.
5. Serve warm.

Nutrition Facts Per Serving:
Calories: 168, Total Fat: 9.8g, Fiber: 2g, Total Carbs: 5.61g, Protein: 14g

Thai Spiced Pork

Prep time: 12 minutes; Cook Time: 7 hrs., Serves: 4

Ingredients:

2 tbsp olive oil	1 tbsp black peppercorns
2 lbs. pork butt, boneless and cubed	2 tbsp garlic, chopped
Salt and black pepper to the taste	2 tbsp five-spice powder
6 eggs, hard-boiled, peeled and sliced	1 and ½ cup of soy sauce
1 tbsp cilantro, chopped	2 tbsp cocoa powder
1 tbsp coriander seeds	1 yellow onion, chopped
1 tbsp ginger, grated	8 cups of water

Instructions:

1. Mix pork with salt, peppercorns, and all other ingredients to the insert of Slow Cooker.
2. Put the cooker's lid on and set the cooking time to 7 hours on Low settings.
3. Serve warm.

Nutrition Facts Per Serving:
Calories: 400, Total Fat: 10g, Fiber: 9g, Total Carbs: 28g, Protein: 22g

Mexican Lamb Fillet

Prep time: 22 minutes; Cook Time: 8 hrs., Serves: 4

Ingredients:

1 chili pepper, deseeded and chopped	1 tsp salt
	1 tsp ground black pepper
1 jalapeno pepper, deseeded and chopped	1 tbsp ground paprika
	1 tsp grated ginger
1 cup sweet corn	1 cup tomato juice
1 cup chicken stock	1 tbsp white sugar
14 oz lamb fillet	

Instructions:

1. Add the peppers, ginger, and ground paprika to the blender jug.
2. Blend this peppers mixture for 30 seconds until smooth.
3. Place the lamb fillet to the insert of the Slow Cooker.
4. Add pepper mixture, tomato juice, white sugar, black pepper, and salt to the lamb.
5. Lastly, add sweet corn and chicken stock.
6. Put the cooker's lid on and set the cooking time to 8 hours on Low settings.
7. Shred the cooked lamb and return the cooker.
8. Mix well and serve warm.

Nutrition Facts Per Serving:
Calories: 348, Total Fat: 18.3g, Fiber: 3g, Total Carbs: 19.26g, Protein: 28g

Roast with Pepperoncini

Prep time: 12 minutes; Cook Time: 8 hrs., Serves: 4

Ingredients:

5 lbs. beef chuck roast	10 pepperoncini's
	1 cup beef stock
1 tbsp soy sauce	2 tbsp butter, melted

Instructions:

1. Add beef roast and all other ingredients to the insert of Slow cooker.
2. Put the cooker's lid on and set the cooking time to 8 hours on Low settings.
3. Shred the cooked meat with the help of 2 forks and return to the cooker.
4. Mix gently and serve warm.

Nutrition Facts Per Serving:
Calories: 362, Total Fat: 4g, Fiber: 8g, Total Carbs: 17g, Protein: 17g

Cider Dipped Pork Roast

Prep time: 12 minutes; Cook Time: 8 hrs., Serves: 6

Ingredients:

1 yellow onion, chopped	Salt and black pepper to the taste
2 tbsp sweet paprika	A pinch of nutmeg, ground
15 oz. canned tomato, roasted and chopped	5 lbs. pork roast
	Juice of 1 lemon
1 tsp cumin, ground	¼ cup apple cider vinegar
1 tsp coconut oil	

Instructions:

1. Place a suitable pan over medium-high heat and add oil.
2. Toss in onions and sauté for few minutes until brown.
3. Transfer the onion to your Slow Cooker then add paprika and remaining ingredients.
4. Put the cooker's lid on and set the cooking time to 8 hours on Low settings.
5. Slice the meat and serve warm with its sauce.
6. Enjoy.

Nutrition Facts Per Serving:
Calories: 350, Total Fat: 5g, Fiber: 2g, Total Carbs: 13g, Protein: 24g

Short Ribs with Tapioca Sauce

Prep time: 12 minutes; Cook Time: 10 hrs., Serves: 6

Ingredients:

3 lbs. beef short ribs	2 tbsp tapioca, crushed
1 fennel bulb, cut into wedges	2 tbsp tomato paste
2 yellow onions, cut into wedges	1 tsp rosemary, dried
1 cup carrot, sliced	Salt and black pepper to the taste
14 oz. canned tomatoes, chopped	4 garlic cloves, minced
1 cup dry red wine	

Instructions:

1. Add short ribs, onion, and all other ingredients to the insert of Slow Cooker.
2. Put the cooker's lid on and set the cooking time to 10 hours on Low settings.
3. Serve warm.

Nutrition Facts Per Serving:
Calories: 432, Total Fat: 14g, Fiber: 6g, Total Carbs: 25g, Protein: 42g

Moroccan Apricot Lamb

Prep time: 25 minutes; Cook Time: 13 hrs., Serves: 8

Ingredients:

2 lb. lamb shoulder	1 tsp chili flakes
1 tsp cumin seeds	4 tbsp tomato paste
1 tsp ground cumin	3 tbsp raisins
1 tsp ground coriander	1 tbsp dried apricots
1 tsp celery root	5 cups of water
1 tsp salt	1 cup onion, chopped

Instructions:

1. Whisk cumin seeds with coriander ground, ground cumin, salt, celery root, and chili flakes in a small bowl.
2. Rub this chili mixture over the lamb shoulder.
3. Brush the seasoned lamb should with tomato paste, then marinate for 10 minutes.
4. Add onion, water, and marinated meat to the insert of the Slow Cooker.
5. Put the cooker's lid on and set the cooking time to 13 hours on Low settings.
6. Serve warm.

Nutrition Facts Per Serving:
Calories: 195, Total Fat: 9.6g, Fiber: 1g, Total Carbs: 4.5g, Protein: 23g

Smoke Infused Lamb

Prep time: 12 minutes; Cook Time: 7 hrs., Serves: 4

Ingredients:

4 lamb chops	1 tsp smoked paprika
1 tsp liquid smoke	2 tbsp garlic, minced
1 cup green onions, chopped	Salt and black pepper to the taste
2 cups canned tomatoes, chopped	3 cups beef stock

Instructions:

1. Add lamb, liquid smoke, and all other ingredients to the insert of Slow Cooker.
2. Put the cooker's lid on and set the cooking time to 7 hours on Low settings.
3. Serve warm.

Nutrition Facts Per Serving:
Calories: 364, Total Fat: 12g, Fiber: 7g, Total Carbs: 29g, Protein: 28g

Soy Dipped Pork Ribs

Prep time: 12 hrs., Cook Time: 6 hrs., Serves: 4

Ingredients:

4 cups vinegar	Salt and black pepper to the taste
4 lbs. pork ribs	A pinch of garlic powder
2 tbsp apple cider vinegar	A pinch of Chinese 5 spice
2 cups of water	
3 tbsp soy sauce	

Instructions:

1. Place pork ribs in a large tray and pour water and white vinegar on top.
2. Cover these ribs and refrigerate them for 12 hours.
3. Drain the marinated ribs and season them with black pepper, garlic powder, Chinese 5 spice, and salt.
4. Transfer the ribs to the insert of the slow cooker along with soy sauce and cider vinegar.
5. Put the cooker's lid on and set the cooking time to 6 hours on High settings.
6. Serve warm.

Nutrition Facts Per Serving:
Calories: 300, Total Fat: 6g, Fiber: 3g, Total Carbs: 15g, Protein: 15g

Sausage with Onion Jam

Prep time: 17 minutes; Cook Time: 3 hrs., Serves: 6

Ingredients:

6 pork sausages	3 oz. water
2 tbsp olive oil	Salt and black pepper to the taste
½ cup onion jam	1 tbsp flour
3 oz. beef stock	

Instructions:

1. Add sausages, onion jam, and all other ingredients to the insert of Slow Cooker.
2. Put the cooker's lid on and set the cooking time to 3 hours on High settings.
3. Serve warm.

Nutrition Facts Per Serving:
Calories: 431, Total Fat: 15g, Fiber: 4g, Total Carbs: 29g, Protein: 13g

Sweet Mongolian Beef

Prep time: 12 minutes; Cook Time: 9 hrs., Serves: 6

Ingredients:

2 lbs. pork steak, sliced	2 oz olive oil
3 tbsp chives, chopped	2 tbsp brown sugar
5 tbsp cornstarch	¼ cup of water
	¼ cup of soy sauce
	8 oz carrot, grated

Instructions:

1. Coat the pork strips with cornstarch and shake off the excess.
2. Transfer the pork strips to the insert of the Slow Cooker.
3. Drizzle olive oil and brown sugar over the pork.
4. Add water, soy sauce, and grated carrot.
5. Put the cooker's lid on and set the cooking time to 2 hours on High settings.
6. Mix well and continue cooking for 7 hours on Low settings.
7. Garnish with chives.

Nutrition Facts Per Serving:
Calories: 557, Total Fat: 38.2g, Fiber: 1g, Total Carbs: 11.9g, Protein: 39g

Maple Rosemary Lamb

Prep time: 12 minutes; Cook Time: 9 hrs., Serves: 4

Ingredients:

3 tbsp mustard	1 tsp dried mint
5 tbsp olive oil	1 tsp salt
3 tbsp fresh rosemary	1 tsp paprika
1 tsp ground coriander	4 tbsp maple syrup
	1 lb. lamb fillet
	2 tbsp water

Instructions:

1. Whisk olive oil with mustard, rosemary, mint, salt, paprika, and coriander in a small bowl.
2. Rub the lamb fillet with the mustard mixture then transfer to the insert of Slow Cooker.
3. Add maple syrup and water to the lamb fillet.
4. Put the cooker's lid on and set the cooking time to 9 hours on Low settings.
5. Slice the cooked lamb and serve warm with the sauce.

Nutrition Facts Per Serving:
Calories: 502, Total Fat: 36.5g, Fiber: 1g, Total Carbs: 14.73g, Protein: 28g

Coconut Meatballs Gravy

Prep time: 20 minutes; Cook Time: 7 hrs; Serves: 8

Ingredients:

3 tbsp coconut	1 egg
1 tbsp curry paste	1 tbsp semolina
1 tsp salt	½ cup onion, chopped
1 cup heavy cream	
1 tbsp flour	1 tsp kosher salt
1 tsp cayenne pepper	3 tbsp bread crumbs
10 oz. ground pork	1 tsp ground black pepper

Instructions:

1. Mix coconut, salt, curry paste, cream, and flour in a bowl until smooth.
2. Add this coconut mixture to the Slow cooker.
3. Put the cooker's lid on and set the cooking time to 1 hour on Low settings.
4. During this time, whisk an egg in a large bowl.
5. Stir in semolina, cayenne pepper, pork, onion, salt, black pepper, and bread crumbs.
6. Mix the pork mixture well then make meatballs out of it.
7. Place the meatball in the coconut gravy in the Slow cooker.
8. Put the cooker's lid on and set the cooking time to 7 hours on Low settings.
9. Serve warm.

Nutrition Facts Per Serving:

Calories 197, Total Fat 10.1g, Fiber 1g, Total Carbs 12.56g, Protein 14g

Chapter 6 Fish & Seafood Recipes

Carp Millet Soup

Prep time: 17 minutes; Cook Time: 6 hrs., Serves: 10

Ingredients:

¼ cup millet	1 tbsp garlic, sliced
8 cups of water	1 carrot, chopped
1 lb. carp, peeled, chopped	1 tbsp salt
1 tsp black peas	1 tsp ground celery root
1 tsp cilantro	1 tsp ground black pepper
¼ cup fresh parsley	

Instructions:

1. Add water, millet, cilantro, carp, and celery root to the insert of the Slow Cooker.
2. Top the millet mixture with carrot, salt, black peas, black pepper, garlic, and parsley.
3. Put the cooker's lid on and set the cooking time to 6 hours on Low settings.
4. Serve warm with sour cream.

Nutrition Facts Per Serving:

Calories: 83, Total Fat: 2.8g, Fiber: 1g, Total Carbs: 5.07g, Protein: 9g

Japanese Pea Shrimp

Prep time: 13 minutes; Cook Time: 1 hr., Serves: 4

Ingredients:

1 lb.'s shrimp, peeled and deveined	¾ cup pineapple juice
2 tbsp soy sauce	1 cup chicken stock
½ lb. pea pods	3 tbsp sugar
3 tbsp vinegar	

Instructions:

1. First, place the pea pods and shrimp in the insert of the Slow cooker.
2. Top the shrimps with the rest of the ingredients.
3. Put the cooker's lid on and set the cooking time to 1 hour on High settings.
4. Serve warm.

Nutrition Facts Per Serving:

Calories: 251, Total Fat: 4g, Fiber: 1g, Total Carbs: 12g, Protein: 30g

Cod with Shrimp Sauce

Prep time: 12 minutes; Cook Time: 2 hrs., Serves: 4

Ingredients:

1 lb. cod fillets, cut into medium pieces	2 eggs, whisked
2 tbsp parsley, chopped	2 oz. butter, melted
	½ pint milk
4 oz. breadcrumbs	½ pint shrimp sauce
2 tsp lemon juice	Salt and black pepper to the taste

Instructions:

1. Toss fish with crumbs, parsley, salt, black pepper, and lemon juice in a suitable bowl.
2. Add butter, milk, egg, and fish mixture to the insert of the Slow Cooker.
3. Put the cooker's lid on and set the cooking time to 2 hours on High settings.
4. Serve warm.

Nutrition Facts Per Serving:

Calories: 231, Total Fat: 3g, Fiber: 5g, Total Carbs: 10g, Protein: 5g

Chili Tamarind Mackerel

Prep time: 12 minutes; Cook Time: 2 hrs., Serves: 4

Ingredients:

18 oz. mackerel, cut into pieces	cut into halves
3 garlic cloves, minced	1 small piece of ginger, chopped
8 shallots, chopped	6 stalks laksa leaves
1 tsp dried shrimp powder	3 and ½ oz. water
1 tsp turmeric powder	5 tbsp vegetable oil
1 tbsp chili paste	1 tbsp tamarind paste mixed with 3 oz. water
2 lemongrass sticks,	Salt to the taste
	1 tbsp sugar

Instructions:

1. Add shallots, garlic, chili paste, shrimp powder, and turmeric powder to a blender jug.
2. Blend it well then add the shallots mixture to the insert of the Slow cooker.
3. Now add fish and all other ingredients to the cooker.
4. Put the cooker's lid on and set the cooking time to 2 hours on High settings.
5. Serve warm.

Nutrition Facts Per Serving:

Calories: 200, Total Fat: 3g, Fiber: 1g, Total Carbs: 20g, Protein: 22g

Chinese Miso Mackerel

Prep time: 12 minutes; Cook Time: 2 hrs., Serves: 4

Ingredients:

2 lbs. mackerel, cut into medium pieces	¼ cup miso
1 cup of water	1 sweet onion, thinly sliced
1 garlic clove, crushed	2 celery stalks, sliced
1 shallot, sliced	1 tbsp rice vinegar
1-inch ginger piece, chopped	1 tsp Japanese hot mustard
1/3 cup sake	Salt to the taste
1/3 cup mirin	1 tsp sugar

Instructions:

1. Add mirin, sake, shallot, garlic, ginger, water, miso, and mackerel to the insert of the Slow cooker.
2. Put the cooker's lid on and set the cooking time to 2 hours on High settings.
3. Soak onion and celery in a bowl filled with ice water.
4. Drain the celery and onion, then toss them with sugar, salt, and mustard.
5. Serve the cooked mackerel with the onion-celery mixture.
6. Enjoy warm.

Nutrition Facts Per Serving:

Calories: 300, Total Fat: 12g, Fiber: 1g, Total Carbs: 14g, Protein: 20g

Dill Shrimp Medley

Prep time: 12 minutes; Cook Time: 1 hr., Serves: 4

Ingredients:

1 lb. shrimp, peeled and deveined	1 cup white wine
2 tbsp olive oil	2 tbsp cornstarch
	¾ cup milk
1 tbsp yellow onion, chopped	1 tbsp dill, chopped

Instructions:

1. Add onion, oil and all other ingredients to the insert of your Slow Cooker.
2. Put the cooker's lid on and set the cooking time to 1 hour on High settings.
3. Serve warm.

Nutrition Facts Per Serving:

Calories: 300, Total Fat: 13g, Fiber: 2g, Total Carbs: 10g, Protein: 10g

Butter Dipped Crab Legs

Prep time: 9 minutes; Cook Time: 1 hr. 30 minutes, Serves: 4
Ingredients:

4 lbs. king crab legs, broken in half	¼ cup butter, melted
3 lemon wedges	½ cup chicken stock

Instructions:
1. Add crab legs, butter, and chicken stock to the insert of the Slow Cooker.
2. Put the cooker's lid on and set the cooking time to 1.5 hours on High settings.
3. Serve warm with lemon wedges.

Nutrition Facts Per Serving:
Calories: 100, Total Fat: 1g, Fiber: 5g, Total Carbs: 12g, Protein: 3g

Semolina Fish Balls

Prep time: 25 minutes; Cook Time: 8 hrs., Serves: 11
Ingredients:

1 cup sweet corn	1 tsp salt
5 tbsp fresh dill, chopped	1 tsp ground black pepper
1 tbsp minced garlic	1 tsp cumin
7 tbsp bread crumbs	1 tsp lemon zest
2 eggs, beaten	¼ tsp cinnamon
10 oz salmon, salmon	3 tbsp almond flour
2 tbsp semolina	3 tbsp scallion, chopped
2 tbsp canola oil	3 tbsp water

Instructions:
1. Mix sweet corn, dill, garlic, semolina, eggs, salt, cumin, almond flour, scallion, cinnamon, lemon zest, and black pepper in a large bowl.
2. Stir in chopped salmon and mix well.
3. Make small meatballs out of this fish mixture then roll them in the breadcrumbs.
4. Place the coated fish ball in the insert of the Slow cooker.
5. Add canola oil and water to the fish balls.
6. Put the cooker's lid on and set the cooking time to 8 hours on Low settings.
7. Serve warm.

Nutrition Facts Per Serving:
Calories: 201, Total Fat: 7.9g, Fiber: 2g, Total Carbs: 22.6g, Protein: 11g

Cider Dipped Clams

Prep time: 12 minutes; Cook Time: 2 hrs., Serves: 4
Ingredients:

2 lbs. clams, scrubbed	cider
3 oz. pancetta	Salt and black pepper to the taste
1 tbsp olive oil	Juice of ½ lemon
3 tbsp butter, melted	1 small green apple, chopped
2 garlic cloves, minced	2 thyme springs, chopped
1 bottle infused	

Instructions:
1. Place a suitable pan over medium-high heat and add oil.
2. Toss in pancetta and sauté for 3 minutes until brown.
3. Transfer the seared pancetta to the insert of the Slow Cooker.
4. Stir in butter, garlic and rest of the ingredients to the cooker.
5. Put the cooker's lid on and set the cooking time to 2 hours on High settings.
6. Serve warm.

Nutrition Facts Per Serving:
Calories: 270, Total Fat: 2g, Fiber: 1g, Total Carbs: 11g, Protein: 20g

Spiced Cod with Peas

Prep time: 15 minutes; Cook Time: 2 hrs., Serves: 4
Ingredients:

16 oz. cod fillets	½ tsp paprika
1 tbsp parsley, chopped	2 garlic cloves, chopped
10 oz. peas	Salt and pepper to the taste
9 oz. wine	
½ tsp oregano, dried	

Instructions:
1. Add garlic, parsley, paprika, oregano, and wine to a blender jug.
2. Blend well, then pour this mixture to the insert of the Slow Cooker.
3. Add black pepper, salt, peas, and fish to the cooker.
4. Put the cooker's lid on and set the cooking time to 2 hours on High settings.
5. Serve warm.

Nutrition Facts Per Serving:
Calories: 251, Total Fat: 2g, Fiber: 6g, Total Carbs: 7g, Protein: 22g

Tuna Mushroom Noodles

Prep time: 5 minutes; Cook Time: 2 hrs., Serves: 4

Ingredients:

14 oz. canned tuna, drained	1 cup peas, frozen
16 oz. egg noodles	3 cups of water
28 oz. cream of mushroom	4 oz. cheddar cheese, grated
	¼ cup breadcrumbs

Instructions:
1. Add paste, water, peas, tuna, and cream to the insert of Slow Cooker.
2. Put the cooker's lid on and set the cooking time to 1 hour on High settings.
3. Top the tuna mixture with breadcrumbs and cheese.
4. Put the cooker's lid on and set the cooking time to 1 hour on High settings.
5. Serve warm.

Nutrition Facts Per Serving:
Calories: 251, Total Fat: 6g, Fiber: 1g, Total Carbs: 20g, Protein: 12g

Indian Fish Curry

Prep time: 12 minutes; Cook Time: 2 hrs., Serves: 6

Ingredients:

6 white fish fillets, cut into medium pieces	ground
1 tomato, chopped	1 tbsp ginger, finely grated
14 oz. coconut milk	½ tsp turmeric, ground
2 yellow onions, sliced	2 tsp cumin, ground
2 red bell peppers, cut into strips	Salt and black pepper to the taste
2 garlic cloves, minced	½ tsp fenugreek, ground
6 curry leaves	1 tsp hot pepper flakes
1 tbsp coriander,	2 tbsp lemon juice

Instructions:
1. Add fish, milk, tomatoes, and rest of the ingredients to the insert of the Slow cooker.
2. Put the cooker's lid on and set the cooking time to 2 hours on High settings.
3. Give it a gentle stir and serve warm.

Nutrition Facts Per Serving:
Calories: 231, Total Fat: 4g, Fiber: 6g, Total Carbs: 16g, Protein: 22g

Tuna Noodles Casserole

Prep time: 21 minutes; Cook Time: 8 hrs., Serves: 12

Ingredients:

8 oz wild mushrooms, chopped	½ cup green peas, frozen
8 oz noodles, cooked	1 tbsp salt
1 lb. tuna, canned	1 tsp ground ginger
3 potatoes, peeled and sliced	½ tsp ground coriander
1 cup cream	½ tsp cilantro
7 oz Parmesan shredded	1 tbsp oregano
1 carrot, peeled, grated	1 tsp olive oil
	1 cup fresh dill, chopped
	1 cup of water

Instructions:
1. Place a suitable pan over medium-high heat and add olive oil.
2. Toss in mushrooms and stir cook for 6 minutes then transfer to the Slow Cooker.
3. Add sliced potatoes, carrot, tuna, cheese, and noodles.
4. Top these layers with green peas, salt, ground ginger, coriander ground, cilantro, dill, water, cream, and oregano.
5. Put the cooker's lid on and set the cooking time to 8 hours on Low settings.
6. Serve warm.

Nutrition Facts Per Serving:
Calories: 296, Total Fat: 5.8g, Fiber: 5g, Total Carbs: 44.39g, Protein: 19g

Italian Parsley Clams

Prep time: 12 minutes; Cook Time: 2 hrs., Serves: 6

Ingredients:

½ cup butter, melted	5 garlic cloves, minced
36 clams, scrubbed	1 tbsp oregano, dried
1 tsp red pepper flakes, crushed	2 cups white wine
1 tsp parsley, chopped	

Instructions:
1. Add clams, butter and rest of the ingredients to the insert of Slow Cooker.
2. Put the cooker's lid on and set the cooking time to 2 hours on High settings.
3. Serve warm.

Nutrition Facts Per Serving:
Calories: 224, Total Fat: 15g, Fiber: 2g, Total Carbs: 7g, Protein: 4g

Dill Crab Cutlets

Prep time: 21 minutes; Cook Time: 1 hour, Serves: 12
Ingredients:

12 oz crab meat, canned	3 tbsp almond flour
4 tbsp fresh dill	¼ cup mashed green peas
1 tsp salt	1 tsp olive oil
½ tsp cilantro	1 large egg
1 tbsp turmeric	1 tsp lemon juice

Instructions:
1. Add crab meat, salt, almond flour, turmeric, cilantro, salt, dill to a blender.
2. Blend this crab mixture then add egg, lemon juice, and mashed green peas.
3. Beat again for 2 minutes until it forms a smooth dough.
4. Make small crab cakes out of this mixture.
5. Grease the insert of Slow cooker with olive oil.
6. Place the crab cakes in the cooker.
7. Put the cooker's lid on and set the cooking time to 1 hour on High settings.
8. Serve warm.

Nutrition Facts Per Serving:
Calories: 45, Total Fat: 1.5g, Fiber: 1g, Total Carbs: 2.3g, Protein: 6g

White Fish with Olives Sauce

Prep time: 12 minutes; Cook Time: 2 hrs., Serves: 4
Ingredients:

4 white fish fillets, boneless	dried
1 cup olives, pitted and chopped	1 garlic clove, minced
1 lb. cherry tomatoes halved	A drizzle of olive oil
A pinch of thyme,	Salt and black pepper to the taste
	¼ cup chicken stock

Instructions:
1. Pour the stock into the insert of the Slow cooker.
2. Add fish, tomatoes, olives, oil, black pepper, salt, garlic, and thyme to the stock.
3. Put the cooker's lid on and set the cooking time to 2 hours on High settings.
4. Serve warm.

Nutrition Facts Per Serving:
Calories: 200, Total Fat: 3g, Fiber: 3g, Total Carbs: 12g, Protein: 20g

Shrimp Chicken Jambalaya

Prep time: 12 minutes; Cook Time: 4 hrs. 30 minutes, Serves: 8
Ingredients:

1 lb. chicken breast, chopped	2 cups green, yellow and red bell peppers, chopped
1 lb. shrimp, peeled and deveined	3 and ½ cups chicken stock
2 tbsp extra virgin olive oil	1 tbsp Creole seasoning
1 lb. sausage, chopped	1 tbsp Worcestershire sauce
2 cups onions, chopped	1 cup tomatoes, crushed
1 and ½ cups of rice	
2 tbsp garlic, chopped	

Instructions:
1. Brush the insert of your Slow cooker with oil.
2. Toss in sausage, chicken, bell peppers, garlic, onion, rice, tomatoes, stock, Worcestershire sauce, and seasoning.
3. Put the cooker's lid on and set the cooking time to 4 hours on High settings.
4. Stir in shrimp and cook for another 30 minutes on High settings.
5. Serve warm.

Nutrition Facts Per Serving:
Calories: 251, Total Fat: 10g, Fiber: 3g, Total Carbs: 20g, Protein: 25g

Maple Mustard Salmon

Prep time: 12 minutes; Cook Time: 2 hrs., Serves: 1
Ingredients:

1 big salmon fillet	2 tbsp mustard
Salt and black pepper to the taste	1 tbsp olive oil
	1 tbsp maple extract

Instructions:
1. Whisk maple extract with mustard in a bowl.
2. Place the salmon in the insert of Slow Cooker.
3. Add salt, black pepper and mustard mixture over the salmon.
4. Put the cooker's lid on and set the cooking time to 2 hours on High settings.
5. Serve warm.

Nutrition Facts Per Serving:
Calories: 240, Total Fat: 7g, Fiber: 1g, Total Carbs: 15g, Protein: 23g

Mackerel Stuffed Tacos

**Prep time: 20 minutes; Cook Time: 2 hrs.,
Serves: 6**
Ingredients:

9 oz mackerel fillet
1 tsp salt
¼ cup fish stock
1 tsp butter
1 tsp paprika
½ tsp ground white

pepper
6 corn tortillas
¼ cup of salsa
1 tsp minced garlic
½ tsp mayo

Instructions:

1. Whisk mayo with butter, garlic, white pepper, salt, and paprika in a small bowl.
2. Rub the mackerel fillet with the mayo garlic mixture.
3. Place this fish in the insert of Slow Cooker and pour in fish stock.
4. Put the cooker's lid on and set the cooking time to 2 hours on Low settings.
5. Meanwhile, layer the corn tortilla with salad evenly.
6. Shred the cooked mackerel fillet and mix it with 2 tsp cooking liquid.
7. Divide the fish shreds on the corn tortillas and wrap them.
8. Serve warm.

Nutrition Facts Per Serving:
Calories: 120, Total Fat: 2.4g, Fiber: 3g,
Total Carbs: 14.37g, Protein: 11g

Rice Stuffed Squid

**Prep time: 12 minutes; Cook Time: 3 hrs.,
Serves: 4**
Ingredients:

3 squids
Tentacles from 1
squid, chopped
1 cup sticky rice
14 oz. dashi stock

2 tbsp sake
4 tbsp soy sauce
1 tbsp mirin
2 tbsp sugar

Instructions:

1. Toss the chopped tentacles with rice and stuff the 3 squids with rice mixture.
2. Seal the squid using toothpicks then place them in the Slow Cooker.
3. Add soy sauce, stock, sugar, sake, and mirin to the squids.
4. Put the cooker's lid on and set the cooking time to 3 hours on High settings.
5. Serve warm.

Nutrition Facts Per Serving:
Calories: 230, Total Fat: 4g, Fiber: 4g, Total
Carbs: 7g, Protein: 11g

Turmeric Coconut Squid

**Prep time: 12 minutes; Cook Time: 3 hrs.,
Serves: 4**
Ingredients:

17 oz. squids
1 and ½ tbsp red
chili powder
Salt and black
pepper to the taste
¼ tsp turmeric
powder
2 cups of water
5 pieces coconut,

shredded
4 garlic cloves,
minced
½ tsp cumin seeds
3 tbsp olive oil
¼ tsp mustard
seeds
1-inch ginger pieces,
chopped

Instructions:

1. Add squids, turmeric, chili powder, water, black pepper, and salt to the insert of the Slow cooker.
2. Put the cooker's lid on and set the cooking time to 2 hours on High settings.
3. Add ginger, garlic, cumin, and oil to a blender jug and blend well.
4. Transfer this ginger-garlic mixture to the squids in the cooker.
5. Cook again for 1 hour on High settings.
6. Serve warm.

Nutrition Facts Per Serving:
Calories: 261, Total Fat: 3g, Fiber: 8g, Total
Carbs: 19g, Protein: 11g

Mussels and Sausage Satay

**Prep time: 5 minutes; Cook Time: 2 hrs.,
Serves: 4**
Ingredients:

2 lbs. mussels,
scrubbed and
debearded
12 oz. amber beer
1 tbsp olive oil

1 yellow onion,
chopped
8 oz. spicy sausage
1 tbsp paprika

Instructions:

1. Grease the insert of your Slow cooker with oil.
2. Toss in mussels, beer, onion, sausage, and paprika.
3. Put the cooker's lid on and set the cooking time to 2 hours on High settings.
4. Discard all the unopened mussels, if any.
5. Serve the rest and enjoy it.

Nutrition Facts Per Serving:
Calories: 124, Total Fat: 3g, Fiber: 1g, Total
Carbs: 7g, Protein: 12g

Flounder Cheese Casserole

Prep time: 20 minutes; Cook Time: 6 hrs., Serves: 11

Ingredients:

8 oz rice noodles	2 tbsp butter, melted
2 cups chicken stock	3 tbsp chives
12 oz flounder fillet, chopped	4 oz shallot, chopped
1 cup carrot, cooked	7 oz cream cheese
½ tsp ground black pepper	5 oz Parmesan, shredded
2 sweet peppers, chopped	½ cup fresh cilantro, chopped
3 sweet potatoes, chopped	1 cup of water

Instructions:

1. Brush the insert of your Slow cooker with melted butter.
2. Place the chopped flounder, carrots, sweet peppers, sweet potatoes, shallots, and chives to the cooker.
3. Add cilantro, stock, black pepper, cream cheese, and water to the flounder.
4. Top the flounder casserole with shredded cheese.
5. Put the cooker's lid on and set the cooking time to 6 hours on Low settings.
6. Serve warm.

Nutrition Facts Per Serving:
Calories: 202, Total Fat: 9.1g, Fiber: 2g, Total Carbs: 19.86g, Protein: 11g

Balsamic-Glazed Salmon

Prep time: 20 minutes; Cook Time: 1.5 hrs., Serves: 7

Ingredients:

5 tbsp brown sugar	pepper
2 tbsp sesame seeds	1 tsp ground paprika
1 tbsp balsamic vinegar	1 tsp turmeric
1 tbsp butter	¼ tsp fresh rosemary
3 tbsp water	1 tsp olive oil
1 tsp salt	21 oz salmon fillet
½ tsp ground black	

Instructions:

1. Whisk rosemary, black pepper, salt, turmeric, and paprika in a small bowl.
2. Rub the salmon fillet with this spice's mixture.
3. Grease a suitable pan with olive oil and place it over medium-high heat.
4. Place the spiced salmon fillet in the hot pan and sear it for 3 minutes per side.
5. Add butter, sesame seeds, brown sugar, balsamic vinegar, and water to the insert of the Slow cooker.
6. Put the cooker's lid on and set the cooking time to 30 minutes on High settings.
7. Stir this sugar mixture occasionally.
8. Place the salmon fillet in the Slow Cooker.
9. Put the cooker's lid on and set the cooking time to 1 hour on Low settings.
10. Serve warm.

Nutrition Facts Per Serving:
Calories: 170, Total Fat: 9.9g, Fiber: 1g, Total Carbs: 1.43g, Protein: 18g

Halibut with Peach Sauce

Prep time: 28 minutes; Cook Time: 1 hr., Serves: 6

Ingredients:

16 oz halibut fillet	½ tsp ground white pepper
4 tbsp peach puree	3 oz tangerines
2 peach, pitted, peeled and chopped	1 tbsp maple syrup
1 tsp salt	1 tsp oregano
1 tsp turmeric	1 tsp olive oil
1 tsp white sugar	1 tsp garlic, sliced
1 tbsp sour cream	½ tsp sage

Instructions:

1. Mix the chopped peaches with peach puree, turmeric, salt, sour cream, and white sugar in a small bowl.
2. Season the halibut fillet with maple syrup, oregano, and white pepper.
3. Grease a suitable pan with olive oil and place it over medium heat.
4. Stir in sage, and sliced garlic, then sauté for 1 minute.
5. Add sage halibut to the pan and cook for 1 minute per side.
6. Pour the peach puree into the insert of the Slow cooker.
7. Add the sear halibut mixture to the peach puree.
8. Put the cooker's lid on and set the cooking time to 1 hour on Low settings.
9. Serve warm.

Nutrition Facts Per Serving:
Calories: 198, Total Fat: 11.7g, Fiber: 1g, Total Carbs: 11.82g, Protein: 12g

Harissa Dipped Cod

Prep time: 25 minutes; Cook Time: 7 hrs., Serves: 6
Ingredients:

2 tbsp harissa, dried
17 oz cod
1 tsp salt
1 tbsp minced garlic
1 tbsp sour cream
¼ cup of soy sauce
1 tbsp oyster sauce
1 tsp chili paste

1 tsp cilantro
1 red onion, peeled and sliced
1 cup fish stock
½ cup canned tomatoes
1 tbsp harissa sauce
4 tbsp orange juice

Instructions:
1. Whisk dried harissa, sour cream, garlic, salt, harissa sauce, orange juice, fish stock, cilantro, chili paste, oyster sauce, and soy sauce in a bowl.
2. Spread the tomatoes in the insert of the Slow Cooker.
3. Place the cod over the tomatoes then add sliced onion on top.
4. Pour in the harissa mixture over the onion layer.
5. Put the cooker's lid on and set the cooking time to 7 hours on Low settings.
6. Give a gentle stir then serve warm.

Nutrition Facts Per Serving:
Calories: 116, Total Fat: 2.9g, Fiber: 1g, Total Carbs: 7.4g, Protein: 15g

Herbed Octopus Mix

Prep time: 1 hr. and 10 minutes; Cook Time: 3 hrs., Serves: 6
Ingredients:

1 octopus, cleaned and prepared
2 rosemary springs
2 tsp oregano, dried
½ yellow onion, roughly chopped
4 thyme sprigs
½ lemon
1 tsp black peppercorns
3 tbsp extra virgin

olive oil
For the marinade:
¼ cup extra virgin olive oil
Juice of ½ lemon
4 garlic cloves, minced
2 thyme sprigs
1 rosemary spring
Salt and black pepper to the taste

Instructions:
1. Place the octopus in the insert of the Slow cooker.
2. Add 2 rosemary springs, salt, peppercorns, lemon, onion, oregano, 3 tbsp olive oil, and 4 thyme springs.

3. Put the cooker's lid on and set the cooking time to 2 hours on High settings.
4. Transfer the cooked octopus to a cutting board and dice it.
5. Put the diced octopus in a suitable bowl then add ¼ cup olive oil, and remaining ingredients.
6. Mix well then transfer the octopus along with marinade to the Slow cooker.
7. Put the cooker's lid on and set the cooking time to 1 hour on High settings.
8. Serve warm.

Nutrition Facts Per Serving:
Calories: 200, Total Fat: 4g, Fiber: 3g, Total Carbs: 10g, Protein: 11g

Japanese Cod Fillet

Prep time: 15 minutes; Cook Time: 1.5 hrs., Serves: 9
Ingredients:

24 oz cod fillet
2 tbsp miso paste
3 oz pickled jalapeno, chopped
2 tbsp oyster sauce
¼ cup of soy sauce

¼ cup fish stock
1 tsp sesame oil
½ tsp chili flakes
¼ tsp cayenne pepper
1 tbsp sugar

Instructions:
1. Whisk miso paste, stock, sesame oil, soy sauce, oyster sauce, sugar, chili flakes, and cayenne pepper in a bowl.
2. Rub this miso mixture over the cod filet liberally.
3. Transfer the miso-seasoned cod to the insert of the Slow cooker.
4. Top the cod with chopped jalapeno and left-over miso paste.
5. Put the cooker's lid on and set the cooking time to 1.5 hours on Low settings.
6. Shred the cooked cod and return to the miso jalapeno sauce.
7. Serve warm.

Nutrition Facts Per Serving:
Calories: 95, Total Fat: 2.5g, Fiber: 1g, Total Carbs: 4.81g, Protein: 13g

Lobster Cheese Soup

Prep time: 12 minutes; Cook Time: 3.5 hrs., Serves: 6

Ingredients:

5 cups fish stock
1 tbsp paprika
½ tsp powdered chili
1 tsp salt
8 oz lobster tails
6 oz Cheddar cheese, shredded
1 tsp ground white

pepper
1/3 cup fresh dill, chopped
1 tbsp almond milk
1 garlic clove, peeled
3 potatoes, peeled and diced

Instructions:

1. Add stock, potatoes, paprika, salt, almond milk, garlic cloves, white pepper, powdered chili to the insert of Slow cooker.
2. Put the cooker's lid on and set the cooking time to 2 hours on High settings.
3. Now add dill, and lobster tails to the cooker.
4. Put the cooker's lid on and set the cooking time to 1.5 hours on High settings.
5. Serve warm with shredded cheese on top.

Nutrition Facts Per Serving:

Calories: 261, Total Fat: 4.8g, Fiber: 5g, Total Carbs: 37.14g, Protein: 19g

Thai Salmon Cakes

Prep time: 12 minutes; Cook Time: 6 hrs., Serves: 10

Ingredients:

6 oz squid, minced
10 oz salmon fillet, minced
2 tbsp chili paste
1 tsp cayenne pepper
2 oz lemon leaves
3 tbsp green peas, mashed
2 tsp fish sauce

2 egg white
1 egg yolk
1 tsp oyster sauce
1 tsp salt
½ tsp ground coriander
1 tsp sugar
2 tbsp butter
¼ cup cream
3 tbsp almond flour

Instructions:

1. Mix seafood with chili paste, cayenne pepper, lemon leaves, mashed green peas, fish sauce, whisked egg yolk and egg whites in a bowl.
2. Stir in sugar, salt, oyster sauce, sugar, almond flour, and ground coriander.

3. Mix well, then make small-sized fish cakes out of this mixture.
4. Add cream and butter to the insert of the Slow cooker.
5. Place the fish cakes in the butter and cream.
6. Put the cooker's lid on and set the cooking time to 5 hours on Low settings.
7. Serve warm with cream mixture.

Nutrition Facts Per Serving:

Calories: 112, Total Fat: 6.7g, Fiber: 1g, Total Carbs: 2.95g, Protein: 10g

Seabass Mushrooms Ragout

Prep time: 21 minutes; Cook Time: 8 hrs., Serves: 8

Ingredients:

6 oz shiitake mushrooms, chopped
8 oz wild mushrooms, chopped
9 oz cremini mushrooms, chopped
2 white onions, chopped
1 tbsp balsamic vinegar
1 lb. seabass,

boneless, cubed
1 tbsp ground celery
1 tsp salt
1 tsp ground nutmeg
2 tbsp sliced garlic
3 carrots, chopped
1 tbsp butter
½ tsp sage, chopped
2 cups of water
3 tbsp fresh dill, chopped
1 tbsp fresh celery, chopped

Instructions:

1. Mix the mushrooms with ground celery, balsamic vinegar, and salt in a bowl.
2. Transfer the mushrooms along with butter to the insert of the Slow Cooker.
3. Put the cooker's lid on and set the cooking time to 1 hour on Low settings.
4. Add seabass, nutmeg, garlic, carrots, sage, celery, dill, and water to the cooker.
5. Put the cooker's lid on and set the cooking time to 7 hours on Low settings.
6. Serve warm.

Nutrition Facts Per Serving:

Calories: 313, Total Fat: 5g, Fiber: 9g, Total Carbs: 55.86g, Protein: 20g

Citrus Glazed Flounder

Prep time: 18 minutes; Cook Time: 8 hrs., Serves: 9

Ingredients:

3 lbs. flounder, peeled
1 lime, sliced
½ cup lemon juice
1 tbsp sugar
1 tsp ground ginger
1 tsp ground cumin
½ tsp ground

coriander
1 tsp ground celery root
2 tsp olive oil
1 tsp garlic, sliced
1/4 tsp nutmeg
1 tsp chili flakes

Instructions:

1. Stuff the flounder with lime slices and place the flounder in a foil sheet.
2. Whisk sugar, ground cumin, ground ginger, nutmeg, chili flakes, ground coriander, and ground celery root in a small bowl.
3. Sprinkle the spice mixture over the flounder and top it with olive oil, garlic, and lemon juice.
4. Wrap the foil around the flounder then place in the Slow cooker.
5. Put the cooker's lid on and set the cooking time to 8 hours on Low settings.
6. Unwrap the flounder and serve warm.

Nutrition Facts Per Serving:
Calories: 113, Total Fat: 3.6g, Fiber: 2g, Total Carbs: 11g, Protein: 10g

Octopus with Mixed Vegetable

Prep time: 1 day, Cook Time: 3 hrs., Serves: 4

Ingredients:

1 octopus, already prepared
1 cup red wine
1 cup white wine
1 cup of water
1 cup olive oil
2 tsp pepper sauce
1 tbsp hot sauce
1 tbsp paprika
1 tbsp tomato sauce

Salt and black pepper to the taste
½ bunch parsley, chopped
2 garlic cloves, minced
1 yellow onion, chopped
4 potatoes, cut into quarters.

Instructions:

1. Add octopus, white wine, half of the oil, water, red wine, hot sauce, tomato paste, parsley, black pepper, salt, hot sauce, and pepper sauce to a suitable bowl.

2. Mix well, then cover octopus for margination. Place this bowl in the refrigerator for 1 day.
3. Add remaining oil to the insert of your Slow cooker.
4. Toss in potatoes, onions, and octopus along with the marinade.
5. Put the cooker's lid on and set the cooking time to 3 hours on High settings.
6. Serve warm.

Nutrition Facts Per Serving:
Calories: 230, Total Fat: 4g, Fiber: 1g, Total Carbs: 7g, Protein: 23g

Lamb Bacon Stew

Prep time: 15 minutes; Cook Time: 7 hrs and 10 minutes, Serves: 6

Ingredients:

2 tbsp flour
2 oz. bacon, cooked and crumbled
1 and ½ lbs. lamb loin, chopped
Salt and black pepper to the taste
1 garlic clove, minced
1 cup yellow onion, chopped
3 and ½ cups veggie

stock
1 cup carrots, chopped
1 cup celery, chopped
2 cups sweet potatoes, chopped
1 tbsp thyme, chopped
1 bay leaf
2 tbsp olive oil

Instructions:

1. Thoroughly mix lamb meat with salt, black pepper, and flour in a bowl.
2. Take oil in a non-stick skillet and heat over medium-high heat.
3. Stir in lamb meat and sauté for 5 minutes.
4. Transfer the sauteed meat to the Slow cooker along with the rest of the ingredients to the cooker.
5. Put the cooker's lid on and set the cooking time to 7 hours on Low settings.
6. Discard the bay leaf and serve warm.

Nutrition Facts Per Serving:
Calories 360, Total Fat 5g, Fiber 3g, Total Carbs 16g, Protein 17g

Crispy Mackerel

Prep time: 12 minutes; Cook Time: 2 hrs., Serves: 4

Ingredients:

4 mackerels	Salt and black
3 oz. breadcrumbs	pepper to the taste
Juice and rind of 1	1 egg, whisked
lemon	1 tbsp butter
1 tbsp chives, finely	1 tbsp vegetable oil
chopped	3 lemon wedges

Instructions:

1. Whisk breadcrumbs with lemon rinds, lemon juice, chives, egg, black pepper, and salt in a small bowl.
2. Coat the mackerel with this breadcrumb's mixture liberally.
3. Brush the insert of your Slow cooker with butter and oil.
4. Place the mackerel along with breadcrumbs mixture to the cooker.
5. Put the cooker's lid on and set the cooking time to 2 hours on High settings.
6. Garnish with lemon wedges.
7. Enjoy.

Nutrition Facts Per Serving:

Calories: 200, Total Fat: 3g, Fiber: 1g, Total Carbs: 3g, Protein: 12g

Clams- Mussels Boil

Prep time: 12 minutes; Cook Time: 2 hrs., Serves: 4

Ingredients:

15 small clams	chopped
30 mussels,	10 oz. beer
scrubbed	2 tbsp parsley,
2 chorizo links,	chopped
sliced	1 tsp olive oil
1 lb. baby red	Lemon wedges for
potatoes, peeled	serving
1 yellow onion,	

Instructions:

1. Grease the insert of Slow cooker with oil.
2. Toss in clams, chorizo, potatoes, onion, parsley, beer, and mussels.
3. Put the cooker's lid on and set the cooking time to 2 hours on High settings.
4. Garnish with lemon wedges.
5. Serve warm.

Nutrition Facts Per Serving:

Calories: 251, Total Fat: 4g, Fiber: 7g, Total Carbs: 10g, Protein: 20g

Shrimp Mushroom Curry

Prep time: 12 minutes; Cook Time: 2 hrs. 30 hrs., Serves: 4

Ingredients:

1 lb. shrimp, peeled	sliced
and deveined	¼ cup yellow onion,
1 cup bouillon	chopped
4 lemon slices	1 tbsp olive oil
Salt and black	½ cup raisins
pepper to the taste	3 tbsp flour
½ tsp curry powder	1 cup milk
¼ cup mushrooms,	

Instructions:

1. Add bouillon, lemon, salt, curry powder, black pepper, onion, milk, and flour to the insert of the Slow cooker.
2. Put the cooker's lid on and set the cooking time to 2 hours on High settings.
3. Toss in raisins and shrimp, then cover again.
4. Cook the shrimp for 30 minutes on High settings.
5. Serve warm.

Nutrition Facts Per Serving:

Calories: 300, Total Fat: 4g, Fiber: 2g, Total Carbs: 30g, Protein: 17g

Mussels Tomato Soup

Prep time: 12 minutes; Cook Time: 2 hrs., Serves: 6

Ingredients:

2 lbs. mussels	minced
28 oz. canned	1 handful parsley,
tomatoes, crushed	chopped
28 oz. canned	1 yellow onion,
tomatoes, chopped	chopped
2 cup chicken stock	Salt and black
1 tsp red pepper	pepper to the taste
flakes, crushed	1 tbsp olive oil
3 garlic cloves,	

Instructions:

1. Toss mussels with tomatoes, stock, parsley, garlic, pepper flakes, oil, black pepper, salt, and onion in the insert of Slow Cooker.
2. Put the cooker's lid on and set the cooking time to 2 hours on High settings.
3. Serve warm.

Nutrition Facts Per Serving:

Calories: 250, Total Fat: 3g, Fiber: 3g, Total Carbs: 8g, Protein: 12g

Sweet Orange Fish

Prep time: 20 minutes; Cook Time: 3 hrs., Serves: 7

Ingredients:

3 oranges, peeled, chopped
2 lb. cod, peeled
1 tbsp honey
1 garlic clove, peeled, sliced
1 tsp ground white

pepper
½ tsp paprika
1 tsp chili flakes
½ tsp salt
2 tbsp lemon juice
1 tsp olive oil
½ tsp honey

Instructions:

1. Season the cod with chili flakes, paprika, white pepper, salt, lemon juice, olive oil, and 1 tbsp honey.
2. Mix oranges with garlic and ½ tsp honey in a bowl.
3. Stuff the fish with this orange mixture then place it over a foil sheet.
4. Wrap the fish in the foil then place it in the insert of the Slow Cooker.
5. Put the cooker's lid on and set the cooking time to 3 hours on High settings.
6. Unwrap and serve fresh.

Nutrition Facts Per Serving:

Calories: 141, Total Fat: 1.4g, Fiber: 2g, Total Carbs: 11.74g, Protein: 21g

Orange Marmalade Salmon

Prep time: 12 minutes; Cook Time: 2 hrs., Serves: 2

Ingredients:

2 lemons, sliced
1 lb. wild salmon, skinless and cubed
¼ cup balsamic vinegar

¼ cup red-orange juice
1 tsp olive oil
1/3 cup orange marmalade

Instructions:

1. Mix orange juice, vinegar, and marmalade in a saucepan.
2. Stir cook this marmalade mixture for 1 minute on a simmer.
3. Transfer this mixture to the insert of the Slow Cooker.
4. Add lemon slices, oil, and salmon to the cooker.
5. Put the cooker's lid on and set the cooking time to 2 hours on High settings.
6. Serve warm.

Nutrition Facts Per Serving:

Calories: 260, Total Fat: 3g, Fiber: 2g, Total Carbs: 16g, Protein: 8g

Vinaigrette Dipped Salmon

Prep time: 2 hrs., Cook Time: 2 hrs., Serves: 6

Ingredients:

6 salmon steaks
2 tbsp olive oil
4 leeks, sliced
2 garlic cloves, minced
2 tbsp parsley, chopped

1 cup clam juice
2 tbsp lemon juice
Salt and white pepper to the taste
1 tsp sherry
1/3 cup dill, chopped

For the raspberry vinegar:

2 pints red raspberries

1-pint cider vinegar

Instructions:

1. Mix raspberries with salmon, and vinegar in a bowl.
2. Cover the raspberry salmon and refrigerate for 2 hours.
3. Add the raspberry mixture along with the remaining ingredients to the insert of the Slow Cooker.
4. Put the cooker's lid on and set the cooking time to 2 hours on High settings.
5. Serve warm.

Nutrition Facts Per Serving:

Calories: 251, Total Fat: 6g, Fiber: 7g, Total Carbs: 16g, Protein: 26g

Salmon with Saffron Rice

Prep time: 5 minutes; Cook Time: 2 hrs., Serves: 2

Ingredients:

2 wild salmon fillets, boneless
Salt and black pepper to the taste
½ cup jasmine rice

1 cup chicken stock
¼ cup veggie stock
1 tbsp butter
A pinch of saffron

Instructions:

1. Add stock, rice, butter, and saffron to the insert of Slow Cooker.
2. Mix well, then add salmon, salt, and black pepper to the cooker.
3. Put the cooker's lid on and set the cooking time to 2 hours on High settings.
4. Serve warm.

Nutrition Facts Per Serving:

Calories: 312, Total Fat: 4g, Fiber: 6g, Total Carbs: 20g, Protein: 22g

Salmon with Lemon Relish

Prep time: 12 minutes; Cook Time: 2 hrs., Serves: 2

Ingredients:

2 medium salmon fillets, boneless	1 big lemon, peeled and cut into wedges
Salt and black pepper to the taste	¼ cup 1 tsp olive oil
1 shallot, chopped	2 tbsp parsley, finely chopped
1 tbsp lemon juice	

Instructions:

1. Rub the salmon fillets with olive, salt, and black pepper.
2. Place the seasoned fillets in the insert of Slow cooker.
3. Add shallots, and lemon juice to the fish.
4. Put the cooker's lid on and set the cooking time to 2 hours on High settings.
5. Shred the cooked salmon and divide it into the two serving bowls.
6. Add remaining oil, lemon wedges, and parsley to the cooker.
7. Mix well then divide in the serving bowls.
8. Enjoy.

Nutrition Facts Per Serving:
Calories: 200, Total Fat: 10g, Fiber: 1g, Total Carbs: 5g, Protein: 20g

Cream White Fish

Prep time: 12 minutes; Cook Time: 2 hrs., Serves: 6

Ingredients:

17 oz. white fish, skinless, boneless and cut into chunks	13 oz. milk
1 yellow onion, chopped	Salt and black pepper to the taste
13 oz. potatoes, peeled and cut into chunks	14 oz. chicken stock
	14 oz. water
	14 oz. half and half cream

Instructions:

1. Add onion, fish, potatoes, water, stock, and milk to the insert of Slow Cooker.
2. Put the cooker's lid on and set the cooking time to 2 hours on High settings.
3. Add half and half cream, black pepper, and salt to the fish.
4. Mix gently, then serve warm.

Nutrition Facts Per Serving:
Calories: 203, Total Fat: 4g, Fiber: 5g, Total Carbs: 20g, Protein: 15g

Cod Bacon Chowder

Prep time: 23 minutes; Cook Time: 3 hrs; Serves: 6

Ingredients:

1 yellow onion, chopped	1 carrot, grated
10 oz. cod, cubed	5 cups of water
3 oz. bacon, sliced	1 tbsp almond milk
1 tsp sage	1 tsp ground coriander
5 oz. potatoes, peeled and cubed	1 tsp salt

Instructions:

1. Place grated carrots and onion in the Slow Cooker.
2. Add almond milk, coriander, water, sage, fish, potatoes, and bacon.
3. Put the cooker's lid on and set the cooking time to 3 hours on High settings.
4. Garnish with chopped parsley.
5. Serve.

Nutrition Facts Per Serving:
Calories 108, Total Fat 4.5g, Fiber 2g, Total Carbs 8.02g, Protein 10g

Chipotle Salmon Fillets

Prep time: 15 minutes; Cook Time: 2 hrs; Serves: 2

Ingredients:

2 medium salmon fillets, boneless	2 tsp sugar
A pinch of nutmeg, ground	1 tsp onion powder
A pinch of cloves, ground	¼ tsp chipotle chili powder
A pinch of ginger powder	½ tsp cayenne pepper
Salt and black pepper to the taste	½ tsp cinnamon, ground
	1/8 tsp thyme, dried

Instructions:

1. Place the salmon fillets in foil wraps.
2. Drizzle ginger, cloves, salt, thyme, cinnamon, black pepper, cayenne, chili powder, onion powder, nutmeg, and coconut sugar on top.
3. Wrap the fish fillet with the aluminum foil.
4. Put the cooker's lid on and set the cooking time to 2 hours on Low settings.
5. Unwrap the fish and serve warm.

Nutrition Facts Per Serving:
Calories 220, Total Fat 4g, Fiber 2g, Total Carbs 7g, Protein 4g

Salmon Tofu Soup

Prep time: 18 minutes; Cook Time: 3 hrs., Serves: 9

Ingredients:

5 cups fish stock
3 cups of water
2 tbsp miso paste
10 oz salmon fillet
4 oz carrot, peeled, chopped
1 white onion, peeled, chopped
1 tbsp fresh dill, chopped
6 oz tofu, chopped
1 tsp salt
½ tsp brown sugar
½ tsp ground coriander

Instructions:

1. Season the salmon fillet with coriander ground and salt.
2. Place the salmon in the insert of Slow cooker then add stock and vegetables.
3. Put the cooker's lid on and set the cooking time to 2 hours on Low settings.
4. Whisk water miso paste with water in a small bowl.
5. Add tofu cheese, brown sugar, and miso paste to the cooker.
6. Put the cooker's lid on and set the cooking time to 1 hour on High settings.
7. Serve warm.

Nutrition Facts Per Serving:
Calories: 148, Total Fat: 7.9g, Fiber: 2g, Total Carbs: 5.82g, Protein: 15g

Seafood Bean Chili

Prep time: 21 minutes; Cook Time: 3.5 hrs., Serves: 8

Ingredients:

1 lb. salmon, diced
7 oz shrimps, peeled
1 tbsp salt
1 cup tomatoes, canned
1 tsp ground white pepper
1 tbsp tomato sauce
2 onions, chopped
1 cup carrot, chopped
1 can red beans
½ cup tomato juice
1 cup fish stock
1 tsp cayenne pepper
1 cup bell pepper, chopped
1 tbsp olive oil
1 tsp coriander
1 cup of water
6 oz Parmesan, shredded
1 garlic clove, sliced

Instructions:

1. Add tomatoes, white pepper, tomato sauce, red beans, carrots, tomato juice, bell pepper, fish stock, cayenne pepper, garlic, water and coriander to the insert of Slow Cooker.

2. Put the cooker's lid on and set the cooking time to 3 hours on High settings.
3. Add olive oil and seafood to a suitable pan, then sauté for 3 minutes.
4. Transfer the sautéed seafood to the slow cooker.
5. Put the cooker's lid on and set the cooking time to 30 minutes on High settings.
6. Serve warm.

Nutrition Facts Per Serving:
Calories: 281, Total Fat: 7.9g, Fiber: 4g, Total Carbs: 22.52g, Protein: 30g

Salmon Chickpea Fingers

Prep time: 27 minutes; Cook Time: 3 hrs., Serves: 8

Ingredients:

2 large eggs
1 cup panko bread crumbs
1 tbsp turmeric
1 tbsp butter
13 oz salmon fillet
1 tsp salt
1 tsp ground black pepper
¼ cup chickpeas, canned
1 tsp onion powder
2 tbsp semolina
¼ tsp ginger

Instructions:

1. Whisk eggs with turmeric, semolina, onion powder, ginger, black pepper, and salt in a bowl.
2. Blend salmon with chickpeas in a blender then stir in the egg mixture.
3. Mix well then make medium finger-shaped logs.
4. Coat the fish fingers with breadcrumbs liberally.
5. Grease the insert of the Slow cooker with melted butter then add fish fingers
6. Put the cooker's lid on and set the cooking time to 3 hours on High settings.
7. Flip the fish fingers when cooked halfway through.
8. Serve warm.

Nutrition Facts Per Serving:
Calories: 149, Total Fat: 6.5g, Fiber: 1g, Total Carbs: 9.72g, Protein: 12g

Shri Lanka Fish Cutlet

Prep time: 30 minutes; Cook Time: 2 hrs., Serves: 14

Ingredients:

16 oz mackerel fillet, minced	1 oz curry powder
1 cup mashed potato	1 tsp salt
1 chili pepper, finely chopped	4 oz tomato sauce
1 cup onion, grated	1 tsp ground thyme
1 tsp minced garlic	4 tsp lime juice
¼ tsp ground ginger	3 large eggs
	1 cup bread crumbs
	1 tsp chives
	1 tbsp onion powder

Instructions:

1. Mix mackerel mince with mashed potato, grated onion, ginger, garlic, curry powder, thyme, lime juice, onion powder, and salt in a suitable bowl.
2. Make small round cutlets out of this mixture.
3. Dip the mackerel cutlets in the whisked egg then coat them with breadcrumbs.
4. Place cutlets in the insert of the slow cooker and top them with tomato sauce.
5. Put the cooker's lid on and set the cooking time to 2 hours on High settings.
6. Serve warm.

Nutrition Facts Per Serving:
Calories: 83, Total Fat: 2g, Fiber: 2g, Total Carbs: 7.67g, Protein: 8g

Cod with Asparagus

Prep time: 15 minutes; Cook Time: 2 hrs; Serves: 4

Ingredients:

4 cod fillets, boneless	Salt and black pepper to the taste
1 bunch asparagus	2 tbsp olive oil
12 tbsp lemon juice	

Instructions:

1. Place the cod fillets in separate foil sheets.
2. Top the fish with asparagus spears, lemon pepper, oil, and lemon juice.
3. Wrap the fish with its foil sheet then place them in Slow Cooker.
4. Put the cooker's lid on and set the cooking time to 2 hours on High settings.
5. Unwrap the fish and serve warm.

Nutrition Facts Per Serving:
Calories 202, Total Fat 3g, Fiber 6g, Total Carbs 7, Protein 3g

Shrimp Potato Boil

Prep time: 12 minutes; Cook Time: 2 hrs. 30 minutes, Serves: 4

Ingredients:

1 and ½ lbs. shrimp, head removed	pepper to the taste
12 oz. Andouille sausage, already cooked and chopped	1 tsp red pepper flakes, crushed
4 ears of corn, each cut into 3 pieces	2 sweet onions, cut into wedges
1 tbsp old bay seasoning	1 lb. potatoes, cut into medium chunks
16 oz. beer	8 garlic cloves, crushed
Salt and black	French baguettes for serving

Instructions:

1. Add beer, old bay seasoning, salt, onion, black pepper, garlic, corn, sausage, potatoes, and red pepper flakes to the insert of Slow Cooker.
2. Put the cooker's lid on and set the cooking time to 2 hours on High settings.
3. Toss in shrimp then cover again to cook for 30 minutes on High settings.
4. Enjoy warm with French baguettes.

Nutrition Facts Per Serving:
Calories: 261, Total Fat: 5g, Fiber: 6g, Total Carbs: 20g, Protein: 16g

Salmon with Green Sauce

Prep time: 13 minutes; Cook Time: 2 hrs and 30 minutes, Serves: 4

Ingredients:

2 garlic cloves, minced	chopped
4 salmon fillets, boneless	3 tbsp lime juice
¾ cup cilantro,	1 tbsp olive oil
	Salt and black pepper to the taste

Instructions:

1. Coat the base of your Slow Cooker with oil.
2. Place salmon along with all other ingredients in the cooker.
3. Put the cooker's lid on and set the cooking time to 2 hours 30minutes on Low settings.
4. Serve warm.

Nutrition Facts Per Serving:
Calories 200, Total Fat 3g, Fiber 2g, Total Carbs 14g, Protein 8g

Lamb Vegetable Curry

Prep time: 17 minutes; Cook Time: 4 hrs; Serves: 4

Ingredients:

1 and ½ tbsp sweet paprika
3 tbsp curry powder
Salt and black pepper to the taste
2 lbs. lamb meat, cubed
2 tbsp olive oil
3 carrots, chopped
4 celery stalks, chopped
1 onion, chopped
4 celery stalks, chopped
1 cup chicken stock
4 garlic cloves minced
1 cup of coconut milk

Instructions:

1. Take oil in a non-stick skillet and heat it over medium-high heat.
2. Stir in lamb meat to sauté until brown.
3. Transfer this meat to the slow cooker along with other ingredients.
4. Put the cooker's lid on and set the cooking time to 4 hours on High settings.
5. Serve warm.

Nutrition Facts Per Serving:

Calories 300, Total Fat 4g, Fiber 4g, Total Carbs 16g, Protein 13g

Spicy Harissa Perch

Prep time: 25 minutes; Cook Time: 4.5 hrs., Serves: 6

Ingredients:

14 oz perch, peeled
1 tsp cayenne pepper
1 chili pepper, chopped
1 onion, peeled and diced
3 garlic cloves, sliced
1 tsp ground ginger
1 tsp cilantro
1 tbsp harissa paste
1 tsp curry paste
1 tsp olive oil
3 tbsp fish sauce
3 tbsp water

Instructions:

1. Season the perch by rubbing it with ground ginger, cayenne pepper, cilantro, curry paste, and harissa paste.
2. Stuff the perch with onion, garlic, and chili pepper.
3. Mix fish sauce with olive oil and water in a small bowl.
4. Layer the insert of the Slow cooker with a foil sheet.
5. Place the stuffed perch in the cooker and pour this fish sauce mixture on top.

6. Put the cooker's lid on and set the cooking time to 4.5 hours on High settings.
7. Serve warm.

Nutrition Facts Per Serving:

Calories: 88, Total Fat: 1.5g, Fiber: 1g, Total Carbs: 4g, Protein: 14g

Fish Potato Cakes

Prep time: 15 minutes; Cook Time: 5 hrs., Serves: 12

Ingredients:

1 lb. trout, minced
6 oz mashed potato
1 carrot, grated
½ cup fresh parsley
1 tsp salt
½ cup panko bread crumbs
1 egg, beaten
1 tsp minced garlic
1 onion, grated
1 tsp olive oil
1 tsp ground black pepper
¼ tsp cilantro

Instructions:

1. Mix minced trout with mashed potatoes, carrot, salt, garlic, cilantro, onion, black pepper, and egg in a bowl.
2. Stir in breadcrumbs and olive oil, then mix well.
3. Make 12 balls out of this mixture then flatten the balls.
4. Place these fish cakes in the insert of Slow cooker.
5. Put the cooker's lid on and set the cooking time to 5 hours on Low settings.
6. Flip all the fish cakes when cooked halfway through.
7. Serve warm.

Nutrition Facts Per Serving:

Calories: 93, Total Fat: 3.8g, Fiber: 1g, Total Carbs: 5.22g, Protein: 9g

Mushrooms Snapper

Prep time: 20 minutes; Cook Time: 6 hrs., Serves: 6

Ingredients:

1 cup sour cream	1 tsp ground
1 onion, diced	coriander
¼ cup almond milk	1 tsp kosher salt
1 tsp salt	1 tbsp lemon juice
7 oz cremini	1 tsp butter
mushrooms	1 lb. snapper,
1 tsp ground thyme	chopped
1 tbsp ground	1 tsp lemon zest
paprika	

Instructions:

1. Season the snapper with thyme, paprika, coriander, salt, lemon zest, and lemon juice in a bowl.
2. Cover the snapper and marinate it for 10 minutes.
3. Grease the insert of Slow cooker with butter and add snapper mixture.
4. Add cremini mushrooms, onion, almond milk, and sour cream.
5. Put the cooker's lid on and set the cooking time to 6 hours on Low settings.
6. Serve warm.

Nutrition Facts Per Serving:

Calories: 248, Total Fat: 6.3g, Fiber: 5g, Total Carbs: 31.19g, Protein: 20g

Rice Stuffed Trout

Prep time: 20 minutes; Cook Time: 4 hrs., Serves: 5

Ingredients:

16 oz whole trout,	1 tsp ground black
peeled	pepper
½ cup sweet corn	½ tsp paprika
¼ cup of rice,	1 tbsp olive oil
cooked	1 tbsp sour cream
1 sweet pepper,	¼ cup cream cheese
chopped	3 lemon wedges
1 tbsp salt	2 tbsp chives
1 tsp thyme	

Instructions:

1. Mix sweet corn, cooked rice, and sweet pepper in a suitable bowl.
2. Whisk chives, salt, sour cream, olive oil, cream cheese, paprika, thyme, black pepper in a separate bowl.
3. Place the trout fish in a foil sheet and brush it with a cream cheese mixture.
4. Stuff the fish with rice mixture and top the fish with lemon wedges.
5. Wrap the stuffed with the foil sheet.
6. Put the cooker's lid on and set the cooking time to 4 hours on High settings.
7. Serve warm.

Nutrition Facts Per Serving:

Calories: 255, Total Fat: 13.9g, Fiber: 2g, Total Carbs: 13.57g, Protein: 22g

Herbed Shrimps

Prep time: 16 minutes; Cook Time: 40 minutes; Serves: 4

Ingredients:

4 tbsp fresh dill	1 lb. shrimp, peeled
¼ cup pineapple	1 tsp ground ginger
juice	½ tsp lemon juice
2 tbsp sugar	1 tbsp tomato juice
3 tbsp mango puree	1 cup of water
1 tbsp butter	½ tsp sage

Instructions:

1. Add shrimp, water, and sage to the insert of Slow Cooker.
2. Put the cooker's lid on and set the cooking time to 20 minutes on High settings.
3. Meanwhile, mix melted butter, mango puree, pineapple juice, sugar, lemon juice, ginger ground, dill and tomatoes juice in a bowl.
4. Add this mixture to the shrimp in the Slow cooker.
5. Put the cooker's lid on and set the cooking time to 20 minutes on High settings.
6. Serve warm.

Nutrition Facts Per Serving:

Calories: 192, Total Fat: 5.4g, Fiber: 2g, Total Carbs: 12.18g, Protein: 24g

Italian Trout Croquettes

**Prep time: 18 minutes; Cook Time: 3 hrs.,
Serves: 8**
Ingredients:

14 oz trout fillet, minced	Seasoning
3 tbsp Worcestershire sauce	1 tsp salt
	1 tsp ground black pepper
7 tbsp flour	6 oz rice, cooked
2 eggs	3 tbsp milk
1 tbsp Italian	1 tsp paprika
	2 tbsp sesame oil

Instructions:
1. Mix trout mince with Worcestershire sauce, flour, salt, Italian seasoning, milk, paprika, cooked rice, and black pepper in a bowl.
2. Whisk in egg and then mix until it forms a smooth mixture.
3. Make small bowls out of this mixture then add to the slow cooker along with sesame oil.
4. Put the cooker's lid on and set the cooking time to 3 hours on High settings.
5. Serve warm.

Nutrition Facts Per Serving:
Calories: 186, Total Fat: 9.6g, Fiber: 1g, Total Carbs: 10.24g, Protein: 14g

Tuna with Chimichurri Sauce

**Prep time: 16 minutes; Cook Time: 1 hr.
15 minutes Serves: 4**
Ingredients:

½ cup cilantro, chopped	and cubed
1/3 cup olive oil	Salt and black pepper to the taste
1 small red onion, chopped	1 tsp red pepper flakes
3 tbsp balsamic vinegar	2 garlic cloves, minced
2 tbsp parsley, chopped	1 tsp thyme, chopped
2 tbsp basil, chopped	A pinch of cayenne pepper
1 jalapeno pepper, chopped	2 avocados, pitted, peeled and sliced
1 lb. tuna steak, boneless, skinless	6 oz. baby arugula

Instructions:
1. Whisk jalapeno, oil, vinegar, cilantro, onion, garlic, basil, pepper flakes, parsley, thyme, black pepper, salt, and

thyme in the Slow cooker.
2. Put the cooker's lid on and set the cooking time to 1 hour on High settings.
3. Now add tuna and cover again to cook for 15 minutes on High settings.
4. Slice the cooked tuna and serve warm with its sauce, arugula, and avocado slices.
5. Enjoy.

Nutrition Facts Per Serving:
Calories: 186, Total Fat: 3g, Fiber: 1g, Total Carbs: 4g, Protein: 20g

Chicken Stuffed Squid

**Prep time: 20 minutes; Cook Time: 7 hrs.,
Serves: 4**
Ingredients:

1 lb. squid tubes	pepper
2 oz capers	1 tsp butter
1 cup tomatoes, chopped	1 tbsp tomato paste
1 tsp salt	1 garlic clove, chopped
1 tsp cayenne pepper	1 cup chicken stock
1 tsp ground black	6 oz ground chicken
	1 tsp cilantro

Instructions:
1. Toss tomatoes with cayenne pepper, salt, black pepper, capers, butter, chicken, cilantro, and garlic in a bowl.
2. Stuff the squid tubes with chicken mixture.
3. Place these stuffed tubes in the insert of Slow cooker and top then with tomato paste and stock.
4. Put the cooker's lid on and set the cooking time to 7 hours on Low settings.
5. Serve warm.

Nutrition Facts Per Serving:
Calories: 216, Total Fat: 7g, Fiber: 1g, Total Carbs: 10.1g, Protein: 28g

Tuna with Potatoes

Prep time: 16 minutes; Cook Time: 4 hrs; Serves: 8

Ingredients:

4 large potatoes, cut in half
8 oz. tuna, canned
½ cup cream cheese
4 oz. Cheddar cheese, shredded
1 garlic clove, minced
1 tsp onion powder
½ tsp salt
1 tsp ground black pepper
1 tsp dried dill

Instructions:

1. Wrap the potatoes with an aluminum foil and put them in the Slow cooker.
2. Put the cooker's lid on and set the cooking time to 2 hours on High settings.
3. Mix cream cheese with tuna, cheese, black pepper, salt, garlic, dill, and onion powder in a separate bowl.
4. Remove the potatoes from the foil and scoop out the flesh from each half.
5. Divide the tuna mixture in the potato shells then return then to the Slow Cooker.
6. Put the cooker's lid on and set the cooking time to 2 hours on High settings.
7. Serve warm.

Nutrition Facts Per Serving:

Calories 247, Total Fat 5.9g, Fiber 4g, Total Carbs 35.31g, Protein 14g

Seafood Medley

Prep time: 15 minutes; Cook Time: 7 hrs; Serves: 4

Ingredients:

28 oz. canned tomatoes, crushed
4 cups veggie stock
3 garlic cloves, minced
1 lb. sweet potatoes, cubed
½ cup yellow onion, chopped
2 lbs. mixed seafood
1 tsp thyme, dried
1 tsp cilantro, dried
1 tsp basil, dried
Salt and black pepper to the taste
A pinch of red pepper flakes, crushed

Instructions:

1. Add sweet potatoes, stock, garlic, tomatoes, basil, red pepper flakes, black pepper, salt, cilantro, thyme, and onion to the Slow Cooker.
2. Put the cooker's lid on and set the cooking time to 6 hours on Low settings.

3. Mix well and add seafood to the veggie mixture.
4. Put the cooker's lid on and set the cooking time to 1 hour on High settings.
5. Serve.

Nutrition Facts Per Serving:

Calories 270, Total Fat 4g, Fiber 4g, Total Carbs 12g, Protein 3g

Shrimp Clam Stew

Prep time: 15 minutes; Cook Time: 4 hrs and 30 minutes, Serves: 8

Ingredients:

29 oz. canned tomatoes, chopped
2 yellow onions, chopped
2 celery ribs, chopped
½ cup fish stock
4 garlic cloves, minced
1 tbsp red vinegar
2 tbsp olive oil
3 lbs. shrimp, peeled and deveined
6 oz. canned clams
2 tbsp cilantro, chopped

Instructions:

1. Add tomatoes, onion, vinegar, stock, celery, and oil to the Slow cooker.
2. Put the cooker's lid on and set the cooking time to 4 hours on Low settings.
3. Stir in cilantro, clams, and shrimp to the cooker.
4. Put the cooker's lid on and set the cooking time to 30 minutes on Low settings.
5. Serve warm.

Nutrition Facts Per Serving:

Calories 255, Total Fat 4g, Fiber 3g, Total Carbs 14g, Protein 26g

Crab with Oyster Sauce

Prep time: 18 minutes; Cook Time: 1 hr., Serves: 6

Ingredients:

15 oz crab	6 cups of water
6 oz fennel bulb, chopped	1 tbsp fresh parsley, chopped
1 lemon	1 oz bay leaf
1 tbsp kosher salt	4 oz shallot, peeled and chopped
1 tbsp oyster sauce	
1 tsp black peas	

Instructions:

1. Add crab, shallot, and fennel bulb to the insert of the Slow Cooker.
2. Stir in black peas, water, bay leaf, and salt to the crab.
3. Put the cooker's lid on and set the cooking time to 1 hour on High settings.
4. Meanwhile, mix lemon juice with parsley and oyster sauce in a small bowl.
5. Peel the cooked crab meat then top this meat with oyster sauce mixture.
6. Serve warm.

Nutrition Facts Per Serving:
Calories: 103, Total Fat: 1.3g, Fiber: 3g, Total Carbs: 9.78g, Protein: 14g

Lamb Potato Stew

Prep time: 15 minutes; Cook Time: 8 hrs; Serves: 4

Ingredients:

1 and ½ lbs. lamb meat, cubed	dried
¼ cup flour	1 onion, sliced
Salt and black pepper to the taste	½ tsp thyme, dried
2 tbsp olive oil	2 cups of water
1 tsp rosemary,	1 cup baby carrots
	2 cups sweet potatoes, chopped

Instructions:

1. First, mix the lamb with flour in a bowl.
2. Take oil in a non-stick pan and place it over medium-high heat.
3. Stir in meat and sauté until brown.
4. Transfer the sauteed meat to the Slow cooker along with the rest of the ingredients.
5. Put the cooker's lid on and set the cooking time to 8 hours on Low settings.
6. Serve warm.

Nutrition Facts Per Serving:
Calories 350, Total Fat 8g, Fiber 3g, Total Carbs 20g, Protein 16g

Trout Capers Piccata

Prep time: 14 minutes; Cook Time: 45 minutes; Serves: 4

Ingredients:

4 oz dry white wine	1 tsp oregano
1 lb. trout fillet	1 tsp cilantro
2 tbsp capers	1 tbsp fresh dill, chopped
3 tbsp olive oil	
3 tbsp flour	1 tsp ground white pepper
1 tsp garlic powder	
1 tsp dried rosemary	1 tsp butter

Instructions:

1. Pour olive oil into the insert of Slow Cooker then place the trout in it.
2. Add garlic powder, dried rosemary, white pepper, cilantro, and oregano over the trout.
3. Put the cooker's lid on and set the cooking time to 30 minutes on High settings.
4. Flip the fish when cooked halfway through.
5. Meanwhile, mix dry wine with flour and add to the cooker.
6. Add butter, capers, and dill on top.
7. Put the cooker's lid on and set the cooking time to 15 minutes on High settings.
8. Serve warm.

Nutrition Facts Per Serving:
Calories: 393, Total Fat: 25.9g, Fiber: 1g, Total Carbs: 8g, Protein: 32g

Chapter 7 Side Dish Recipes

Asian Sesame Asparagus

Prep Time: 24 minutes Cook Time: 4 hrs. Serves: 4

Ingredients:

1 tbsp sesame seeds	1 tsp salt
1 tsp miso paste	1 tsp chili flakes
¼ cup of soy sauce	1 tsp oregano
1 cup fish stock	1 cup of water
8 oz. asparagus	

Instructions:

1. Fill the insert of the slow cooker with water and add asparagus.
2. Put the cooker's lid on and set the cooking time to 3 hours on High settings.
3. During this time, mix miso paste with soy sauce, fish stock, and sesame seeds in a suitable bowl.
4. Stir in oregano, chili flakes, and salt, then mix well.
5. Drain the slow-cooked asparagus then return it to the slow cooker.
6. Pour the miso-stock mixture over the asparagus.
7. Put the cooker's lid on and set the cooking time to 1 hour on High settings.
8. Serve warm.

Nutrition Facts Per Serving:
Calories: 85, Total Fat: 4.8g, Fiber: 2g, Total Carbs: 7.28g, Protein: 4g

Blueberry Spinach Salad

Prep time: 14 minutes Cook Time: 1 hour Serves: 3

Ingredients:

¼ cup pecans, chopped	1 tbsp olive oil
½ tsp sugar	4 cups spinach
2 tsp maple syrup	2 oranges, peeled and cut into segments
1 tbsp white vinegar	
2 tbsp orange juice	
	1 cup blueberries

Instructions:

1. Add pecans, maple syrup, and rest of the ingredients to the Slow cooker.
2. Put the cooker's lid on and set the cooking time to 1 hour on High settings.
3. Serve warm.

Nutrition Facts Per Serving:
Calories: 140, Total Fat: 4g, Fiber: 3g, Total Carbs: 10g, Protein: 3g

Baked Potato

Prep time: 23 minutes Cook Time: 8 hours Serves: 6

Ingredients:

6 large potatoes, peeled and cubed	½ tsp salt
3 oz. mushrooms, chopped	½ tsp minced garlic
	1 tsp sour cream
1 onion, chopped	½ tsp turmeric
1 tsp butter	1 tsp olive oil

Instructions:

1. Grease the insert of the slow cooker with olive oil.
2. Toss in potatoes, onion, mushrooms, and rest of the ingredients.
3. Put the cooker's lid on and set the cooking time to 8 hours on Low settings.
4. Serve warm.

Nutrition Facts Per Serving:
Calories: 309, Total Fat: 1.9g, Fiber: 9g, Total Carbs: 66.94g, Protein: 8g

Slow-Cooked White Onions

Prep time: 23 minutes Cook Time: 9 hours Serves: 5

Ingredients:

½ cup bread crumbs	1 tbsp salt
5 oz. Romano cheese, shredded	5 large white onions, peeled and wedges
¼ cup cream cheese	1 tsp ground black pepper
¼ cup half and half	
3 oz. butter	1 tsp garlic powder

Instructions:

1. Add onion wedges to the insert of the slow cooker.
2. Mix breadcrumbs and shredded cheese in a suitable bowl.
3. Whisk the half and half cream with remaining ingredients.
4. Spread this mixture over the onion and then top it with breadcrumbs mixture.
5. Put the cooker's lid on and set the cooking time to 9 hours on Low settings.
6. Serve warm.

Nutrition Facts Per Serving:
Calories: 349, Total Fat: 25.3g, Fiber: 3g, Total Carbs: 19.55g, Protein: 13g

Broccoli Filling

Prep time: 16 minutes Cook Time: 5 hrs. Serves: 6

Ingredients:

10 oz. broccoli, chopped
7 oz. Cheddar cheese, shredded
4 eggs
½ cup onion, chopped
1 cup heavy cream
3 tbsp mayo sauce
3 tbsp butter
½ cup bread crumbs

Instructions:

1. Spread broccoli in the insert of the Slow cooker and top it with ½ cup cream.
2. Put the cooker's lid on and set the cooking time to 3 hours on High settings.
3. Beat eggs with onion, mayo sauce, butter, and remaining cream in a bowl.
4. Mash the cooked broccoli and stir in the mayo-eggs mixture.
5. Spread the breadcrumbs over the broccoli mixture.
6. Put the cooker's lid on and set the cooking time to 2 hours on High settings.
7. Serve warm.

Nutrition Facts Per Serving:

Calories: 289, Total Fat: 22.9g, Fiber: 2g, Total Carbs: 9.07g, Protein: 13g

Garlicky Black Beans

Prep time: 14 minutes Cook Time: 7 hours Serves: 8

Ingredients:

1 cup black beans, soaked overnight, drained and rinsed
1 cup of water
Salt and black pepper to the taste
1 spring onion, chopped
2 garlic cloves, minced
½ tsp cumin seeds

Instructions:

1. Add beans, salt, black pepper, cumin seeds, garlic, and onion to the Slow cooker.
2. Put the cooker's lid on and set the cooking time to 7 hours on Low settings.
3. Serve warm.

Nutrition Facts Per Serving:

Calories: 300, Total Fat: 4g, Fiber: 6g, Total Carbs: 20g, Protein: 15g

Balsamic-Glazed Beets

Prep time: 23 minutes Cook Time: 2 hours Serves: 6

Ingredients:

1 lb. beets, sliced
5 oz. orange juice
3 oz. balsamic vinegar
3 tbsp almonds
6 oz. goat cheese
1 tsp minced garlic
1 tsp olive oil

Instructions:

1. Toss the beets with balsamic vinegar, orange juice, and olive oil in the insert of Slow cooker.
2. Put the cooker's lid on and set the cooking time to 7 hours on Low settings.
3. Toss goat cheese with minced garlic and almonds in a bowl.
4. Spread this cheese garlic mixture over the beets.
5. Put the cooker's lid on and set the cooking time to 10 minutes on High settings.
6. Serve warm.

Nutrition Facts Per Serving:

Calories: 189, Total Fat: 11.3g, Fiber: 2g, Total Carbs: 12g, Protein: 10g

Beets Salad

Prep time: 14 minutes Cook Time: 7 hours Serves: 12

Ingredients:

5 beets, peeled and sliced
¼ cup balsamic vinegar
1/3 cup honey
1 tbsp rosemary,
chopped
2 tbsp olive oil
Salt and black pepper to the taste
2 garlic cloves, minced

Instructions:

1. Add beets, oil, vinegar, salt, black pepper, honey, garlic, and rosemary to the Slow cooker.
2. Put the cooker's lid on and set the cooking time to 7 hours on Low settings.
3. Serve warm.

Nutrition Facts Per Serving:

Calories: 70, Total Fat: 3g, Fiber: 2g, Total Carbs: 17g, Protein: 3g

Buttery Artichokes

Prep time: 18 minutes Cook Time: 6 hrs. Serves: 5

Ingredients:

13 oz. artichoke heart halved
1 tsp salt
4 cups chicken stock
1 tsp turmeric
1 garlic clove, peeled
4 tbsp butter
4 oz. Parmesan, shredded

Instructions:

1. Add artichoke, stock, salt, and turmeric to the Slow cooker.
2. Put the cooker's lid on and set the cooking time to 6 hours on Low settings.
3. Drain and transfer the cooked artichoke to the serving plates.
4. Drizzle, cheese, and butter over the artichoke.
5. Serve warm.

Nutrition Facts Per Serving:

Calories: 272, Total Fat: 12.8g, Fiber: 4g, Total Carbs: 24.21g, Protein: 17g

Orange Squash

Prep time: 17 minutes Cook Time: 5 hours Serves: 6

Ingredients:

1 lb. butternut squash, peeled and diced
1 Poblano pepper,chopped
1 tsp brown sugar
1 tsp ground
cinnamon
1 tbsp salt
1 cup heavy cream
1 orange, sliced
¼ tsp ground cardamom

Instructions:

1. Toss the butternut squash with poblano pepper, salt, cream, cardamom, sugar, and cardamom.
2. Spread the orange slices in the insert of the Slow cooker.
3. Spread the butternut squash-poblano pepper mixture over the orange slices.
4. Put the cooker's lid on and set the cooking time to 5 hours on Low settings.
5. Serve warm.

Nutrition Facts Per Serving:

Calories: 105, Total Fat: 7.6g, Fiber: 2g, Total Carbs: 9g, Protein: 2g

Carrot Beet Salad

Prep time: 14 minutes Cook Time: 7 hours Serves: 6

Ingredients:

½ cup walnuts, chopped
¼ cup lemon juice
½ cup olive oil
1 shallot, chopped
1 tsp Dijon mustard
1 tbsp brown sugar
Salt and black
pepper to the taste
2 beets, peeled and cut into wedges
2 carrots, peeled and sliced
1 cup parsley
5 oz. arugula

Instructions:

1. Add beets, carrots, and rest of the ingredients to the Slow Cooker.
2. Put the cooker's lid on and set the cooking time to 7 hours on Low settings.
3. Serve warm.

Nutrition Facts Per Serving:

Calories: 100, Total Fat: 3g, Fiber: 3g, Total Carbs: 7g, Protein: 3g

Cornbread Cream Pudding

Prep time: 18 minutes Cook Time: 8 hours Serves: 8

Ingredients:

11 oz. cornbread mix
1 cup corn kernels
3 cups heavy cream
1 cup sour cream
3 eggs
1 chili pepper
1 tsp salt
1 tsp ground black pepper
2 oz. pickled jalapeno
¼ tbsp sugar
1 tsp butter

Instructions:

1. Whisk eggs in a suitable bowl and add cream and cornbread mix.
2. Mix it well then add salt, chili pepper, sour cream, sugar, butter, and black pepper.
3. Add corn kernels and pickled jalapeno then mix well to make a smooth dough.
4. Spread this dough in the insert of a Slow cooker.
5. Put the cooker's lid on and set the cooking time to 8 hours on Low settings.
6. Slice and serve.

Nutrition Facts Per Serving:

Calories: 398, Total Fat: 27.9g, Fiber: 2g, Total Carbs: 29.74g, Protein: 9g

Cauliflower Carrot Gratin

Prep time: 14 minutes Cook Time: 7 hours Serves: 12

Ingredients:

16 oz. baby carrots
6 tbsp butter, soft
1 cauliflower head, florets separated
Salt and black pepper to the taste
1 yellow onion, chopped

1 tsp mustard powder
1 and ½ cups of milk
6 oz. cheddar cheese, grated
½ cup breadcrumbs

Instructions:

1. Add carrots, cauliflower, and rest of the ingredients to the Slow cooker.
2. Put the cooker's lid on and set the cooking time to 7 hours on Low settings.
3. Serve warm.

Nutrition Facts Per Serving:

Calories: 182, Total Fat: 4g, Fiber: 7g, Total Carbs: 9g, Protein: 4g

Mac Cream Cups

Prep time: 27 minutes Cook Time: 8 hours Serves: 6

Ingredients:

6 oz. puff pastry
1 cup fresh basil
7 oz. elbow macaroni, cooked
1 egg
¼ cup heavy cream

1 tbsp flour
1 tbsp cornstarch
1 tsp salt
1 tbsp turmeric
1 tsp olive oil

Instructions:

1. Roll the puff pastry and cut it into 6 squares.
2. Layer a muffin tray with olive oil and place one square into each muffin cup.
3. Press the puff pastry square into the muffin cup.
4. Beat egg with cream, flour, salt, cornstarch, and turmeric in a suitable bowl.
5. Stir in macaroni then divide this mixture into the muffin cups.
6. Place this muffin tray in the Slow cooker.
7. Put the cooker's lid on and set the cooking time to 8 hours on Low settings.
8. Serve warm.

Nutrition Facts Per Serving:

Calories: 270, Total Fat: 15.4g, Fiber: 2g, Total Carbs: 26.67g, Protein: 6g

Rainbow Carrots

Prep time: 17 minutes Cook Time: 7 hours Serves: 9

Ingredients:

3 lb. rainbow carrot
3 tbsp sesame oil
1 tsp coriander
¼ cup coriander

ground
1 tbsp sour cream
½ tsp salt
½ tsp sugar

Instructions:

1. Add carrots along with cream, sesame oil, salt and rest of the ingredients to the Slow cooker.
2. Put the cooker's lid on and set the cooking time to 6 hours on Low settings.
3. Serve warm.

Nutrition Facts Per Serving:

Calories: 95, Total Fat: 5g, Fiber: 5g, Total Carbs: 13g, Protein: 1g

Herbed Eggplant Cubes

Prep time: 18 minutes Cook Time: 4 hrs Serves: 8

Ingredients:

17 oz. eggplants, peeled and cubed
1 tbsp salt
1 tsp ground black pepper
1 tsp cilantro

4 cups of water
7 tbsp mayo
1 tsp onion powder
1 tsp garlic powder
1 tbsp nutmeg
3 tbsp butter

Instructions:

1. Add eggplant, salt, and water to the Slow cooker.
2. Put the cooker's lid on and set the cooking time to 1 hour on High settings.
3. Meanwhile, mix remaining spices, butter, and mayo in a bowl.
4. Drain the cooked eggplants and return them to the Slow cooker.
5. Now add the butter-mayo mixture to the eggplants.
6. Put the cooker's lid on and set the cooking time to 3 hours on Low settings.
7. Serve warm.

Nutrition Facts Per Serving:

Calories: 67, Total Fat: 4.8g, Fiber: 2g, Total Carbs: 6.09g, Protein: 1g

Creamy Butter Parsnips

Prep time: 17 minutes Cook Time: 7 hours Serves: 5

Ingredients:

1 cup cream
2 tsp butter
1 lb. parsnip, peeled and chopped
1 carrot, chopped
1 yellow onion, chopped
1 tbsp chives,
chopped
1 tsp salt
1 tsp ground white pepper
½ tsp paprika
1 tbsp salt
¼ tsp sugar

Instructions:

1. Add parsnips, carrot, and rest of the ingredients to the Slow cooker.
2. Put the cooker's lid on and set the cooking time to 7 hours on Low settings.
3. Serve warm.

Nutrition Facts Per Serving:

Calories: 190, Total Fat: 11.2g, Fiber: 4g, Total Carbs: 22g, Protein: 3g

Cheesy Rice

Prep time: 14 minutes Cook Time: 4 hrs. Serves: 6

Ingredients:

2 garlic cloves, minced
2 tbsp olive oil
¾ cup yellow onion, chopped
1 and ½ cups Arborio rice
½ cup white wine
12 oz. spinach, chopped
3 and ½ cups hot veggie stock
Salt and black pepper to the taste
4 oz. goat cheese, soft and crumbled
2 tbsp lemon juice
1/3 cup pecans, toasted and chopped

Instructions:

1. Add spinach, garlic, oil, onion, rice, salt, black, stock, and wine to the Slow cooker.
2. Put the cooker's lid on and set the cooking time to 4 hours on Low settings.
3. Stir in goat cheese and lemon juice.
4. Serve warm.

Nutrition Facts Per Serving:

Calories: 300, Total Fat: 12g, Fiber: 4g, Total Carbs: 20g, Protein: 15g

Muffin Corn Pudding

Prep time: 14 minutes Cook Time: 8 hrs. Serves: 8

Ingredients:

6 oz. muffin mix
12 oz. corn kernels
1 cup heavy cream
1 tsp salt
1 tsp ground black
pepper
3 oz. Parmesan cheese
1 tbsp cilantro
1 tsp ground cumin

Instructions:

1. Whisk muffin mix with cream, salt, ground cumin, black pepper, and cilantro in a suitable bowl.
2. Stir in corn kernel then mix until smooth.
3. Spread this muffin corn mixture in the insert of Slow cooker.
4. Put the cooker's lid on and set the cooking time to 8 hours on Low settings.
5. Top with parmesan cheese and slice.
6. Serve.

Nutrition Facts Per Serving:

Calories: 180, Total Fat: 9.6g, Fiber: 2g, Total Carbs: 18.8g, Protein: 6g

Cinnamon Applesauce

Prep time: 18 minutes Cook Time: 6 hrs. Serves: 5

Ingredients:

1 lb. red apples, peeled and chopped
2 oz. cinnamon stick
1 tsp ground ginger
½ tsp nutmeg
1 tsp ground cinnamon
4 oz. water
½ tsp salt
1 tbsp lime juice

Instructions:

1. Add red apples, cinnamon stick, salt, cinnamon ground, water, lime juice, nutmeg, and ginger to the Slow cooker.
2. Put the cooker's lid on and set the cooking time to 6 hours on High settings.
3. Discard the cinnamon sticks from the apples.
4. Serve fresh.
5. Transfer the dish to the serving bowls and serve it or keep in the fridge for not more than 3 days. Enjoy!

Nutrition Facts Per Serving:

Calories: 86, Total Fat: 0.4g, Fiber: 9g, Total Carbs: 22.93g, Protein: 1g

Carrot Shallots Medley

Prep time: 17 minutes Cook Time: 6 minutes Serves: 7

Ingredients:

1 large carrot, cut into strips	1 tsp ground black pepper
1 lb. shallots, chopped	1 tsp cilantro
1 cup heavy cream	1 tbsp butter, unsalted
1 tbsp sugar	1 tbsp minced garlic
1 tsp salt	

Instructions:

1. Add carrot and shallots to the Slow cooker.
2. Whisk cream with sugar, salt, black pepper, cilantro, butter, and garlic.
3. Pour this mixture over the veggies.
4. Put the cooker's lid on and set the cooking time to 6 hours on Low settings.
5. Serve warm.

Nutrition Facts Per Serving:

Calories: 133, Total Fat: 8.1g, Fiber: 3g, Total Carbs: 14.5g, Protein: 2g

Honey Glazed Vegetables

Prep time: 18 minutes Cook Time: 6 hrs. Serves: 12

Ingredients:

4 large carrots, peeled and chopped	½ cup brown sugar
3 red onions, chopped	1 tbsp salt
1 lb. potato, peeled and diced	1 tsp coriander
3 sweet potatoes, peeled and diced	1 tsp cilantro
	2 tbsp dried dill
	1 tbsp sesame oil
	3 oz. honey

Instructions:

1. Toss onions, carrots, potato, and sweet potatoes with the rest of the ingredients in a Slow Cooker.
2. Put the cooker's lid on and set the cooking time to 6 hours on Low settings.
3. Serve warm.

Nutrition Facts Per Serving:

Calories: 148, Total Fat: 1.4g, Fiber: 3g, Total Carbs: 33g, Protein: 2g

Butter Glazed Yams

Prep time: 24 minutes Cook Time: 4 hrs. Serves: 7

Ingredients:

2 lb. yams, peeled and diced	4 oz. white sugar
5 tbsp butter, melted	½ tsp salt
5 oz. brown sugar	1 tsp vanilla extract
	2 tbsp cornstarch

Instructions:

1. Add melted butter, brown sugar, yams, white sugar, salt, and vanilla extract to the Slow cooker.
2. Put the cooker's lid on and set the cooking time to 4 hours on High settings.
3. Toss well, then stir in cornstarch, continue cooking for 10 minutes on High.
4. Mix well and serve.

Nutrition Facts Per Serving:

Calories: 404, Total Fat: 16.4g, Fiber: 6g, Total Carbs: 63.33g, Protein: 3g

Pumpkin Nutmeg Rice

Prep time: 14 minutes Cook Time: 5 hours Serves: 4

Ingredients:

2 oz. olive oil	ground
1 small yellow onion, chopped	1 tsp thyme, chopped
2 garlic cloves, minced	½ tsp ginger, grated
12 oz. risotto rice	½ tsp cinnamon powder
4 cups chicken stock	½ tsp allspice, ground
6 oz. pumpkin puree	4 oz. heavy cream
½ tsp nutmeg,	

Instructions:

1. Add rice, pumpkin puree, and all other ingredients except the cream to the Slow cooker.
2. Put the cooker's lid on and set the cooking time to 4 hours 30 minutes on Low settings.
3. Stir in cream and cover again to the cook for 30 minutes on the low setting.
4. Serve warm.

Nutrition Facts Per Serving:

Calories: 251, Total Fat: 4g, Fiber: 3g, Total Carbs: 30g, Protein: 5g

Beans and Red Peppers

Prep time: 14 minutes Cook Time: 2 hrs. Serves: 2
Ingredients:

2 cups green beans, halved
1 red bell pepper, cut into strips
Salt and black
pepper to the taste
1 tbsp olive oil
1 and ½ tbsp honey mustard

Instructions:
1. Add green beans, honey mustard, red bell pepper, oil, salt, and black to Slow cooker.
2. Put the cooker's lid on and set the cooking time to 2 hours on High settings.
3. Serve warm.

Nutrition Facts Per Serving:
Calories: 50, Total Fat: 0g, Fiber: 4g, Total Carbs: 8g, Protein: 2g

Butter Green Beans

Prep time: 14 minutes Cook Time: 2 hrs. Serves: 6
Ingredients:

22 oz. green beans
2 garlic cloves, minced
¼ cup butter, soft
2 tbsp parmesan, grated

Instructions:
1. Add green beans, butter, garlic, and parmesan to the Slow cooker.
2. Put the cooker's lid on and set the cooking time to 2 hours on High settings.
3. Serve.

Nutrition Facts Per Serving:
Calories: 60, Total Fat: 4g, Fiber: 1g, Total Carbs: 3g, Protein: 1g

Herbed Balsamic Beets

Prep time: 14 minutes Cook Time: 7 hours Serves: 4
Ingredients:

6 medium assorted-color beets, peeled and cut into wedges
2 tbsp balsamic vinegar
2 tbsp olive oil
2 tbsp chives,
chopped
1 tbsp tarragon, chopped
Salt and black pepper to the taste
1 tsp orange peel, grated

Instructions:
1. Add beets, tarragon, and rest of the ingredients to the Slow cooker.

2. Put the cooker's lid on and set the cooking time to 7 hours on Low settings.
3. Serve warm.

Nutrition Facts Per Serving:
Calories: 144, Total Fat: 3g, Fiber: 1g, Total Carbs: 17g, Protein: 3g

Squash and Peppers Mix

Prep time: 14 minutes Cook Time: 1 hr 30 minutes Serves: 4
Ingredients:

12 small squash, peeled and cut into wedges
2 red bell peppers, cut into wedges
2 green bell peppers, cut into wedges
1/3 cup Italian dressing
1 red onion, cut into wedges
Salt and black pepper to the taste
1 tbsp parsley, chopped

Instructions:
1. Add squash, peppers, and rest of the ingredients to the Slow cooker.
2. Put the cooker's lid on and set the cooking time to 1.5 hours on High settings.
3. Garnish with parsley.
4. Serve warm.

Nutrition Facts Per Serving:
Calories: 80, Total Fat: 2g, Fiber: 3g, Total Carbs: 11g, Protein: 2g

Lemony Honey Beets

Prep time: 14 minutes Cook Time: 8 hrs Serves: 6
Ingredients:

6 beets, peeled and cut into medium wedges
2 tbsp honey
2 tbsp olive oil
2 tbsp lemon juice
Salt and black pepper to the taste
1 tbsp white vinegar
½ tsp lemon peel, grated

Instructions:
1. Add beets, honey, oil, salt, black pepper, lemon peel, vinegar, and lemon juice to the Slow cooker.
2. Put the cooker's lid on and set the cooking time to 8 hours on Low settings.
3. Serve warm.

Nutrition Facts Per Serving:
Calories: 80, Total Fat: 3g, Fiber: 4g, Total Carbs: 8g, Protein: 4g

Jalapeno Meal

Prep time: 14 minutes Cook Time: 6 hrs. Serves: 6

Ingredients:

12 oz. jalapeno pepper, cut in half and deseeded
2 tbsp olive oil
1 tbsp balsamic vinegar

1 onion, sliced
1 garlic clove, sliced
1 tsp ground coriander
4 tbsp water

Instructions:

1. Place the jalapeno peppers in the Slow cooker.
2. Top the pepper with olive oil, balsamic vinegar, onion, garlic, coriander, and water.
3. Put the cooker's lid on and set the cooking time to 6 hours on Low settings.
4. Serve warm.

Nutrition Facts Per Serving:

Calories: 67, Total Fat: 4.7g, Fiber: 2g, Total Carbs: 6.02g, Protein: 1g

Garlic Mushrooms

Prep time: 14 minutes Cook Time: 8 hrs. Serves: 6

Ingredients:

2 lbs. cremini mushrooms, quartered
1 lemon, chopped
½ cup fresh parsley
1 tsp salt
1 tsp ground black

pepper
1/3 cup half and half
1 tsp thyme
1 tsp coriander
1 tsp turmeric
3 tbsp garlic, chopped

Instructions:

1. Spread the mushrooms in the insert of Slow cooker.
2. Whisk the half and half cream with remaining ingredients.
3. Top the mushrooms with the cream sauce.
4. Put the cooker's lid on and set the cooking time to 8 hours on Low settings.
5. Serve warm.

Nutrition Facts Per Serving:

Calories: 55, Total Fat: 0.8g, Fiber: 2g, Total Carbs: 9.43g, Protein: 6g

Cream Cheese Macaroni

Prep time: 17 minutes Cook Time: 3.5 hours Serves: 6

Ingredients:

12 oz. elbow macaroni
1 cup cream cheese
3 tbsp fresh parsley
1 tbsp fresh dill

3 cups chicken stock
1 tsp salt
1 egg
¼ tsp turmeric

Instructions:

1. Whisk egg with cream cheese and chicken stock in a mixer.
2. Spread the macaroni in the slow cooker then pour the stock mixture on top.
3. Drizzle parsley, dill, turmeric, and salt on top.
4. Put the cooker's lid on and set the cooking time to 3.5 hours on High settings.
5. Serve warm.

Nutrition Facts Per Serving:

Calories: 398, Total Fat: 15.5g, Fiber: 2g, Total Carbs: 48.96g, Protein: 15g

Nut Berry Salad

Prep time: 14 minutes Cook Time: 1 hour Serves: 4

Ingredients:

2 cups strawberries, halved
2 tbsp mint, chopped
1/3 cup raspberry vinegar
2 tbsp honey
1 tbsp canola oil

Salt and black pepper to the taste
4 cups spinach, torn
½ cup blueberries
¼ cup walnuts, chopped
1 oz. goat cheese, crumbled

Instructions:

1. Toss strawberries with walnuts, spinach, honey, oil, salt, black pepper, blueberries, vinegar, and mint in the Slow cooker.
2. Put the cooker's lid on and set the cooking time to 1 hour on High settings.
3. Serve warm with cheese on top.

Nutrition Facts Per Serving:

Calories: 200, Total Fat: 12g, Fiber: 4g, Total Carbs: 17g, Protein: 15g

Turmeric Potato Strips

Prep time: 14 minutes Cook Time: 5 hours Serves: 8

Ingredients:

3 lbs. potato, peeled and cut into strips	1 sweet pepper, chopped
2 tomatoes, chopped	1 tsp salt
1 tbsp paprika	½ tsp turmeric
	2 tbsp sesame oil

Instructions:

1. Season the potato strips with salt, paprika, and turmeric.
2. Add oil and seasoned potatoes to the Slow cooker and toss them well.
3. Put the cooker's lid on and set the cooking time to 3 hours on High settings.
4. Meanwhile, you can blend tomatoes with sweet pepper in a blender jug.
5. Pour this puree into the Slow cooker.
6. Put the cooker's lid on and set the cooking time to 2 hours on High settings.
7. Serve warm.

Nutrition Facts Per Serving:
Calories: 176, Total Fat: 3.8g, Fiber: 5g, Total Carbs: 32.97g, Protein: 4g

Green Beans with Mushrooms

Prep time: 14 minutes Cook Time: 3 hours Serves: 4

Ingredients:

1 lb. fresh green beans, trimmed	1 cup chicken stock
1 small yellow onion, chopped	8 oz. mushrooms, sliced
6 oz. bacon, chopped	Salt and black pepper to the taste
1 garlic clove, minced	A splash of balsamic vinegar

Instructions:

1. Add green beans, onion, stock and rest of the ingredients to the Slow cooker.
2. Put the cooker's lid on and set the cooking time to 3 hours on Low settings.
3. Serve warm.

Nutrition Facts Per Serving:
Calories: 162, Total Fat: 4g, Fiber: 5g, Total Carbs: 8g, Protein: 4g

Saucy Macaroni

Prep time: 14 minutes Cook Time: 3.5 hours Serves: 6

Ingredients:

8 oz. macaroni	1 cup heavy cream
1 cup tomatoes, chopped	3 cups of water
1 garlic clove, peeled	1 tbsp salt
1 tsp butter	6 oz. Parmesan, shredded
	1 tbsp dried basil

Instructions:

1. Add macaroni, salt, and water to the Slow cooker.
2. Put the cooker's lid on and set the cooking time to 3 hours on High settings.
3. Meanwhile, puree tomatoes in a blender then add cheese, cream, butter, and dried basil.
4. Drain the cooked macaroni and return them to the Slow cooker.
5. Pour in the tomato-cream mixture.
6. Put the cooker's lid on and set the cooking time to 30 minutes on High settings.
7. Serve warm.

Nutrition Facts Per Serving:
Calories: 325, Total Fat: 10.1g, Fiber: 2g, Total Carbs: 41.27g, Protein: 17g

Zucchini Onion Pate

Prep time: 19 minutes Cook Time: 6 hours Serves: 6

Ingredients:

3 medium zucchinis, peeled and chopped	1 tsp butter
2 red onions, grated	1 tbsp brown sugar
6 tbsp tomato paste	½ tsp ground black pepper
½ cup fresh dill	1 tsp paprika
1 tsp salt	¼ chili pepper

Instructions:

1. Add zucchini to the food processor and blend for 3 minutes until smooth.
2. Transfer the zucchini blend to the Slow cooker.
3. Stir in onions and all other ingredients.
4. Put the cooker's lid on and set the cooking time to 6 hours on Low settings.
5. Serve warm.

Nutrition Facts Per Serving:
Calories: 45, Total Fat: 0.8g, Fiber: 2g, Total Carbs: 9.04g, Protein: 1g

Creamy Red Cabbage

Prep time: 17 minutes Cook Time: 8 hours Serves: 9

Ingredients:

17 oz. red cabbage, sliced	1 tsp salt
1 cup fresh cilantro, chopped	1 tbsp tomato paste
3 red onions, diced	1 tsp ground black pepper
1 tbsp sliced almonds	1 tsp cumin
1 cup sour cream	½ tsp thyme
½ cup chicken stock	2 tbsp butter
	1 cup green peas

Instructions:

1. Add cabbage, onion and all other ingredients to the Slow Cooker.
2. Put the cooker's lid on and set the cooking time to 8 hours on Low settings.
3. Serve warm.

Nutrition Facts Per Serving:

Calories: 112, Total Fat: 5.9g, Fiber: 3g, Total Carbs: 12.88g, Protein: 4g

Refried Black Beans

Prep time: 17 minutes Cook Time: 9 hours Serves: 10

Ingredients:

5 oz. white onion, peeled and chopped	10 cups water
4 cups black beans	1 tsp salt
1 chili pepper, chopped	½ tsp ground black pepper
1 oz. minced garlic	¼ tsp cilantro, chopped

Instructions:

1. Add onion, black beans and all other ingredients to the Slow Cooker.
2. Put the cooker's lid on and set the cooking time to 9 hours on Low settings.
3. Strain all the excess liquid out of the beans while leaving only ¼ cup of the liquid.
4. Transfer the beans-onion mixture to a food processor and blend until smooth.
5. Serve fresh.

Nutrition Facts Per Serving:

Calories: 73, Total Fat: 1.5g, Fiber: 4g, Total Carbs: 12.34g, Protein: 3g

Rice with Artichokes

Prep time: 14 minutes Cook Time: 4 hrs Serves: 4

Ingredients:

1 tbsp olive oil	15 oz. canned artichoke hearts, chopped
5 oz. Arborio rice	
2 garlic cloves, minced	16 oz. cream cheese
1 and ¼ cups chicken stock	1 tbsp parmesan, grated
1 tbsp white wine	1 and ½ tbsp thyme, chopped
6 oz. graham crackers, crumbled	Salt and black pepper to the taste
1 and ¼ cups of water	

Instructions:

1. Add oil, rice, artichokes, garlic, water, wine, crackers, and stock to the Slow cooker.
2. Put the cooker's lid on and set the cooking time to 4 hours on Low settings.
3. Stir in cream cheese, salt, parmesan, thyme, and black pepper.
4. Mix well and serve warm.

Nutrition Facts Per Serving:

Calories: 230, Total Fat: 3g, Fiber: 5g, Total Carbs: 30g, Protein: 4g

Farro Rice Pilaf

Prep time: 14 minutes Cook Time: 5 hours Serves: 12

Ingredients:

1 shallot, chopped	pepper to the taste
1 tsp garlic, minced	1 tbsp parsley and sage, chopped
A drizzle of olive oil	
1 and ½ cups whole grain farro	½ cup hazelnuts, toasted and chopped
¾ cup wild rice	¾ cup cherries, dried
6 cups chicken stock	
Salt and black	

Instructions:

1. Add farro, rice, stock, and rest of the ingredients to the Slow cooker.
2. Put the cooker's lid on and set the cooking time to 5 hours on Low settings.
3. Serve warm.

Nutrition Facts Per Serving:

Calories: 120, Total Fat: 2g, Fiber: 7g, Total Carbs: 20g, Protein: 3g

Beans Risotto

Prep time: 23 minutes Cook Time: 5 hours Serves: 6

Ingredients:

1 lb. red kidney beans, soaked overnight and drained
Salt to the taste
1 tsp olive oil
1 lb. smoked sausage, roughly chopped
1 yellow onion, chopped
1 celery stalk, chopped
4 garlic cloves, chopped
1 green bell pepper, chopped
1 tsp thyme, dried
2 bay leaves
5 cups of water
2 green onions, minced
2 tbsp parsley, minced

Instructions:

1. Add red beans, oil, sausage, and rest of the ingredients to the Slow cooker.
2. Put the cooker's lid on and set the cooking time to 5 hours on Low settings.
3. Serve warm.

Nutrition Facts Per Serving:

Calories: 200, Total Fat: 5g, Fiber: 6g, Total Carbs: 20g, Protein: 5g

Veggies Rice Pilaf

Prep time: 6 minutes Cook Time: 5 hours Serves: 4

Ingredients:

2 cups basmati rice
1 cup mixed carrots, peas, corn, and green beans
2 cups of water
½ tsp green chili, minced
½ tsp ginger, grated
3 garlic cloves, minced
2 tbsp butter
1 cinnamon stick
1 tbsp cumin seeds
2 bay leaves
3 whole cloves
5 black peppercorns
2 whole cardamoms
1 tbsp sugar
Salt to the taste

Instructions:

1. Add water, rice, veggies and all other ingredients to the Slow cooker.
2. Put the cooker's lid on and set the cooking time to 5 hours on Low settings.
3. Discard the cinnamon and serve warm.

Nutrition Facts Per Serving:

Calories: 300, Total Fat: 4g, Fiber: 3g, Total Carbs: 40g, Protein: 13g

Cider Dipped Farro

Prep time: 14 minutes Cook Time: 5 hours Serves: 6

Ingredients:

1 tbsp apple cider vinegar
1 cup whole-grain farro
1 tsp lemon juice
Salt to the taste
3 cups of water
1 tbsp olive oil
½ cup cherries, dried and chopped
¼ cup green onions, chopped
10 mint leaves, chopped
2 cups cherries, pitted and halved

Instructions:

1. Add water and farro to the Slow cooker.
2. Put the cooker's lid on and set the cooking time to 5 hours on Low settings.
3. Toss the cooker farro with salt, cherries, mint, green onion, lemon juice, and oil in a bowl.
4. Serve fresh.

Nutrition Facts Per Serving:

Calories: 162, Total Fat: 3g, Fiber: 6g, Total Carbs: 12g, Protein: 4g

Mexican Avocado Rice

Prep time: 14 minutes Cook Time: 4 hrs Serves: 8

Ingredients:

1 cup long-grain rice
1 and ¼ cups veggie stock
½ cup cilantro, chopped
½ avocado, pitted,
peeled and chopped
Salt and black pepper to the taste
¼ cup green hot sauce

Instructions:

1. Add rice and stock to the Slow cooker.
2. Put the cooker's lid on and set the cooking time to 4 hours on Low settings.
3. Meanwhile, blend avocado flesh with hot sauce, cilantro, salt, and black pepper.
4. Serve the cooked rice with avocado sauce on top.

Nutrition Facts Per Serving:

Calories: 100, Total Fat: 3g, Fiber: 6g, Total Carbs: 18g, Protein: 4g

Hasselback Potatoes

Prep time: 17 minutes Cook Time: 8 hours Serves: 7

Ingredients:

7 potatoes	1 tbsp dried dill
2 oz. butter	1 tsp salt
1 tbsp olive oil	1 tsp paprika

Instructions:

1. Use a knife to make 4 slits on top of each potato.
2. Mix butter, dill, olive oil, paprika, and salt in a bowl.
3. Layer the insert of the slow cooker with a foil sheet.
4. Place the potatoes inside and pour the butter-dill mixture on top of them.
5. Put the cooker's lid on and set the cooking time to 8 hours on Low settings.
6. Serve warm.

Nutrition Facts Per Serving:

Calories: 363, Total Fat: 9g, Fiber:8g, Total Carbs: 65.17g, Protein: 8g

Scalloped Cheese Potatoes

Prep time: 27 minutes Cook Time: 7 hours Serves: 12

Ingredients:

2 lbs. potato, peeled and sliced	unsalted
	4 tbsp flour
1 lb. sweet potato, peel	1 tbsp minced garlic
	4 cups of milk
1 tbsp salt	¼ tsp nutmeg
1 tsp ground black pepper	4 oz. Parmesan
	5 oz. Cheddar
1/3 cup butter,	cheese

Instructions:

1. Toss potatoes with salt and black pepper to season them.
2. Spread the potatoes and sweet potatoes in the Slow cooker in layers.
3. Whisk butter with flour, nutmeg, milk, garlic, parmesan, and cheddar cheese in a suitable bowl.
4. Pour this milk-flour mixture over the potatoes.
5. Put the cooker's lid on and set the cooking time to 7 hours on Low settings.
6. Serve warm.

Nutrition Facts Per Serving:

Calories: 422, Total Fat: 21.6g, Fiber: 5g, Total Carbs: 46g, Protein: 11g

Eggplants with Mayo Sauce

Prep time: 14 minutes Cook Time: 5 hours Serves: 8

Ingredients:

2 tbsp minced garlic	1 tsp salt
1 chili pepper, chopped	½ tsp ground black pepper
1 sweet pepper, chopped	18 oz. eggplants, peeled and diced
4 tbsp mayo	2 tbsp sour cream
1 tsp olive oil	

Instructions:

1. Blend chili pepper, sweet peppers, salt, garlic, and black pepper in a blender until smooth.
2. Add eggplant and this chili mixture to the Slow cooker then toss them well.
3. Now mix mayo with sour cream and spread on top of eggplants.
4. Put the cooker's lid on and set the cooking time to 5 hours on High settings.
5. Serve warm

Nutrition Facts Per Serving:

Calories: 40, Total Fat: 1.1g, Fiber: 3g, Total Carbs: 7.5g, Protein: 1g

Corn Cucumber Salad

Prep time: 23 minutes Cook Time: 5 hours Serves: 6

Ingredients:

1 cup corn kernels	2 cucumbers, diced
5 oz. dried tomatoes, cut into strips	1 red onion, diced
	1 tsp ground paprika
	1 cup fresh parsley
1 tsp salt	1 carrot, grated
1 cup heavy cream	1 tsp olive oil

Instructions:

1. Add corn kernels, dried tomatoes, cream, paprika, onion, and salt to the Slow cooker.
2. Put the cooker's lid on and set the cooking time to 5 hours on Low settings.
3. Transfer this corn mixture to a salad bowl.
4. Toss in parsley, carrot, and cucumbers.
5. Serve fresh.

Nutrition Facts Per Serving:

Calories: 123, Total Fat: 8.9g, Fiber: 2g, Total Carbs: 10.4g, Protein: 2g

Tamale Side Dish

Prep time: 27 minutes Cook Time: 7 hours Serves: 5

Ingredients:

12 oz. masa harina	1 onion, chopped
1 cup chicken stock	5 tbsp olive oil
½ tsp salt	5 corn husks
1 tsp onion powder	5 cups of water

Instructions:

1. Chicken Mix masa harina with chicken salt, salt, onion powder.
2. Stir in the chopped onion, and olive oil, then knead this dough.
3. Soak corn husks for 15 minutes in water then drain.
4. Spread the corn husks on the working surface.
5. Divide the masa harina mixture over the corn husks.
6. Roll the corn husk around the filling, then place these rolls in the Slow cooker.
7. Put the cooker's lid on and set the cooking time to 7 hours on Low settings.
8. Serve fresh.

Nutrition Facts Per Serving:
Calories: 214, Total Fat: 14.8g, Fiber: 2g, Total Carbs: 18g, Protein: 3g

Ramen Noodles

Prep time: 7 minutes Cook Time: 25 minutes Serves: 5

Ingredients:

1 tbsp ramen seasoning	1 tsp salt
10 oz. ramen noodles	3 tbsp soy sauce
	1 tsp paprika
4 cups chicken stock	1 tbsp butter

Instructions:

1. Add chicken stock, butter, ramen, paprika, noodles and all other ingredients to the Slow cooker.
2. Put the cooker's lid on and set the cooking time to 25 minutes on High settings.
3. Serve warm.

Nutrition Facts Per Serving:
Calories: 405, Total Fat: 19.2g, Fiber: 6g, Total Carbs: 49.93g, Protein: 15g

Tangy Red Potatoes

Prep time: 18 minutes Cook Time: 8 hours Serves: 4

Ingredients:

1 lb. red potato	1 tsp minced garlic
2 tbsp olive oil	3 tbsp fresh dill, chopped
1 garlic clove	
1 tsp sage	1 tsp paprika
4 tbsp mayo	

Instructions:

1. Add potatoes, olive oil, garlic cloves, garlic, and sage to the Slow Cooker.
2. Put the cooker's lid on and set the cooking time to 8 hours on Low settings.
3. Whisk mayo and minced garlic in a suitable bowl.
4. Transfer the slow-cooked potatoes to a bowl and mash them using a fork.
5. Stir in the mayo-garlic mixture then mix well.
6. Serve fresh.

Nutrition Facts Per Serving:
Calories: 164, Total Fat: 7.8g, Fiber: 4g, Total Carbs: 22.87g, Protein: 3g

Dill Mixed Fennel

Prep time: 14 minutes Cook Time: 3 hour Serves: 7

Ingredients:

10 oz. fennel bulbs, diced	1 tsp oregano
	1 tsp basil
2 tbsp olive oil	3 tbsp white wine
1 tsp ground black pepper	1 tsp salt
	2 garlic cloves
1 tsp paprika	1 tsp dried dill
1 tsp cilantro	

Instructions:

1. Add fennel bulbs and all other ingredients to the Slow cooker.
2. Put the cooker's lid on and set the cooking time to 3.5 hours on High settings.
3. Serve warm.

Nutrition Facts Per Serving:
Calories: 53, Total Fat: 4.1g, Fiber: 2g, Total Carbs: 4g, Protein: 1g

Millet with Dill

Prep time: 14 minutes Cook Time: 5 hours Serves: 6

Ingredients:

2 tbsp butter	1 tsp basil
½ cup half and half	4 cups of water
1 tsp salt	4 cups millet
½ cup fresh dill	1 tsp olive oil

Instructions:
1. Add water, millet, olive oil, half and half cream, salt, and basil to the Slow Cooker.
2. Put the cooker's lid on and set the cooking time to 5 hours on Low settings.
3. Garnish with dill and serve.

Nutrition Facts Per Serving:
Calories: 557, Total Fat: 10.5g, Fiber: 11g, Total Carbs: 98.98g, Protein: 15g

Sweet Red Onions

Prep time: 17 minutes Cook Time: 6 hours Serves: 6

Ingredients:

17 oz. red onion, sliced	¼ cup cream cheese
1 tbsp brown sugar	1 tsp lemon juice
½ tsp salt	½ tbsp lemon zest
1 tbsp paprika	1 apple, peeled and grated
3 tbsp butter	

Instructions:
1. Add sliced onion, apple, and rest of the ingredients to the Slow Cooker.
2. Put the cooker's lid on and set the cooking time to 6 hours on Low settings.
3. Serve fresh.

Nutrition Facts Per Serving:
Calories: 138, Total Fat: 8.9g, Fiber: 3g, Total Carbs: 14.44g, Protein: 2g

Summer Squash Medley

Prep time: 18 minutes Cook Time: 2 hrs Serves: 4

Ingredients:

¼ cup olive oil	2 tsp mustard
2 tbsp basil, chopped	Salt and black pepper to the taste
2 tbsp balsamic vinegar	3 summer squash, sliced
2 garlic cloves, minced	2 zucchinis, sliced

Instructions:
1. Add squash, zucchinis, and all other ingredients to the Slow cooker.
2. Put the cooker's lid on and set the cooking time to 2 hours on High settings.
3. Serve.

Nutrition Facts Per Serving:
Calories: 179, Total Fat: 13g, Fiber: 2g, Total Carbs: 10g, Protein: 4g

Lemony Pumpkin Wedges

Prep time: 17 minutes Cook Time: 6 hours Serves: 4

Ingredients:

15 oz. pumpkin, peeled and cut into wedges	1 tsp honey
	½ tsp ground cardamom
1 tbsp lemon juice	1 tsp lime juice
1 tsp salt	

Instructions:
1. Add pumpkin, lemon juice, honey, lime juice, cardamom, and salt to the Slow cooker.
2. Put the cooker's lid on and set the cooking time to 6 hours on Low settings.
3. Serve fresh.

Nutrition Facts Per Serving:
Calories: 35, Total Fat: 0.1g, Fiber: 1g, Total Carbs: 8.91g, Protein: 1g

Thyme Mixed Beets

Prep time: 14 minutes Cook Time: 6 hrs Serves: 8

Ingredients:

12 small beets, peeled and sliced	1 tsp thyme, dried
¼ cup of water	Salt and black pepper to the taste
4 garlic cloves, minced	1 tbsp fresh thyme, chopped
2 tbsp olive oil	

Instructions:
1. Add water, beets, garlic and rest of the ingredients to the Slow cooker.
2. Put the cooker's lid on and set the cooking time to 6 hours on Low settings.
3. Serve warm.

Nutrition Facts Per Serving:
Calories: 66, Total Fat: 4g, Fiber: 1g, Total Carbs: 8g, Protein: 1g

Tomato Okra Mix

Prep time: 14 minutes Cook Time: 7 hours Serves: 6

Ingredients:

2 lb. okra, frozen
1 cup tomato sauce
4 oz. water
1 onion, chopped
1 tsp minced garlic
¼ tbsp salt
1 tsp sugar

Instructions:

1. Add frozen okra, tomato sauce, water, onion, garlic, sugar, and salt to the Slow cooker.
2. Put the cooker's lid on and set the cooking time to 7 hours on Low settings.
3. Serve warm.

Nutrition Facts Per Serving:

Calories: 107, Total Fat: 0.4g, Fiber: 8g, Total Carbs: 22.55g, Protein: 4g

Eggplant Salad

Prep time: 14 minutes Cook Time: 2 hrs Serves: 4

Ingredients:

2 garlic cloves, minced
½ cup olive oil
¼ cup basil, chopped
Salt and black pepper to the taste
1 red bell pepper, chopped
1 eggplant, roughly chopped
1 summer squash, cubed
1 Vidalia onion, cut into wedges
1 zucchini, sliced
1 green bell pepper, chopped

Instructions:

1. Add red bell pepper, squash, and rest of the ingredients to the Slow cooker.
2. Put the cooker's lid on and set the cooking time to 2 hours on High settings.
3. Serve warm.

Nutrition Facts Per Serving:

Calories: 165, Total Fat: 11g, Fiber: 3g, Total Carbs: 15g, Protein: 2g

Turmeric Buckwheat

Prep time: 27 minutes Cook Time: 4 hrs Serves: 6

Ingredients:

4 tbsp milk powder
2 tbsp butter
1 carrot
4 cup buckwheat
4 cups chicken stock
1 tbsp salt
1 tbsp turmeric
1 tsp paprika

Instructions:

1. Whisk milk powder with buckwheat, stock, salt, turmeric, and paprika in the Slow cooker.
2. Stir in carrot strips and mix gently.
3. Put the cooker's lid on and set the cooking time to 4 hours on High settings.
4. Stir in butter then serve warm.

Nutrition Facts Per Serving:

Calories: 238, Total Fat: 6.6g, Fiber: 4g, Total Carbs: 37.85g, Protein: 9g

Chicken with Sweet Potato

Prep Time: 23 minutes Cook Time: 3 hours Serves: 6

Ingredients:

16 oz. sweet potato, peeled and diced
3 cups chicken stock
1 tbsp salt
3 tbsp margarine
2 tbsp cream cheese

Instructions:

1. Add sweet potato, chicken stock, and salt to the Slow Cooker.
2. Put the cooker's lid on and set the cooking time to 5 hours on High settings.
3. Drain the slow-cooked potatoes and transfer them to a suitable bowl.
4. Mash the sweet potatoes and stir in cream cheese and margarine.
5. Serve fresh.

Nutrition Facts Per Serving:

Calories: 472, Total Fat: 31.9g, Fiber: 6.7g, Total Carbs: 43.55g, Protein: 3g

Pink Salt Rice

Prep time: 14 minutes Cook Time: 5 hours Serves: 8

Ingredients:

1 tsp salt
2 and ½ cups of
water
2 cups pink rice

Instructions:

1. Add rice, salt, and water to the Slow cooker.
2. Put the cooker's lid on and set the cooking time to 5 hours on Low settings.
3. Serve warm.

Nutrition Facts Per Serving:

Calories: 120, Total Fat: 3g, Fiber: 3g, Total Carbs: 16g, Protein: 4g

Berry Wild Rice

Prep time: 14 minutes Cook Time: 5 hours 30 minutes Serves: 4

Ingredients:

2 cups wild rice	1 tbsp chives
4 cups of water	1 tbsp butter
1 tsp salt	2 tbsp heavy cream
6 oz. cherries, dried	

Instructions:

1. Add wild rice, salt, water, and dried cherries to the Slow cooker.
2. Put the cooker's lid on and set the cooking time to 5 hours on High settings.
3. Stir in cream and butter, then cover again to cook for 30 minutes on the low setting.
4. Serve.

Nutrition Facts Per Serving:
Calories: 364, Total Fat: 6.6g, Fiber: 6g, Total Carbs: 66.97g, Protein: 12g

Zucchini Crackers Casserole

Prep time: 14 minutes Cook Time: 2 hrs Serves: 10

Ingredients:

7 cups zucchini, sliced	cheese, shredded
2 cups crackers, crushed	1 cup chicken stock
	1/3 cup sour cream
2 tbsp melted butter	Salt and black
1/3 cup yellow onion, chopped	pepper to the taste
1 cup cheddar	1 tbsp parsley, chopped
	Cooking spray

Instructions:

1. Grease the insert of your Slow cooker with cooking spray.
2. Spread the zucchini and onion in the cooker.
3. Top the veggies with stock, sour cream, butter, black pepper, and salt.
4. Spread cheese and crackers over the veggies.
5. Put the cooker's lid on and set the cooking time to 2 hours on High settings.
6. Garnish with parsley.
7. Serve warm.

Nutrition Facts Per Serving:
Calories: 180, Total Fat: 6g, Fiber: 1g, Total Carbs: 14g, Protein: 4g

Chapter 8 Snack Recipes

Apple Sausage Snack

Prep time: 14 minutes Cook Time: 2 hrs Serves: 15

Ingredients:

2 lbs. sausages, sliced	18 oz. apple jelly
	9 oz. Dijon mustard

Instructions:

1. Add sausage slices, apple jelly, and mustard to the Slow cooker.
2. Put the cooker's lid on and set the cooking time to 2 hours on Low settings.
3. Serve fresh.

Nutrition Facts Per Serving:
Calories: 200, Total Fat: 3g, Fiber: 1g, Total Carbs: 9g, Protein: 10g

Carrot Broccoli Fritters

Prep time: 24 minutes Cook Time: 4 hrs Serves: 12

Ingredients:

2 large carrots, grated	pepper
	1 tsp paprika
4 oz. broccoli, chopped	1 tsp butter
	4 tbsp fresh cilantro, chopped
1 tbsp cream cheese	
¼ cup flour	1 egg
1 tsp salt	3 oz. celery stalk
1 tsp ground black	

Instructions:

1. Whisk egg with cream cheese, salt, flour, cilantro, black pepper, and paprika in a bowl.
2. Stir in celery stalk, carrots and broccoli, and mix to well to form a dough.
3. Divide the broccoli dough into 2 or 4 pieces and roll them into fritters.
4. Grease the base of slow cooker with butter and these fritters inside.
5. Put the cooker's lid on and set the cooking time to 3 hours on High settings.
6. Flip the slow cooker fritters and again cover to cook for another 1 hour.
7. Serve fresh

Nutrition Facts Per Serving:
Calories: 37, Total Fat: 1.6g, Fiber: 1g, Total Carbs: 4.22g, Protein: 2g

Bean Pesto Dip

Prep time: 14 minutes Cook Time: 6 hrs
Serves: 8
Ingredients:

10 oz. refried beans	1 tsp paprika
1 tbsp pesto sauce	1 cup of salsa
1 tsp salt	4 tbsp sour cream
7 oz. Cheddar	2-oz. cream cheese
cheese, shredded	1 tsp dried dill

Instructions:

1. Mix pesto with salt, salsa, sour cream, dill, beans, cheese, paprika, and cream cheese in the Slow Cooker.
2. Put the cooker's lid on and set the cooking time to 6 hours on Low settings.
3. Once slow cooker, blend the mixture using a hand blender.
4. Serve fresh.

Nutrition Facts Per Serving:
Calories: 102, Total Fat: 6.3g, Fiber: 1g, Total Carbs: 7.43g, Protein: 5g

Thyme Pepper Shrimp

Prep time: 17 minutes Cook Time: 25 minutes Serves: 5
Ingredients:

1 tsp sage	2 tbsp heavy cream
1 tbsp Piri Piri sauce	1 tsp salt
1 tsp thyme	¼ cup butter
1 tbsp cayenne	1 lb. shrimp, peeled
pepper	½ cup fresh parsley

Instructions:

1. Blend butter with Piri Piri, thyme, sage, cayenne pepper, salt, and cream in a blender until smooth.
2. Add this buttercream mixture to the Slow cooker.
3. Put the cooker's lid on and set the cooking time to 10 minutes on High settings.
4. Now add the shrimp to the Slow cooker and cover again to cook for another 15 minutes.
5. Serve warm.

Nutrition Facts Per Serving:
Calories: 199, Total Fat: 12.9g, Fiber: 1g, Total Carbs: 1.28g, Protein: 19g

Beef Tomato Meatballs

Prep time: 14 minutes Cook Time: 8 hrs
Serves: 8
Ingredients:

1 and ½ lbs. beef, ground	chopped
	2 garlic cloves, minced
1 egg, whisked	1 yellow onion, chopped
16 oz. canned tomatoes, crushed	Salt and black pepper to the taste
14 oz. canned tomato puree	
¼ cup parsley,	

Instructions:

1. Mix beef with parsley, egg, garlic, onion, and black pepper in a bowl.
2. Make 16 small meatballs out of this beef mixture.
3. Add tomato puree, tomatoes, and meatballs to the Slow cooker.
4. Put the cooker's lid on and set the cooking time to 8 hours on Low settings.
5. Serve warm.

Nutrition Facts Per Serving:
Calories: 160, Total Fat: 5g, Fiber: 3g, Total Carbs: 10g, Protein: 7g

Cheeseburger Cream Dip

Prep time: 14 minutes Cook Time: 3 hours Serves: 10
Ingredients:

1 lb. beef, ground	12 oz. cream cheese, soft
1 tsp garlic powder	1 cup sour cream
Salt and black pepper to the taste	2 tbsp ketchup
2 tbsp Worcestershire sauce	2 tbsp mustard
8 bacon strips, chopped	10 oz. canned tomatoes and chilies, chopped
3 garlic cloves, minced	1 and ½ cup cheddar cheese, shredded
1 yellow onion, chopped	1 cup mozzarella, shredded

Instructions:

1. Add beef, Worcestershire sauce and all other ingredients to the Slow cooker.
2. Put the cooker's lid on and set the cooking time to 3 hours on Low settings.
3. Serve fresh.

Nutrition Facts Per Serving:
Calories: 251, Total Fat: 5g, Fiber: 8g, Total Carbs: 16g, Protein: 4g

Bean Salsa Salad

Prep time: 14 minutes Cook Time: 4 hrs Serves: 6

Ingredients:

1 tbsp soy sauce
½ tsp cumin, ground
1 cup canned black beans
1 cup of salsa
6 cups romaine lettuce leaves
½ cup avocado, peeled, pitted and mashed

Instructions:

1. Add black beans, cumin, soy sauce, and salsa to the Slow Cooker.
2. Put the cooker's lid on and set the cooking time to 4 hours on Low settings.
3. Transfer the beans to a salad bowl and toss in lettuce leaves, and mashed avocado.
4. Mix well then serve.

Nutrition Facts Per Serving:

Calories: 221, Total Fat: 4g, Fiber: 7g, Total Carbs: 12g, Protein: 3g

Caramel Milk Dip

Prep time: 14 minutes Cook Time: 2 hours Serves: 4

Ingredients:

1 cup butter
12 oz. condensed milk
2 cups brown sugar
1 cup of corn syrup

Instructions:

1. Add butter, milk, corn syrup, and sugar to the Slow Cooker.
2. Put the cooker's lid on and set the cooking time to 2 hours on High settings.
3. Serve warm.

Nutrition Facts Per Serving:

Calories: 172, Total Fat: 2g, Fiber: 6g, Total Carbs: 12g, Protein: 4g

Cashew Hummus Dip

Prep time: 14 minutes Cook Time: 3 hours Serves: 10

Ingredients:

1 cup of water
1 cup cashews
10 oz. hummus
¼ tsp garlic powder
¼ tsp onion powder
A pinch of salt and
black pepper
¼ tsp mustard powder
1 tsp apple cider vinegar

Instructions:

1. Add water, cashews, black pepper, and salt to the Slow cooker.
2. Put the cooker's lid on and set the cooking time to 3 hours on High settings.
3. Drain and transfer the cooked cashews to a blender jug.
4. Add onion powder, vinegar, mustard powder, garlic powder, and hummus.
5. Blend the cashews hummus mixture well until smooth.
6. Serve.

Nutrition Facts Per Serving:

Calories: 192, Total Fat: 7g, Fiber: 7g, Total Carbs: 12g, Protein: 4g

Butter Stuffed Chicken Balls

Prep Time: 21 minutes Cook Time: 3.5 hours Serves: 9

Ingredients:

3 oz. butter, cubed
1 tbsp mayonnaise
1 tsp cayenne pepper
1 tsp ground black pepper
1 tsp salt
1 egg
2 oz. white bread
4 tbsp milk
1 tsp olive oil
1 tbsp almond flour
1 tsp dried dill
14 oz. ground chicken
½ tsp olive oil

Instructions:

1. Whisk mayonnaise with black pepper, dill, chicken, salt, and cayenne pepper in a bowl.
2. Stir in egg, milk, and white bread then mix well.
3. Grease the base of the Slow cooker with cooking oil.
4. Make small meatballs our of this mixture and insert one butter cubes into each ball.
5. Dust the meatballs with almond then place them in the Slow cooker.
6. Put the cooker's lid on and set the cooking time to 3.5 hours on High settings.
7. Serve warm.

Nutrition Facts Per Serving:

Calories: 181, Total Fat: 14.1g, Fiber: 1g, Total Carbs: 4.02g, Protein: 10g

Cordon Bleu Dip

Prep time: 14 minutes Cook Time: 1 hour 30 minutes Serves: 6
Ingredients:

16 oz. cream cheese	3 garlic cloves, minced
2 chicken breasts, baked and shredded	6 oz. ham, chopped
1 cup cheddar cheese, shredded	2 tbsp green onions
1 cup Swiss cheese, shredded	Salt and black pepper to the taste

Instructions:
1. Add cream cheese, chicken and all other ingredients to the Slow cooker.
2. Put the cooker's lid on and set the cooking time to 1.5 hours on Low settings.
3. Serve warm.

Nutrition Facts Per Serving:
Calories: 243, Total Fat: 5g, Fiber: 8g, Total Carbs: 15g, Protein: 3g

Zucchini Sticks

Prep time: 17 minutes Cook Time: 2 hours Serves: 13
Ingredients:

9 oz. green zucchini, cut into thick sticks	1 tsp salt
4 oz. Parmesan, grated	1 tsp ground white pepper
1 egg	1 tsp olive oil
	2 tbsp milk

Instructions:
1. Grease of the base of your Slow cooker with olive oil.
2. Whisk egg with milk, white pepper, and salt in a bowl.
3. Dip the prepared zucchini sticks in the egg mixture then place them in the Slow cooker.
4. Put the cooker's lid on and set the cooking time to 2 hours on High settings.
5. Spread the cheese over the zucchini sticks evenly.
6. Put the cooker's lid on and set the cooking time to 2 hours on High settings.
7. Serve.

Nutrition Facts Per Serving:
Calories: 51, Total Fat: 1.7g, Fiber: 0g, Total Carbs: 4.62g, Protein: 5g

Cheesy Chili Pepper Dip

Prep time: 17 minutes Cook Time: 9 hours Serves: 8
Ingredients:

4 chili pepper, sliced and deseeded	3 tbsp dried dill
7 oz. Monterey cheese	3 oz. butter
3 tbsp cream cheese	1 tbsp cornstarch
1 tbsp onion powder	1 tbsp flour
	¼ tsp salt

Instructions:
1. Add chili peppers to a blender and add salt, butter, onion powder, and dill.
2. Blend the chili peppers well then transfer to the Slow cooker.
3. Stir in flour, cornstarch, cream cheese, and Monterey cheese.
4. Put the cooker's lid on and set the cooking time to 6 hours on Low settings.
5. Serve.

Nutrition Facts Per Serving:
Calories: 212, Total Fat: 18.2g, Fiber: 1g, Total Carbs: 6.06g, Protein: 8g

Apple Wedges with Peanuts

Prep time: 17 minutes Cook Time: 2 hours Serves: 5
Ingredients:

1 tbsp peanut butter	½ tsp cinnamon
3 tbsp peanut, crushed	1 tbsp butter
6 green apples, cut into wedges	2 tsp water
	1 tsp lemon zest
	1 tsp lemon juice

Instructions:
1. Toss the peanuts with peanut butter, butter, lemon zest, cinnamon, and lemon juice in a bowl.
2. Stir in apple wedges and mix well to coat them.
3. Transfer the apple to the slow cooker along with 2 tsp water.
4. Put the cooker's lid on and set the cooking time to 2 hours on High settings.
5. Serve.

Nutrition Facts Per Serving:
Calories: 20, Total Fat: 6.9g, Fiber: 6g, Total Carbs: 35.16g, Protein: 4g

Dill Butter Muffins

Prep time: 23 minutes Cook Time: 9 hours Serves: 6

Ingredients:

2 egg	1 tsp cilantro
5 tbsp butter	1 cup milk
1 cup fresh dill	2 cups flour
1 tsp baking soda	1 tsp salt
1 tbsp lemon juice	¼ tsp cooking spray

Instructions:

1. Whisk eggs with butter, baking soda, lemon juice, flour, salt, milk, dill, and cilantro in a bowl.
2. Divide this dill batter into a greased muffin tray.
3. Place the muffin tray in the Slow cooker.
4. Put the cooker's lid on and set the cooking time to 9 hours on Low settings.
5. Serve.

Nutrition Facts Per Serving:

Calories: 306, Total Fat: 14.6g, Fiber: 1g, Total Carbs: 34.37g, Protein: 9g

Egg Bacon Muffins

Prep time: 27 minutes Cook Time: 6 hours Serves: 8

Ingredients:

6 eggs	3 tbsp almond flour
½ cup flour	2 tbsp butter, melted
1 tsp baking powder	5 oz. bacon, chopped, roasted
1 tsp vinegar	¼ tsp cooking spray
1 tsp salt	

Instructions:

1. Whisk eggs with baking powder, salt, flour, vinegar, butter, and almond flour in a mixer.
2. Fold in bacon and mix gently until smooth.
3. Knead the dough well and grease the muffin tray with cooking spray.
4. Divide the sticky dough into the muffin cups.
5. Pour ½ cup water into the slow cooker and place the muffin tray in it.
6. Put the cooker's lid on and set the cooking time to 6 hours on Low settings.
7. Serve.

Nutrition Facts Per Serving:

Calories: 210, Total Fat: 15.7g, Fiber: 1g, Total Carbs: 8.24g, Protein: 10g

Eggplant Zucchini Dip

Prep time: 14 minutes Cook Time: 4 hrs 10 minutes Serves: 4

Ingredients:

1 eggplant	1 celery stick, chopped
1 zucchini, chopped	1 tomato, chopped
2 tbsp olive oil	2 tbsp tomato paste
2 tbsp balsamic vinegar	1 and ½ tsp garlic, minced
1 tbsp parsley, chopped	A pinch of sea salt
1 yellow onion, chopped	Black pepper to the taste

Instructions:

1. Rub the eggplant with cooking oil and grill it for 5 minutes per side on a preheated grill.
2. Chop the grilled eggplant and transfer it to the Slow cooker.
3. Add tomato, parsley and all other ingredients to the cooker.
4. Put the cooker's lid on and set the cooking time to 4 hours on High settings.
5. Serve.

Nutrition Facts Per Serving:

Calories: 110, Total Fat: 1g, Fiber: 2g, Total Carbs: 7g, Protein: 5g

Eggplant Capers Salsa

Prep time: 14 minutes Cook Time: 7 hours Serves: 4

Ingredients:

1 and ½ cups tomatoes, chopped	minced
3 cups eggplant, cubed	2 tsp balsamic vinegar
2 tsp capers	1 tbsp basil, chopped
6 oz. green olives, pitted and sliced	Salt and black pepper to the taste
4 garlic cloves,	

Instructions:

1. Add eggplant cubes and all other ingredients to the Slow cooker.
2. Put the cooker's lid on and set the cooking time to 7 hours on Low settings.
3. Serve.

Nutrition Facts Per Serving:

Calories: 200, Total Fat: 6g, Fiber: 5g, Total Carbs: 9g, Protein: 2g

Fajita Chicken Dip

Prep time: 14 minutes Cook Time: 4 hrs Serves: 6

Ingredients:

3 chicken breasts, skinless and boneless	8 oz. pepper jack cheese, shredded
8 oz. root beer	16 oz. sour cream
3 red bell peppers, chopped	2 fajita seasoning mix packets
1 yellow onion, chopped	1 tbsp olive oil
8 oz. cream cheese	Salt and black pepper to the taste

Instructions:

1. Add root beer, chicken and all other ingredients to the Slow cooker.
2. Put the cooker's lid on and set the cooking time to 4 hours on High settings.
3. Shred the slow-cooked chicken with the help of two forks.
4. Mix well with its sauce and serve.

Nutrition Facts Per Serving:

Calories: 261, Total Fat: 4g, Fiber: 6g, Total Carbs: 17g, Protein: 5g

Fava Bean Onion Dip

Prep time: 14 minutes Cook Time: 5 hours Serves: 6

Ingredients:

1 lb. fava bean, rinsed	1 bay leaf
1 cup yellow onion, chopped	¼ cup olive oil
4 and ½ cups of water	1 garlic clove, minced
	2 tbsp lemon juice
	Salt to the taste

Instructions:

1. Add 4 cups water, bay leaf, salt, and fava beans to the Slow cooker.
2. Put the cooker's lid on and set the cooking time to 3 hours on low settings.
3. Drain the slow cooker beans and discard the bay leaf.
4. Return the cooked beans to the cooker and add onion, garlic, and ½ cup water.
5. Put the cooker's lid on and set the cooking time to 2 hours on Low settings.
6. Blend the slow-cooked beans with lemon juice and olive oil.
7. Serve.

Nutrition Facts Per Serving:

Calories: 300, Total Fat: 3g, Fiber: 1g, Total Carbs: 20g, Protein: 6g

Pork Stuffed Tamales

Prep Time: 14 minutes Cook Time: 8 hrs 30 minutes Serves: 24

Ingredients:

8 oz. dried corn husks, soaked for 1 day and drained	1 tbsp chipotle chili powder
4 cups of water	2 tbsp chili powder
3 lbs. pork shoulder, boneless and chopped	Salt and black pepper to the taste
1 yellow onion, chopped	1 tsp cumin, ground
2 garlic cloves, crushed	4 cups masa harina
	¼ cup of corn oil
	¼ cup shortening
	1 tsp baking powder

Instructions:

1. Add 2 cups water, onion, black pepper, salt, garlic, chili powder, pork, cumin, and chipotle powder to the Slow cooker.
2. Put the cooker's lid on and set the cooking time to 7 hours on Low settings.
3. Shred the slow-cooked meat using 2 forks then mix it with 1 tbsp cooking liquid, black pepper, and salt.
4. Mix masa harina with baking powder, oil, shortening, black pepper, and salt in a mixer.
5. Add the cooking liquid from the cooker and blend well until smooth.
6. Spread the corn husks on the working surface and add ¼ cup harina mixture to the top of each husk.
7. Add 1 tbsp shredded pork to each husk and fold it from the top, bottom, and sideways to make a roll.
8. Place these tamales in the Slow cooker and pour in the remaining water.
9. Put the cooker's lid on and set the cooking time to 1.5 hours on High settings.
10. Serve.

Nutrition Facts Per Serving:

Calories: 162, Total Fat: 4g, Fiber: 3g, Total Carbs: 10g, Protein: 5g

Pork Tostadas

Prep Time: 14 minutes Cook Time: 4 hrs
Serves: 4
Ingredients:

4 lbs. pork shoulder, boneless and cubed
Salt and black pepper to the taste
2 cups coca cola
1/3 cup brown sugar
½ cup hot sauce
2 tsp chili powder
2 tbsp tomato paste
¼ tsp cumin, ground
1 cup enchilada sauce
Corn tortillas, toasted for a few minutes in the oven
Mexican cheese, shredded for serving
4 shredded lettuce leaves, for serving
Salsa
Guacamole for serving

Instructions:
1. Add 1 cup coke, salsa, sugar, chili powder, cumin, pork, hot sauce, and tomato paste to the Slow cooker.
2. Put the cooker's lid on and set the cooking time to 4 hours on Low settings.
3. Drain the cooked pork and shred it finely.
4. Mix well the shredded pork with enchilada sauce and remaining coke.
5. Divide the pork in the tortillas and top it with lettuce leaves, guacamole, and Mexican cheese.
6. Serve.

Nutrition Facts Per Serving:
Calories: 162, Total Fat: 3g, Fiber: 6g, Total Carbs: 12g, Protein: 5g

Slow-Cooked Lemon Peel

Prep time: 24 minutes Cook Time: 4 hrs
Serves: 80 pieces
Ingredients:

5 big lemons, peel cut into strips
2 and ¼ cups white sugar
5 cups of water

Instructions:
1. Spread the lemon peel in the Slow cooker and top it with sugar and water.
2. Put the cooker's lid on and set the cooking time to 4 hours on Low settings.
3. Drain the cooked peel and serve.

Nutrition Facts Per Serving:
Calories: 7, Total Fat: 1g, Fiber: 1g, Total Carbs: 2g, Protein: 1g

Garlicky Bacon Slices

Prep time: 17 minutes Cook Time: 4 hrs
Serves: 9
Ingredients:

10 oz. Canadian bacon, sliced
2 tbsp garlic powder
2 garlic cloves, peeled and sliced
2 tbsp whipped cream
1 tsp dried dill
1 tsp chili flakes
½ tsp salt

Instructions:
1. Season the bacon with garlic powder and spread it in the Slow cooker.
2. Whisk the cream with garlic, dill, salt, and chili flakes in a bowl.
3. Spread this cream mixture over the bacon strips and leave for 10 minutes.
4. Put the cooker's lid on and set the cooking time to 3 hours on High settings.
5. Flip the bacon slices and remove excess liquid out of the cooker.
6. Put the cooker's lid on and set the cooking time to 1 hour on High settings.
7. Serve.

Nutrition Facts Per Serving:
Calories: 51, Total Fat: 1.6g, Fiber: 0g, Total Carbs: 2.59g, Protein: 7g

Garlic Parmesan Dip

Prep time: 17 minutes Cook Time: 6 hours Serves: 7
Ingredients:

10 oz. garlic cloves, peeled
5 oz. Parmesan
1 cup cream cheese
1 tsp cayenne
pepper
1 tbsp dried dill
1 tsp turmeric
½ tsp butter

Instructions:
1. Add garlic cloves, cream cheese and all other ingredients to the Slow cooker.
2. Put the cooker's lid on and set the cooking time to 6 hours on Low settings.
3. Mix well and blend the dip with a hand blender.
4. Serve.

Nutrition Facts Per Serving:
Calories: 244, Total Fat: 11.5g, Fiber: 1g, Total Carbs: 23.65g, Protein: 13g

Maple Glazed Turkey Strips

Prep time: 17 minutes Cook Time: 3.5 hours Serves: 8

Ingredients:

15 oz. turkey fillets, cut into strips
2 tbsp honey
1 tbsp maple syrup
1 tsp cayenne pepper
1 tbsp butter
1 tsp paprika
1 tsp oregano
1 tsp dried dill
2 tbsp mayo

Instructions:

1. Place the turkey strips in the Slow cooker.
2. Add all other spices, herbs, and mayo on top of the turkey.
3. Put the cooker's lid on and set the cooking time to 3 hours on High settings.
4. During this time, mix honey with maples syrup and melted butter in a bowl.
5. Pour this honey glaze over the turkey evenly.
6. Put the cooker's lid on and set the cooking time to 30 minutes on High settings.
7. Serve warm.

Nutrition Facts Per Serving:
Calories: 295, Total Fat: 25.2g, Fiber: 0g, Total Carbs: 6.82g, Protein: 10g

Spinach Mussels Salad

Prep time: 14 minutes Cook Time: 1 hour Serves: 4

Ingredients:

2 lbs. mussels, cleaned and scrubbed
1 radicchio, cut into thin strips
1 white onion, chopped
1 lb. baby spinach
½ cup dry white wine
1 garlic clove, crushed
½ cup of water
A drizzle of olive oil

Instructions:

1. Add mussels, onion, water, oil, garlic, and wine to the Slow cooker.
2. Put the cooker's lid on and set the cooking time to 1 hour on High settings.
3. Spread the radicchio and spinach in the serving plates.
4. Divide the cooked mussels over the spinach leaves.
5. Serve.

Nutrition Facts Per Serving:
Calories: 59, Total Fat: 4g, Fiber: 1g, Total Carbs: 1g, Protein: 1g

Tomato Mussels Salad

Prep time: 14 minutes Cook Time: 1 hour Serves: 4

Ingredients:

28 oz. canned tomatoes, crushed
½ cup white onion, chopped
2 jalapeno peppers, chopped
¼ cup dry white wine
¼ cup extra virgin olive oil
¼ cup balsamic vinegar
2 lbs. mussels, cleaned and scrubbed
2 tbsp red pepper flakes
2 garlic cloves, minced
Salt to the taste
½ cup basil, chopped
Lemon wedges for serving

Instructions:

1. Add mussels, tomatoes and all other ingredients to the Slow cooker.
2. Put the cooker's lid on and set the cooking time to 1 hour on High settings.
3. Discard those mussels which remained unopened.
4. Serve the rest with lemon wedges.

Nutrition Facts Per Serving:
Calories: 100, Total Fat: 1g, Fiber: 1g, Total Carbs: 7g, Protein: 2g

Ginger Chili Peppers

Prep time: 17 minutes Cook Time: 3 hours Serves: 7

Ingredients:

2 tbsp balsamic vinegar
10 oz. red chili pepper, chopped
4 garlic cloves, peeled and sliced
1 white onion, chopped
3 tbsp water
1 tsp oregano
1 tsp ground black pepper
4 tbsp olive oil
1 tsp ground nutmeg
½ tsp ground ginger

Instructions:

1. Spread the red chili peppers in the slow cooker.
2. Mix onion and garlic with remaining ingredients and spread on top of chili peppers.
3. Put the cooker's lid on and set the cooking time to 3 hours on High settings.
4. Serve.

Nutrition Facts Per Serving:
Calories: 96, Total Fat: 8g, Fiber: 1g, Total Carbs: 5.87g, Protein: 1g

Jalapeno Chorizo Poppers

Prep time: 14 minutes Cook Time: 3 hours Serves: 4

Ingredients:

½ lb. chorizo, chopped
10 jalapenos, tops cut off and deseeded
1 small white onion, chopped

½ lb. beef, ground
¼ tsp garlic powder
1 tbsp maple syrup
1 tbsp mustard
1/3 cup water

Instructions:

1. Mix beef with onion, garlic powder, and chorizo in a bowl.
2. Divide this beef filling into the jalapenos.
3. Add water and stuffed jalapenos to the base of the Slow cooker.
4. Put the cooker's lid on and set the cooking time to 3 hours on High settings.
5. Meanwhile, mix maple syrup with mustard in a bowl.
6. Serve the jalapeno popper with maple sauce on top.

Nutrition Facts Per Serving:

Calories: 214, Total Fat: 2g, Fiber: 3g, Total Carbs: 8g, Protein: 3g

Blue Cheese Parsley Dip

Prep time: 14 minutes Cook Time: 7 hours Serves: 7

Ingredients:

1 cup parsley, chopped
8 oz. celery stalk, chopped
6 oz. Blue cheese, chopped
1 tbsp apple cider vinegar

6 oz. cream
1 tsp minced garlic
1 tsp paprika
¼ tsp ground red pepper
1 onion, peeled and grated

Instructions:

1. Whisk the cream with cream cheese in a bowl and add to the Slow cooker.
2. Toss in parsley, celery stalk, garlic, onion, apple cider vinegar, and red pepper ground.
3. Put the cooker's lid on and set the cooking time to 7 hours on Low settings.
4. Mix the dip after 4 hours of cooking then resume cooked.
5. Serve.

Nutrition Facts Per Serving:

Calories: 151, Total Fat: 11.9g, Fiber: 1g, Total Carbs: 5.14g, Protein: 7g

Marsala Cheese Mushrooms

Prep time: 17 minutes Cook Time: 8 hours 20 minutes Serves: 6

Ingredients:

4 oz. marsala
8 oz. button mushrooms
½ cup fresh dill
2 oz. shallot, chopped
3 oz. chicken stock
5 oz. cream,

whipped
1 oz. corn starch
3 garlic cloves, chopped
3 oz. Cheddar cheese
1 tsp salt
½ tsp paprika

Instructions:

1. Add mushrooms to the base of the Slow cooker.
2. Mix Marsala wine with chicken stock and pour over the mushrooms.
3. Now add shallot, salt, and paprika to the cooker.
4. Put the cooker's lid on and set the cooking time to 8 hours on Low settings.
5. Whisk cream with dill, cornstarch, and cheese.
6. Add this cream-cheese mixture to the cooked mushrooms.
7. Put the cooker's lid on and set the cooking time to 20 minutes on High settings.
8. Serve.

Nutrition Facts Per Serving:

Calories: 254, Total Fat: 10.3g, Fiber: 5g, Total Carbs: 35.7g, Protein: 9g

Cheese Onion Dip

Prep time: 14 minutes Cook Time: 1 hour Serves: 6

Ingredients:

8 oz. cream cheese, soft
¾ cup sour cream
1 cup cheddar cheese, shredded

10 bacon slices, cooked and chopped
2 yellow onions, chopped

Instructions:

1. Add cream cheese, bacon and all other ingredients to the Slow cooker.
2. Put the cooker's lid on and set the cooking time to 1 hour on High settings.
3. Serve.

Nutrition Facts Per Serving:

Calories: 222, Total Fat: 4g, Fiber: 6g, Total Carbs: 17g, Protein: 4g

Cheese Stuffed Meat Balls

Prep time: 23 minutes Cook Time: 9 hours Serves: 9

Ingredients:

10 oz. ground pork	cheese, cut into cubes
1 tbsp minced garlic	
1 tsp ground black pepper	1 cup panko bread crumbs
1 tsp salt	1 tsp chili flakes
1 tsp paprika	1 egg
1 tsp oregano	2 tsp milk
6 oz. Romano	1 tsp olive oil

Instructions:

1. Mix ground pork with oregano, chili flakes, paprika, salt, garlic, and black pepper in a bowl.
2. Stir in beaten egg and milk, then mix well with your hands.
3. Make golf ball-sized meatballs out of this beef mixture and insert one cheese cubes into each ball.
4. Roll each meatball in the bread crumbs to coat well.
5. Place these cheese-stuffed meatballs in the Slow Cooker.
6. Put the cooker's lid on and set the cooking time to 9 hours on Low settings.
7. Serve warm.

Nutrition Facts Per Serving:

Calories: 167, Total Fat: 9.2g, Fiber: 0g, Total Carbs: 3.92g, Protein: 17g

Jalapeno Salsa Snack

Prep time: 14 minutes Cook Time: 3 hours Serves: 6

Ingredients:

10 Roma tomatoes, chopped	tomatoes
2 jalapenos, chopped	3 garlic cloves, minced
1 sweet onion, chopped	1 bunch cilantro, chopped
28 oz. canned plum	Salt and black pepper to the taste

Instructions:

1. Add Roma tomatoes, onion, and all other ingredients to the Slow cooker.
2. Put the cooker's lid on and set the cooking time to 3 hours on High settings.
3. Mix well and serve.

Nutrition Facts Per Serving:

Calories: 162, Total Fat: 4g, Fiber: 6g, Total Carbs: 12g, Protein: 3g

Mozzarella Basil Tomatoes

Prep time: 14 minutes Cook Time: 30 minutes Serves: 8

Ingredients:

3 tbsp fresh basil	sliced
1 tsp chili flakes	1 tbsp olive oil
5 oz. Mozzarella, sliced	1 tsp minced garlic
4 large tomatoes,	½ tsp onion powder
	½ tsp cilantro

Instructions:

1. Whisk olive oil with onion powder, cilantro, garlic, and chili flakes in a bowl.
2. Rub all the tomato slices with this cilantro mixture.
3. Top each tomato slice with cheese slice and then place another tomato slice on top to make a sandwich.
4. Insert a toothpick into each tomato sandwich to seal it.
5. Place them in the base of the Slow cooker.
6. Put the cooker's lid on and set the cooking time to 20 minutes on High settings.
7. Garnish with basil.
8. Enjoy.

Nutrition Facts Per Serving:

Calories: 59, Total Fat: 1.9g, Fiber: 2g, Total Carbs: 4.59g, Protein: 7g

Cheesy Mushroom Dip

Prep time: 14 minutes Cook Time: 4 hrs Serves: 6

Ingredients:

2 cups green bell peppers, chopped	chopped
1 cup yellow onion, chopped	28 oz. tomato sauce
3 garlic cloves, minced	½ cup goat cheese, crumbled
1 lb. mushrooms,	Salt and black pepper to the taste

Instructions:

1. Add mushrooms, bell peppers and all other ingredients to the Slow cooker.
2. Put the cooker's lid on and set the cooking time to 4 hours on Low settings.
3. Serve.

Nutrition Facts Per Serving:

Calories: 255, Total Fat: 4g, Fiber: 7g, Total Carbs: 9g, Protein: 3g

Jalapeno Onion Dip

Prep time: 14 minutes Cook Time: 4 hrs Serves: 6
Ingredients:

7 cups tomatoes, chopped
1 yellow onion, chopped
1 red onion, chopped
3 jalapenos, chopped
1 red bell pepper, chopped
1 green bell pepper, chopped
¼ cup apple cider vinegar
1 tbsp cilantro, chopped
1 tbsp sage, chopped
3 tbsp basil, chopped
Salt to the taste

Instructions:

1. Add tomatoes, onion and all other ingredients to the Slow Cooker.
2. Put the cooker's lid on and set the cooking time to 4 hours on Low settings.
3. Puree the cooked mixture in a blender until smooth.
4. Serve.

Nutrition Facts Per Serving:
Calories: 162, Total Fat: 7g, Fiber: 4g, Total Carbs: 7g, Protein: 3g

Peanut Butter Chicken

Prep time: 17 minutes Cook Time: 6 hours Serves: 7
Ingredients:

3 tbsp peanut butter, melted
1 lb. chicken breast, boneless, cut into strips
1 tsp paprika
1 tsp salt
1 tsp olive oil
2 tbsp almond flour
1 tsp cayenne pepper

Instructions:

1. Mix the chicken strips with cayenne pepper, salt, and paprika.
2. Dust these with almond flour to coat.
3. Add olive oil and coated chicken strips to the Slow cooker.
4. Put the cooker's lid on and set the cooking time to 4 hours on High settings.
5. Flip the cooked chicken strips and cook for another 2 hours on the LOW setting.
6. Serve.

Nutrition Facts Per Serving:
Calories: 161, Total Fat: 9.5g, Fiber: 1g, Total Carbs: 3.15g, Protein: 16g

Black Eyes Peas Dip

Prep time: 14 minutes Cook Time: 5 hours Serves: 4
Ingredients:

1 ½ cups black-eyed peas
3 cups of water
1 tsp Cajun seasoning
½ cup pecans, toasted
½ tsp garlic powder
½ tsp jalapeno powder
Salt and black pepper to the taste
¼ tsp liquid smoke
½ tsp Tabasco sauce

Instructions:

1. Add water, salt, Cajun seasoning, black pepper, and black eye peas to the Slow cooker.
2. Put the cooker's lid on and set the cooking time to 5 hours on High settings.
3. Drain and transfer the black-eyed peas to a blender jug.
4. Add jalapeno powder, tabasco sauce, pecans, garlic, liquid smoke, salt and black pepper, to taste.
5. Blend this black-eyes pea dip until smooth.
6. Serve.

Nutrition Facts Per Serving:
Calories: 221, Total Fat: 4g, Fiber: 7g, Total Carbs: 16g, Protein: 4g

Chickpea Hummus

Prep time: 14 minutes Cook Time: 8 hrs Serves: 10
Ingredients:

1 cup chickpeas, dried
2 tbsp olive oil
3 cup of water
A pinch of salt and
black pepper
1 garlic clove, minced
1 tbsp lemon juice

Instructions:

1. Add chickpeas, salt, water, and black pepper to the Slow cooker.
2. Put the cooker's lid on and set the cooking time to 8 hours on Low settings.
3. Drain and transfer the chickpeas to a blender jug.
4. Add salt, black pepper, lemon juice, garlic, and olive oil.
5. Blend the chickpeas dip until smooth.
6. Serve.

Nutrition Facts Per Serving:
Calories: 211, Total Fat: 6g, Fiber: 7g, Total Carbs: 8g, Protein: 4g

Herbed Pecans Snack

Prep time: 14 minutes Cook Time: 2 hrs 15 minutes Serves: 5

Ingredients:

1 lb. pecans halved	¼ tsp garlic powder
2 tbsp olive oil	1 tsp thyme, dried
1 tsp basil, dried	½ tsp onion powder
1 tbsp chili powder	A pinch of cayenne
1 tsp oregano, dried	pepper

Instructions:

1. Add pecans, basil, and all other ingredients to the Slow cooker.
2. Put the cooker's lid on and set the cooking time to 2 hours on Low settings.
3. Mix well and serve.

Nutrition Facts Per Serving:
Calories: 78, Total Fat: 3g, Fiber: 2g, Total Carbs: 9g, Protein: 2g

Cheesy Pork Rolls

Prep time: 23 minutes Cook Time: 7 hours Serves: 8

Ingredients:

3 oz. Monterey cheese, sliced	1 tsp ground pepper
6 oz. ground pork	5 oz. Cheddar cheese, sliced
2 oz. onion, chopped	1 tbsp pesto sauce
1 tbsp sliced garlic	8 flour tortilla
1 tsp salt	1 tsp olive oil

Instructions:

1. Grease the base of your Slow cooker with olive oil.
2. Add ground pepper with onion, pesto sauce, ground pork, and onion to the Slow cooker.
3. Put the cooker's lid on and set the cooking time to 5 hours on High settings.
4. Mix well, then divide this beef mixture into each tortilla.
5. Drizzle chopped cheese over the tortilla filling.
6. Roll all the tortilla and place them in the Slow cooker.
7. Put the cooker's lid on and set the cooking time to 2 hours on High settings.
8. Serve.

Nutrition Facts Per Serving:
Calories: 270, Total Fat: 10.8g, Fiber: 1g, Total Carbs: 27.52g, Protein: 16g

Cheesy Potato Dip

Prep time: 17 minutes Cook Time: 5 hours Serves: 12

Ingredients:

1 cup heavy cream	1 cup fresh cilantro
1 cup milk	1 tsp salt
2 tbsp cornstarch	1 tsp black pepper
5 medium potatoes, peeled and diced	1 tsp paprika
	½ tsp onion powder
5 oz. Cheddar cheese, chopped	1 tbsp garlic powder
	¼ tsp oregano

Instructions:

1. Add milk, cream, potatoes, salt, paprika, onion powder, oregano, garlic powder, and black pepper to the Slow cooker.
2. Put the cooker's lid on and set the cooking time to 3 hours on High settings.
3. Stir in cilantro and cheese to the cooked potatoes.
4. Put the cooker's lid on and set the cooking time to 2 hours on High settings.
5. Mix well and serve.

Nutrition Facts Per Serving:
Calories: 196, Total Fat: 5.6g, Fiber: 4g, Total Carbs: 31.58g, Protein: 6g

Potato Onion Salsa

Prep time: 14 minutes Cook Time: 8 hrs Serves: 6

Ingredients:

1 sweet onion, chopped	potatoes, cut into medium cubes
¼ cup white vinegar	¼ cup dill, chopped
2 tbsp mustard	1 cup celery, chopped
Salt and black pepper to the taste	Cooking spray
1 and ½ lbs. gold	

Instructions:

1. Grease the base of the Slow cooker with cooking spray.
2. Add onion, potatoes and all other ingredients to the cooker.
3. Put the cooker's lid on and set the cooking time to 8 hours on Low settings.
4. Mix well and serve.

Nutrition Facts Per Serving:
Calories: 251, Total Fat: 6g, Fiber: 7g, Total Carbs: 12g, Protein: 7g

Bacon Fingerling Potatoes

Prep time: 16 minutes Cook Time: 8 hours Serves: 15

Ingredients:

2 lb. fingerling potatoes	1 tsp garlic powder
8 oz. bacon	1 tsp paprika
1 tsp onion powder	3 tbsp butter
1 tsp chili powder	1 tsp dried dill
	1 tbsp rosemary

Instructions:

1. Grease the base of your slow cooker with butter.
2. Spread the fingerling potatoes in the buttered cooker.
3. Mix all the spices, herbs, and bacon in a bowl.
4. Spread bacon-spice mixture over the lingering potatoes.
5. Put the cooker's lid on and set the cooking time to 8 hours on Low settings.
6. Serve warm.

Nutrition Facts Per Serving:

Calories: 117, Total Fat: 6.9g, Fiber: 2g, Total Carbs: 12.07g, Protein: 3g

Peanut Bombs

Prep time: 17 minutes Cook Time: 6 hours Serves: 9

Ingredients:

1 cup peanut	1 tsp salt
½ cup flour	1 tsp turmeric
1 egg	4 tbsp milk
1 tsp butter, melted	¼ tsp nutmeg

Instructions:

1. First, blend the peanuts in a blender then stir in flour.
2. Beat egg with milk, nutmeg, turmeric, and salt in a bowl.
3. Stir in the peanut-flour mixture and mix well to form a dough.
4. Grease the base of the Slow cooker with melted butter.
5. Divide the dough into golf ball-sized balls and place them the cooker.
6. Put the cooker's lid on and set the cooking time to 6 hours on Low settings.
7. Serve.

Nutrition Facts Per Serving:

Calories: 215, Total Fat: 12.7g, Fiber: 2g, Total Carbs: 17.4g, Protein: 10g

Sausage Cream Dip

Prep time: 14 minutes Cook Time: 5 hours Serves: 8

Ingredients:

8 oz. sausage, cooked, chopped	½ cup cream cheese
4 tbsp sour cream	3 tbsp chives
2 tbsp Tabasco sauce	5 oz. salsa
	4 oz. Monterey Cheese

Instructions:

1. Mix chopped sausages with sour cream in the Slow cooker.
2. Stir in Tabasco sauce, cream cheese, salsa, chives, and Monterey cheese.
3. Put the cooker's lid on and set the cooking time to 5 hours on Low settings.
4. Continue mixing the dip after every 30 minutes of cooking.
5. Serve.

Nutrition Facts Per Serving:

Calories: 184, Total Fat: 14.4g, Fiber: 1g, Total Carbs: 5.11g, Protein: 10g

Pesto Pitta Pockets

Prep time: 18 minutes Cook Time: 4 hrs Serves: 6

Ingredients:

6 pita bread	chopped
2 sweet peppers, deseeded and chopped	1 tsp salt
	2 tbsp vinegar
1 chili pepper, chopped	1 tbsp olive oil
	1 tbsp garlic, sliced
1 red onion,	2 tbsp pesto

Instructions:

1. Add sweet peppers and all other ingredients, except for pesto and pita bread to the Slow cooker.
2. Put the cooker's lid on and set the cooking time to 4 hours on Low settings.
3. Layer the pocket of each pita bread with pesto.
4. Mix the cooked sweet peppers filling and divide in the pita bread pockets.
5. Serve.

Nutrition Facts Per Serving:

Calories: 153, Total Fat: 6.1g, Fiber: 3g, Total Carbs: 22.42g, Protein: 4g

Creamy Mushroom Bites

Prep Time: 27 minutes Cook Time: 5 hours Serves: 10

Ingredients:

7 oz. shiitake mushroom, chopped	1 tsp salt
2 eggs	½ tsp chili flakes
1 tbsp cream cheese	1 tsp olive oil
3 tbsp panko bread crumbs	1 tsp ground coriander
2 tbsp flour	½ tsp nutmeg
1 tsp minced garlic	1 tbsp almond flour
	1 tsp butter, melted

Instructions:

1. Toss the mushrooms with salt, chili flakes, olive oil, ground coriander, garlic, and nutmeg in a skillet.
2. Stir cook for 5 minutes approximately on medium heat.
3. Whisk eggs with flour, cream cheese, and bread crumbs in a suitable bowl.
4. Stir in sauteed mushrooms and butter then mix well.
5. Knead this mushroom dough and divide it into golf ball-sized balls.
6. Pour the oil from the skillet in the Slow cooker.
7. Add the mushroom dough balls to the cooker.
8. Put the cooker's lid on and set the cooking time to 3 hours on High settings.
9. Flip the balls and cook for another 2 hours on high heat.
10. Serve.

Nutrition Facts Per Serving:
Calories: 65, Total Fat: 3.5g, Fiber: 1g, Total Carbs: 6.01g, Protein: 3g

Basic Pepper Salsa

Prep time: 14 minutes Cook Time: 5 hours Serves: 6

Ingredients:

7 cups tomatoes, chopped	¼ cup apple cider vinegar
1 green bell pepper, chopped	1 tsp coriander, ground
1 red bell pepper, chopped	1 tbsp cilantro, chopped
2 yellow onions, chopped	3 tbsp basil, chopped
4 jalapenos, chopped	Salt and black pepper to the taste

Instructions:

1. Add jalapenos, tomatoes and all other ingredients to the Slow cooker.
2. Put the cooker's lid on and set the cooking time to 5 hours on Low settings.
3. Mix gently and serve.

Nutrition Facts Per Serving:
Calories: 172, Total Fat: 3g, Fiber: 5g, Total Carbs: 8g, Protein: 4g

Chicken Taco Nachos

Prep Time: 24 minutes Cook Time: 4 hrs Serves: 10

Ingredients:

1 tbsp taco seasoning	1 tsp minced garlic
16 oz. chicken breast, boneless, diced	4 tbsp tomato sauce
1 tsp salt	1 tsp thyme
1 tsp paprika	1 tbsp chives, chopped
1 onion, chopped	6 oz. Cheddar cheese, shredded
1 chili pepper, chopped	7 oz. tortilla chips
2 tbsp salsa	1 avocado, pitted, peeled and diced

Instructions:

1. Mix taco seasoning, salt, thyme, and paprika in a shallow bowl.
2. Set the chicken in the Slow cooker and drizzle the taco mixture over it.
3. Add tomato sauce, salsa, garlic, chili pepper, and onion to the cooker.
4. Put the cooker's lid on and set the cooking time to 2 hours on High settings.
5. Use two forks and shred the slow-cooked chicken.
6. Spread the tortilla chip on the serving plate and top
7. Place the tortilla chips on the serving plate and top them with shredded chicken.
8. Add chives, cheese, and avocado pieces.
9. Serve.

Nutrition Facts Per Serving:
Calories: 249, Total Fat: 11.8g, Fiber: 3g, Total Carbs: 21.56g, Protein: 14g

Mixed Nuts

Prep time: 27 minutes Cook Time: 40 minutes Serves: 6

Ingredients:

½ tsp cooking spray	1 tsp salt
1 tsp chili flakes	1 cup peanuts
1 tsp ground cinnamon	1 cup cashew
2 oz. butter, melted	1 cup walnuts
	3 tbsp maple syrup

Instructions:

1. Toss cashew, peanuts, and walnuts in a baking sheet and bake for 10 minutes at 350 degrees F.
2. Toss the nuts after every 2 minutes of cooking.
3. Mix chili flakes, salt, and cinnamon ground in a bowl.
4. Transfer the nuts to the Slow cooker and drizzle spice mixture on top.
5. Whisk maple syrup and melted butter in a bowl and pour over the nuts.
6. Put the cooker's lid on and set the cooking time to 20 minutes on High settings.
7. Stir the nuts well, then continue cooking for another 20 minutes on High setting.
8. Serve.

Nutrition Facts Per Serving:

Calories: 693, Total Fat: 55.4g, Fiber: 5g, Total Carbs: 39.16g, Protein: 20g

Spicy Mussels

Prep time: 18 minutes Cook Time: 1 hour Serves: 4

Ingredients:

2 lbs. mussels, scrubbed and debearded	flakes
2 tbsp olive oil	14 oz. tomatoes, chopped
1 yellow onion, chopped	2 tsp garlic, minced
½ tsp red pepper	½ cup chicken stock
	2 tsp oregano, dried

Instructions:

1. Add onions, mussels, and other ingredients to the Slow cooker.
2. Put the cooker's lid on and set the cooking time to 1 hour on High settings.
3. Mix well and serve.

Nutrition Facts Per Serving:

Calories: 83, Total Fat: 2g, Fiber: 2g, Total Carbs: 8g, Protein: 3g

Crumbly Chickpeas Snack

Prep time: 18 minutes Cook Time: 4 hrs Serves: 9

Ingredients:

1 lb. chickpea, canned, drained	coriander
4 oz. white onion, peeled and grated	1 tsp salt
1 tbsp minced garlic	12 oz. chicken stock
1 tbsp chili flakes	½ cup fresh dill, chopped
½ tsp thyme	1 tsp butter, melted
½ tsp ground	3 tbsp bread crumbs

Instructions:

1. Mix onion with garlic, salt, butter, cinnamon, thyme, and chili flakes.
2. Spread the chickpeas in the slow cooker and top it with onion mixture.
3. Pour the chicken stock over the chickpeas.
4. Put the cooker's lid on and set the cooking time to 4 hours on High settings.
5. Strain the cooked chickpeas and transfer to the bowl.
6. Top them with breadcrumbs and chopped dill.
7. Serve.

Nutrition Facts Per Serving:

Calories: 270, Total Fat: 5.3g, Fiber: 7g, Total Carbs: 44.09g, Protein: 13g

Apple Chutney

Prep time: 17 minutes Cook Time: 9 hours Serves: 10

Ingredients:

1 cup wine vinegar	1 tsp ground cardamom
4 oz. brown sugar	½ tsp ground cinnamon
2 lbs. apples, chopped	1 tsp chili flakes
4 oz. onion, chopped	
1 jalapeno pepper	

Instructions:

1. Mix brown sugar with wine vinegar in the Slow cooker.
2. Put the cooker's lid on and set the cooking time to 1 hour on High settings.
3. Add chopped apples and all other ingredients to the cooker.
4. Put the cooker's lid on and set the cooking time to 8 hours on Low settings.
5. Mix well and mash the mixture with a fork.

6. Serve.

Nutrition Facts Per Serving:
Calories: 101, Total Fat: 0.2g, Fiber: 3g,
Total Carbs: 25.04g, Protein: 0g

Spinach Cream Dip

**Prep time: 16 minutes Cook Time: 3 hrs
20 minutes Serves: 8**
Ingredients:

2 cups cream cheese	7 oz. Mozzarella, cut
2 cups fresh	into strips
spinach, chopped	1 onion, peeled and
1 tsp salt	chopped
1 tsp ground black	1 tbsp Tabasco
pepper	sauce
1 tsp paprika	1 tbsp butter
1 tsp ground white	3 tbsp milk
pepper	

Instructions:
1. Whisk cream cheese, black pepper, salt, white pepper, paprika, cream cheese, milk, and Tabasco sauce in a bowl.
2. Stir in onion and transfer this mixture to the Slow cooker.
3. Put the cooker's lid on and set the cooking time to 20 minutes on High settings.
4. Stir in spinach and mozzarella strips.
5. Put the cooker's lid on and set the cooking time to 3 hours on High settings.
6. Serve.

Nutrition Facts Per Serving:
Calories: 241, Total Fat: 18.9g, Fiber: 1g,
Total Carbs: 6.03g, Protein: 13g

Potato Cups

**Prep time: 17 minutes Cook Time: 8
hours Serves: 8**
Ingredients:

5 tbsp mashed	3 tbsp sour cream
potato	1 tsp minced garlic
1 carrot, boiled,	7 oz. puff pastry
cubed	1 egg yolk, beaten
3 tbsp green peas	4 oz. Parmesan,
1 tsp paprika	shredded

Instructions:
1. Mix mashed potato with carrot cubes in a bowl.
2. Stir in sour cream, paprika, green peas, and garlic, then mix well.

3. Spread the puff pastry and slice it into 2x2 inches squares.
4. Place the puff pastry square in the muffin cups of the muffin tray.
5. Press the puff pastry and in the muffin cups and brush it with egg yolk.
6. Divide the potatoes mixture into the muffin cups
7. Place the muffin tray in the Slow cooker.
8. Put the cooker's lid on and set the cooking time to 8 hours on Low settings.
9. Serve.

Nutrition Facts Per Serving:
Calories: 387, Total Fat: 11.5g, Fiber: 6g,
Total Carbs: 59.01g, Protein: 13g

Mixed Vegetable Spread

**Prep time: 14 minutes Cook Time: 7
hours Serves: 4**
Ingredients:

1 cup carrots, sliced	1 tsp garlic powder
1 and ½ cups	Salt and black
cauliflower florets	pepper to the taste
1/3 cup cashews	¼ tsp smoked
½ cup turnips,	paprika
chopped	¼ tsp mustard
2 ½ cups of water	powder
1 cup almond milk	A pinch of salt

Instructions:
1. Add cauliflower, carrots, turnips, cashews, and water to the Slow cooker.
2. Put the cooker's lid on and set the cooking time to 7 hours on Low settings.
3. Drain the cooked veggies and cashews and transfer to a blender.
4. Add garlic powder, mustard powder, black pepper, salt, paprika, almond milk, then blend until smooth.
5. Serve.

Nutrition Facts Per Serving:
Calories: 291, Total Fat: 7g, Fiber: 4g, Total
Carbs: 14g, Protein: 3g

Chapter 9 Dessert Recipes

Avocado Peppermint Pudding

Prep time: 2 hrs., Cook Time: 1 hr., Serves: 3
Ingredients:

½ cup vegetable oil
½ tbsp sugar

1 tbsp cocoa powder

For the pudding:

1 tsp peppermint oil
14 oz. coconut milk
1 avocado, pitted,

peeled and chopped
1 tbsp sugar

Instructions:

1. Start by mixing vegetable oil, ½ tbsp sugar, and cocoa powder in a bowl.
2. Spread this mixture in a container and refrigerate for 1 hour.
3. Blend this mixture with coconut milk, avocado, 1 tbsp sugar, peppermint oil in a blender.
4. Transfer this mixture to the insert of the Slow Cooker.
5. Put the cooker's lid on and set the cooking time to 1 hour on Low settings.
6. Stir in chocolate chips then divide the pudding the serving bowls.
7. Refrigerate for 1 hour then enjoy.

Nutrition Facts Per Serving:
Calories: 140, Total Fat: 3g, Fiber: 2g, Total Carbs: 3g, Protein: 4g

Mixed-Berry Marmalade

Prep time: 12 minutes; Cook Time: 3 hrs., Serves: 12
Ingredients:

1 lb. cranberries
1 lb. strawberries
½ lb. blueberries
3.5 oz. black currant

2 lbs. sugar
Zest of 1 lemon
2 tbsp water

Instructions:

1. Toss all the berries with sugar, water, and lemon zest in the insert of Slow cooker.
2. Put the cooker's lid on and set the cooking time to 3 hours on High settings.
3. Divide the marmalade mixture into the jars and allow it to cool.
4. Serve.

Nutrition Facts Per Serving:
Calories: 100, Total Fat: 4g, Fiber: 3g, Total Carbs: 12g, Protein: 3g

Spongy Banana Bread

Prep time: 12 minutes; Cook Time: 3 hrs., Serves: 6
Ingredients:

¾ cup of sugar
1/3 cup butter, soft
1 tsp vanilla extract
1 egg
2 bananas, mashed
1 tsp baking powder

1 and ½ cups flour
½ tsp baking soda
1/3 cupmilk
1 and ½ tsp cream of tartar
Cooking spray

Instructions:

1. Whisk milk with cream of tartar, sugar, egg, butter, bananas, and vanilla in a bowl.
2. Beat well, then add flour, baking soda, baking powder, and salt.
3. Again, mix well until it forms a smooth tartar-banana batter,
4. Grease the insert of Slow cooker with cooking spray and spread the bread batter in it.
5. Put the cooker's lid on and set the cooking time to 3 hours on High settings.
6. Slice and serve.

Nutrition Facts Per Serving:
Calories: 300, Total Fat: 3g, Fiber: 4g, Total Carbs: 28g, Protein: 5g

Banana Almond Foster

Prep time: 17 minutes; Cook Time: 4 hrs., Serves: 4
Ingredients:

1 lb. banana, peeled and chopped
3 oz butter
1 cup white sugar
2 tsp rum
1 tsp ground

cinnamon
3 tbsp coconut flakes
½ tsp vanilla extract
4 tbsp almond, crushed

Instructions:

1. Add bananas, white sugar, rum, coconut flakes, ground cinnamon, crushed almonds, and vanilla extract to the insert of Slow Cooker.
2. Put the cooker's lid on and set the cooking time to 4 hours on Low settings.
3. Serve with whipped cream.

Nutrition Facts Per Serving:
Calories: 689, Total Fat: 30.7g, Fiber: 13g, Total Carbs: 109.32g, Protein: 6g

Butternut Squash Pudding

Prep time: 12 minutes; Cook Time: 3 hrs., Serving: 8

Ingredients:

2 lbs. butternut squash, steamed, peeled and mashed	powder
	½ tsp ginger powder
	¼ tsp cloves, ground
2 eggs	1 tbsp cornstarch
1 cupmilk	Whipped cream for serving
¾ cup maple syrup	
1 tsp cinnamon	

Instructions:

1. Toss squash with milk, eggs, maple syrup, cornstarch, cinnamon, cloves ground, and ginger in the insert of Slow Cooker.
2. Put the cooker's lid on and set the cooking time to 2 hours on Low settings.
3. Serve with whipped cream on top.

Nutrition Facts Per Serving:

Calories: 152, Total Fat: 3g, Fiber: 4g, Total Carbs: 16g, Protein: 4g

Creamy Caramel Dessert

Prep time: 12 minutes; Cook Time: 2 hrs., Serves: 2

Ingredients:

1 and ½ tsp caramel extract	For the caramel sauce:
1 cup of water	2 tbsp sugar
2 oz. cream cheese	2 tbsp butter, melted
2 eggs	¼ tsp caramel extract
1 and ½ tbsp sugar	

Instructions:

1. Blend cream cheese with 1 ½ tbsp sugar, 1 ½ tsp caramel extract, water, and eggs in a blender.
2. Transfer this mixture to the insert of Slow Cooker.
3. Put the cooker's lid on and set the cooking time to 2 hours on High settings.
4. Divide this cream cheese mixture into the serving cups.
5. Now mix melted butter with caramel extract and sugar in a bowl.
6. Pour this caramel sauce over the cream cheese mixture.
7. Refrigerate the caramel cream for 1 hour.
8. Serve.

Nutrition Facts Per Serving:

Calories: 254, Total Fat: 24g, Fiber: 1g, Total Carbs: 6g, Protein: 8g

Vanilla Cheesecake

Prep time: 27 minutes; Cook Time: 3 hrs., Serves: 8

Ingredients:

2 cups cream cheese	½ cup butter, melted
½ cup sour cream	1 cup of sugar
5 eggs	1 tsp vanilla extract
8 oz graham cookies	1 tsp lemon zest

Instructions:

1. Whisk cream cheese, sour cream, sugar, lemon zest, and vanilla extract in a mixing bowl.
2. Add eggs to the mixture while beating it with a hand mixer.
3. Mix melted butter and crushed graham cookies in a blender.
4. Spread this mixture in a pan lined with a parchment sheet.
5. Fill this crust with the cream cheese mixture.
6. Add 1 cup water into the insert of Slow cooker and place steel rack inside.
7. Place the baking pan with the prepared cheesecake batter in the Slow Cooker.
8. Put the cooker's lid on and set the cooking time to 3 hours on Low settings.
9. Slice and serve when chilled.

Nutrition Facts Per Serving:

Calories: 551, Total Fat: 39.2g, Fiber: 1g, Total Carbs: 38.36g, Protein: 12g

Choco Liquor Crème

Prep time: 12 minutes; Cook Time: 2 hrs., Serves: 4

Ingredients:

3.5 oz. crème Fraiche	chunks
	1 tsp liquor
3.5 oz. dark chocolate, cut into	1 tsp sugar

Instructions:

1. Whisk crème Fraiche with sugar, liquor, and chocolate in the insert of Slow Cooker.
2. Put the cooker's lid on and set the cooking time to 2 hours on High settings.
3. Serve chilled.

Nutrition Facts Per Serving:

Calories: 200, Total Fat: 12g, Fiber: 4g, Total Carbs: 6g, Protein: 3g

Citron Vanilla Bars

Prep time: 25 minutes; Cook Time: 4 hrs., Serves: 10
Ingredients:

6 tbsp sugar	1 tbsp lemon zest
9 tbsp butter	¼ tsp olive oil
1 ½ cup flour	1 large egg, beaten
7 oz lemon curd	1 tsp vanilla extract

Instructions:
1. Mix softened butter with lemon zest, egg, sugar, and flour in a bowl.
2. Stir in vanilla extract, then mix well until it forms a smooth dough.
3. Spread this dough into a sheet then place this dough in the insert of Slow Cooker.
4. Add lemon curd over the dough evenly.
5. Put the cooker's lid on and set the cooking time to 4 hours on High settings.
6. Slice and serve.

Nutrition Facts Per Serving:
Calories: 191, Total Fat: 11.2g, Fiber: 1g, Total Carbs: 20.69g, Protein: 2g

Candied Sweet Lemon

Prep time: 20 minutes; Cook Time: 4 hrs., Serves: 4
Ingredients:

5 lemons, peeled and cut into medium segments	3 cups white sugar
	3 cups of water

Instructions:
1. Add lemons, sugar, and water to the insert of Slow Cooker.
2. Put the cooker's lid on and set the cooking time to 4 hours on Low settings.
3. Serve once chilled.

Nutrition Facts Per Serving:
Calories: 62, Total Fat: 3g, Fiber: 5g, Total Carbs: 3g, Protein: 4g

Nutty Caramel Apples

Prep time: 8 minutes; Cook Time: 4 hrs., Serves: 6
Ingredients:

6 gala apples, cut in half and deseeded	5 tbsp water
	3 tbsp walnuts, crushed
8 oz caramel, package	

Instructions:
1. Toss the apples with water, caramel, and walnuts in an insert of Slow Cooker.
2. Put the cooker's lid on and set the cooking time to 3 hours on Low settings.
3. Serve when chilled.

Nutrition Facts Per Serving:
Calories: 307, Total Fat: 12g, Fiber: 5g, Total Carbs: 47.17g, Protein: 4g

Cocoa Vanilla Cake

Prep time: 2 minutes; Cook Time: 2 hrs., Serves: 3
Ingredients:

10 tbsp flour	4 eggs
3 tbsp butter, melted	¼ tsp vanilla extract
4 tsp sugar	½ tsp baking powder
1 tbsp cocoa powder	

Instructions:
1. Beat butter with eggs, cocoa powder, and all other ingredients in a mixer.
2. Spread this cocoa batter in the insert of Slow Cooker.
3. Put the cooker's lid on and set the cooking time to 2 hours on High settings.
4. Slice and serve.

Nutrition Facts Per Serving:
Calories: 240, Total Fat: 34g, Fiber: 7g, Total Carbs: 10g, Protein: 20g

Green Tea Avocado Pudding

Prep time: 14 minutes; Cook Time: 1 hr., Serves: 2
Ingredients:

½ cup of coconut milk	2 tbsp green tea powder
1 and ½cup avocado, pitted and peeled	2 tsp lime zest, grated
	1 tbsp sugar

Instructions:
1. Mix coconut milk with tea powder and rest of the ingredients in the insert of Slow cooker.
2. Put the cooker's lid on and set the cooking time to 1 hour on Low settings.
3. Divide the pudding into the serving cups and allow it to cool.
4. Serve.

Nutrition Facts Per Serving:
Calories: 107, Total Fat: 5g, Fiber: 3g, Total Carbs: 6g, Protein: 8g

Creamy Dark Chocolate Dessert

Prep time: 4 minutes, Cook Time: 1 hr., Serves: 6

Ingredients:

½ cup heavy cream
4 oz. dark chocolate, unsweetened and chopped

Instructions:

1. Add cream with chocolate in the insert of Slow Cooker.
2. Put the cooker's lid on and set the cooking time to 1 hour on High settings.
3. Allow this mixture to cool.
4. Serve.

Nutrition Facts Per Serving:
Calories: 78, Total Fat: 1g, Fiber: 1g, Total Carbs: 2g, Protein: 1g

Cocoa Peanut Candies

Prep time: 26 minutes; Cook Time: 2.5 hrs., Serves: 11

Ingredients:

6 tbsp, peanuts, roasted and crushed
8 oz dark chocolate, crushed
¼ cup of cocoa
powder
4 tbsp chocolate chips
3 tbsp heavy cream

Instructions:

1. Add roasted peanuts and rest of the ingredients to the insert of Slow Cooker.
2. Put the cooker's lid on and set the cooking time to 2.5 hours on Low settings.
3. Divide this chocolate mixture into a silicone candy molds tray.
4. Place this tray in the refrigerator for 2 hours.
5. Serve.

Nutrition Facts Per Serving:
Calories: 229, Total Fat: 15.8g, Fiber: 3g, Total Carbs: 19.02g, Protein: 5g

Apricot Rice Pudding

Prep time: 21 minutes; Cook Time: 3 hrs., Serves: 3

Ingredients:

3 tbsp coconut flakes
1 cup of rice
1 cup almond milk
1 tsp vanilla extract
1 tbsp butter
2 tsp sugar
1 tbsp dried apricots, chopped

Instructions:

1. Coconut flakes, rice, milk and all other ingredients to the insert of Slow Cooker.
2. Put the cooker's lid on and set the cooking time to 3 hours on Low settings.
3. Allow it cool down.
4. Serve.

Nutrition Facts Per Serving:
Calories: 182, Total Fat: 7.6g, Fiber: 1g, Total Carbs: 25.5g, Protein: 3g

Coconut Vanilla Pudding

Prep time: 18 minutes; Cook Time: 1 hr., Serves: 4

Ingredients:

1 and 2/3 cups of coconut milk
1 tbsp gelatin
6 tbsp sugar
3 egg yolks
½ tsp vanilla extract

Instructions:

1. Whisk gelatin with 1 tbsp coconut milk in a bowl.
2. Transfer this gelatin mixture to the insert of Slow Cooker.
3. Stir in milk, egg yolks, sugar, and vanilla.
4. Put the cooker's lid on and set the cooking time to 1 hour on High settings.
5. Serve chilled.

Nutrition Facts Per Serving:
Calories: 170, Total Fat: 2g, Fiber: 0g, Total Carbs: 6g, Protein: 2g

Vanilla Blueberry Cream

Prep time: 18 minutes; Cook Time: 1 hr., Serves: 4

Ingredients:

14 oz. canned coconut milk
1 tsp vanilla extract
2 tbsp sugar
4 oz. blueberries
2 tbsp walnuts, chopped

Instructions:

1. Whisk coconut milk, vanilla extract, and sugar in a mixer.
2. Transfer this mixture to the insert of the Slow cooker.
3. Stir in berries and walnuts, then mix them gently.
4. Put the cooker's lid on and set the cooking time to 1 hour on Low settings.
5. Allow it to cool then serve.

Nutrition Facts Per Serving:
Calories: 160, Total Fat: 23g, Fiber: 4g, Total Carbs: 6g, Protein: 7g

Cinnamon Cream Dessert

Prep time: 1 hr., Cook Time: 1 hr., Serves: 6

Ingredients:

2 cups fresh cream
1 tsp cinnamon powder
6 egg yolks
5 tbsp white sugar
Zest of 1 orange, grated
A pinch of nutmeg for serving
4 tbsp sugar
2 cups of water

Instructions:

1. Whisk cream with orange zest, nutmeg, and cinnamon in a bowl.
2. Beat egg yolks with sugar in another.
3. Stir in cream mixture and mix it gently.
4. Divide this cream mixture into the ramekins.
5. Place these ramekins in the insert of Slow Cooker then pour 2 cups of water into it.
6. Put the cooker's lid on and set the cooking time to 1 hour on Low settings.
7. Allow it to cool and serve.

Nutrition Facts Per Serving:

Calories: 200, Total Fat: 4g, Fiber: 5g, Total Carbs: 15g, Protein: 5g

Tangerine Cream Pie

Prep time: 21 minutes; Cook Time: 4.5 hrs. Serves: 6

Ingredients:

8 oz tangerines, peeled and separated into pieces
1 tsp baking soda
1 tbsp vinegar
1 cup sour cream
1 cup flour
¼ tsp salt
5 tbsp white sugar
1 tsp vanilla extract
2 eggs
1 tsp butter

Instructions:

1. Grease the insert of Slow Cooker with butter and place tangerine pieces in it.
2. Whisk flour, baking soda, salt, sour cream whisked eggs, and vinegar in a bowl until smooth.
3. Spread this sour cream batter over the tangerines.
4. Put the cooker's lid on and set the cooking time to 4.5 hours on High settings.
5. Serve when chilled.

Nutrition Facts Per Serving:

Calories: 201, Total Fat: 8.7g, Fiber: 1g, Total Carbs: 23.21g, Protein: 7g

Latte Vanilla Cake

Prep time: 25 minutes; Cook Time: 7 hrs., Serves: 7

Ingredients:

½ cup pumpkin puree
3 cups flour
4 eggs
1 cup sugar, brown
½ cup of coconut milk
4 tbsp olive oil
3 tbsp espresso powder
2 tbsp maple syrup
1 tbsp vanilla extract
4 tbsp liquid honey
¼ tsp cooking spray

Instructions:

1. Beat eggs with pumpkin puree, espresso powder, and brown sugar in a bowl.
2. Stir in olive oil, coconut milk, vanilla extract, liquid honey, flour, and maple syrup.
3. Whisk this pumpkin batter using a hand mixer until smooth.
4. Use cooking to grease the insert of your Slow Cooker and pour the batter in it.
5. Put the cooker's lid on and set the cooking time to 7 hours on Low settings.
6. Slice and serve when chilled.

Nutrition Facts Per Serving:

Calories: 538, Total Fat: 22g, Fiber: 2g, Total Carbs: 71.97g, Protein: 14g

Cinnamon Apple Butter

Prep time: 12 minutes; Cook Time: 6 hrs. Serves: 6

Ingredients:

1 lb. sweet apples, peeled and chopped
6 oz white sugar
2 oz cinnamon stick
¼ tsp salt
¼ tsp ground ginger

Instructions:

1. Add apples, white sugar, cinnamon stick, salt, and ground ginger to the insert of Slow Cooker.
2. Put the cooker's lid on and set the cooking time to 3.5 hours on High settings.
3. Discard the cinnamon stick and blend the remaining apple mixture.
4. Put the cooker's lid on and set the cooking time to 3 hours on Low settings.
5. Serve when chilled.

Nutrition Facts Per Serving:

Calories: 222, Total Fat: 14.1g, Fiber: 9g, Total Carbs: 27.15g, Protein: 3g

Cinnamon Pear Toasts

**Prep time: 27 minutes; Cook Time: 3 hrs.
Serves: 8**
Ingredients:

4 pears, cut in half and deseeds.	3 tbsp butter
4 tsp brown sugar	½ tsp cooking spray
1 tsp vanilla extract	1 egg yolk, whisked
8 oz puff pastry	1 tsp cinnamon

Instructions:
1. Start by rolling the puff pastry and cut it into 8 equal parts.
2. Brush the puff pastry parts with butter and drizzle the cinnamon on top.
3. Place one pear half on each piece of puff pastry.
4. Brush the pears with whisked egg yolk.
5. Grease the insert of Slow Cooker with cooking spray and layer with parchment sheet.
6. Place the puff pastry boats in the insert of Slow Cooker.
7. Put the cooker's lid on and set the cooking time to 3 hours on High settings.
8. Serve.

Nutrition Facts Per Serving:
Calories: 238, Total Fat: 15.9g, Fiber: 3g, Total Carbs: 21.95g, Protein: 3g

Pear Apple Jam

**Prep time: 12 minutes; Cook Time: 3 hrs.
Serves: 12**
Ingredients:

8 pears, cored and cut into quarters	½ cup apple juice
2 apples, peeled, cored and quartered	1 tsp cinnamon, ground

Instructions:
1. Toss pears, apples, apple juice, and cinnamon in the insert of Slow Cooker.
2. Put the cooker's lid on and set the cooking time to 3 hours on High settings.
3. Blend this cooked pears-apples mixture to make a jam.
4. Allow it to cool them divide in the jars.
5. Serve.

Nutrition Facts Per Serving:
Calories: 100, Total Fat: 1g, Fiber: 2g, Total Carbs: 20g, Protein: 3g

Coffee Cinnamon Roll

**Prep time: 25 minutes; Cook Time: 4 hrs.,
Serves: 4**
Ingredients:

3 tbsp butter	½ tsp yeast
3 tbsp ground cinnamon	¼ cup whey
1 tbsp instant coffee powder	½ cup flour
1 tsp vanilla extract	¼ tsp salt
3 tbsp sugar, brown	1 tsp white sugar
	1 egg yolk
	½ tsp canola oil

Instructions:
1. Whisk yeast with sugar and whey in a bowl.
2. Stir in flour, salt, vanilla, and enough water to make a smooth dough.
3. Roll this dough into ¼ inch thick sheet.
4. Mix cinnamon with coffee powder, brown sugar, and butter in a small bowl.
5. Spread this cinnamon-butter mixture over the dough sheet.
6. Start rolling the dough from one to make a cinnamon roll.
7. Grease the insert of your Slow Cooker with canola oil and place the cinnamon roll it.
8. Brush the top of this roll with whisked egg yolk.
9. Put the cooker's lid on and set the cooking time to 4 hours on High settings.
10. Slice the roll and serve.

Nutrition Facts Per Serving:
Calories: 203, Total Fat: 10.8g, Fiber: 4g, Total Carbs: 24.52g, Protein: 3g

Lemony Orange Marmalade

**Prep time: 12 minutes; Cook Time: 3 hrs.,
Serves: 8**
Ingredients:

Juice of 2 lemons	peeled and cut into segments
3 lbs. sugar	1-pint water
1 lb. oranges,	

Instructions:
1. Whisk lemon juice, sugar, water, and oranges in the insert of Slow Cooker.
2. Put the cooker's lid on and set the cooking time to 3 hours on High settings.
3. Serve when chilled.

Nutrition Facts Per Serving:
Calories: 100, Total Fat: 4g, Fiber: 4g, Total Carbs: 12g, Protein: 4g

Cornmeal Apricot Pudding

Prep time: 21 minutes; Cook Time: 7 hrs., Serves: 6

Ingredients:

4 oz. cornmeal	1 tsp vanilla extract
10 oz. milk	1/3 tsp ground ginger
¼ tsp salt	
2 oz. butter	3 tbsp dried apricots, chopped
1 egg	
2 oz. molasses	

Instructions:

1. Grease the insert of your Slow cooker with butter.
2. Put the cooker's lid on and set the cooking time to 10 minutes on High settings.
3. Mix milk with cornmeal in a separate bowl.
4. Stir in vanilla extract, salt, ground ginger, molasses, and whisked egg then mix until smooth.
5. Spread this cornmeal batter in the greased insert of Slow Cooker.
6. Add dried apricots on top of this batter.
7. Put the cooker's lid on and set the cooking time to 7 hours on Low settings.
8. Serve when chilled.

Nutrition Facts Per Serving:

Calories: 234, Total Fat: 11.2g, Fiber: 1g, Total Carbs: 28.97g, Protein: 5g

Lemon Cream Dessert

Prep time: 16 minutes; Cook Time: 1 hr., Serves: 4

Ingredients:

1 cup heavy cream	¼ cup lemon juice
1 tsp lemon zest, grated	8 oz. mascarpone cheese

Instructions:

1. Whisk cream with mascarpone, lemon juice, and lemon zest in the Slow Cooker.
2. Put the cooker's lid on and set the cooking time to 1 hour on Low settings.
3. Divide the cream in serving glasses then refrigerate for 4 hours.
4. Serve.

Nutrition Facts Per Serving:

Calories: 165, Total Fat: 7g, Fiber: 0g, Total Carbs: 7g, Protein: 4g

Cardamom Lemon Pie

Prep time: 20 minutes; Cook Time: 7 hrs., Serves: 6

Ingredients:

3 lemons, sliced	2 cups flour
1 tsp ground cardamom	1 tsp baking powder
5 eggs, whisked	1 tbsp lemon juice
1 cup whey	1 cup of sugar
½ cup cottage cheese	1 tsp lime zest
	2 tsp ground ginger

Instructions:

1. Start by mixing whey, lemon juice, baking powder, cottage cheese, sugar, ground cardamom, lime zest, and ground ginger in a mixer.
2. Stir in flour and whisk until it forms a smooth whey batter.
3. Fold in the sliced lemons and mix gently.
4. Layer the base of the insert of Slow Cooker with a parchment sheet.
5. Spread the lemon-whey batter in the insert of Slow Cooker.
6. Put the cooker's lid on and set the cooking time to 7 hours on Low settings.
7. Slice and serve chilled.

Nutrition Facts Per Serving:

Calories: 363, Total Fat: 9.5g, Fiber: 1g, Total Carbs: 54.92g, Protein: 14g

Wine Dipped Pears

Prep time: 12 minutes; Cook Time: 1 hr. 30 minutes, Serves: 6

Ingredients:

6 green pears	A pinch of cinnamon
1 vanilla pod	7 oz. sugar
1 clove	1 glass red wine

Instructions:

1. Add pears, cinnamon, vanilla, wine, cloves, and sugar to the insert of Slow Cooker.
2. Put the cooker's lid on and set the cooking time to 1.5 hours on High settings.
3. Serve the pears with wine sauce.

Nutrition Facts Per Serving:

Calories: 162, Total Fat: 4g, Fiber: 3g, Total Carbs: 6g, Protein: 3g

Cheesecake with Lime Filling

Prep time: 16 minutes; Cook Time: 1 hr., Serves: 10

Ingredients:

2 tbsp butter, melted	¼ cup coconut, shredded
2 tsp sugar	Cooking spray
4 oz. almond meal	

For the filling:

1 lb. cream cheese	2 sachets lime jelly
Zest of 1 lime	2 cup hot water
Juice from 1 lime	

Instructions:

1. Whisk coconut with butter, sugar, and almond meal in a bowl.
2. Grease the insert of Slow cooker with cooking spray.
3. Spread the coconut mixture in the greased cooker.
4. Now beat cream cheese with lime zest, lime juice, and jelly in a separate bowl.
5. Spread this cream cheese mixture over the coconut crust.
6. Put the cooker's lid on and set the cooking time to 1 hour on High settings.
7. Refrigerate the cooked cheesecake for 2 hours.
8. Slice and serve.

Nutrition Facts Per Serving:
Calories: 300, Total Fat: 23g, Fiber: 2g, Total Carbs: 5g, Protein: 7g

Berry-Berry Mascarpone Cream

Prep time: 18 minutes; Cook Time: 1 hr., Serves: 12

Ingredients:

8 oz. mascarpone cheese	1 cup whipping cream
¾ tsp vanilla extract	½ pint blueberries
1 tbsp sugar	½ pint strawberries

Instructions:

1. Whisk cream with sugar, mascarpone, and vanilla in the insert of Slow Cooker.
2. Stir in strawberries and blueberries, mix gently.
3. Put the cooker's lid on and set the cooking time to 1 hour on High settings.
4. Mix well and serve when chilled.

Nutrition Facts Per Serving:
Calories: 143, Total Fat: 12g, Fiber: 1g, Total Carbs: 6g, Protein: 2g

Maple Chocolate Fondue

Prep time: 12 minutes; Cook Time: 4 hrs., Serves: 5

Ingredients:

1 pinch salt	½ cup milk
1 cup milk chocolate chips	1 tbsp butter
1 cup dark chocolate chips	¼ tsp nutmeg
	2 tsp maple syrup

Instructions:

1. Add milk, chocolate chips, and rest of the ingredients to the insert of Slow Cooker.
2. Put the cooker's lid on and set the cooking time to 4 hrs. on Low settings.
3. Serve when chilled.

Nutrition Facts Per Serving:
Calories: 571, Total Fat: 28.7g, Fiber: 0g, Total Carbs: 74.85g, Protein: 7g

Spiced Peach Crisp

Prep time: 20 minutes; Cook Time: 3.5 hrs., Serves: 6

Ingredients:

1 lb. peaches, pitted and sliced	1 tsp vinegar
¼ cup of sugar	1/3 cup flour
4 tbsp lemon juice	3 tbsp butter
1 tsp vanilla extract	1 tsp ground ginger
5 oz oats	½ tsp pumpkin pie seasoning
1 tsp baking soda	

Instructions:

1. Grease the insert of Slow cooker with butter.
2. Place the peach slices in the insert and top them with sugar and lemon juice.
3. Toss oats with vanilla extract, vinegar, baking soda, flour, ground ginger, pumpkin pie seasoning in a bowl.
4. Spread this oats spice mixture on top of the peaches.
5. Put the cooker's lid on and set the cooking time to 1.5 hours on High settings.
6. Remove the lid and stir the cooked mixture well.
7. Cover again and continue cooking for another 2 hours on High settings.
8. Serve.

Nutrition Facts Per Serving:
Calories: 212, Total Fat: 7.6g, Fiber: 5g, Total Carbs: 41.26g, Protein: 5g

Mango Cream Dessert

Preparation time: 11 minutes; Cook Time: 1 hr., Serves: 4

Ingredients:

1 mango, sliced
14 oz. coconut cream

Instructions:

1. Add mango and cream to the insert of Slow Cooker.
2. Put the cooker's lid on and set the cooking time to 1 hour on High settings.
3. Serve.

Nutrition Facts Per Serving:

Calories: 150, Total Fat: 12g, Fiber: 2g, Total Carbs: 6g, Protein: 1g

Raspberry Nutmeg Cake

Prep time: 25 minutes; Cook Time: 7 hrs. Serves: 8

Ingredients:

4 eggs	1/3 cup sugar, brown
1 cup sugar	1 tbsp butter
1 cup flour	¼ tsp nutmeg
1 tsp vanilla extract	1 tbsp cornstarch
1 cup raspberry	

Instructions:

1. Separate the egg yolks from egg whites and keep them in a separate bowl.
2. Beat egg yolks with sugar, vanilla extract, cornstarch and nutmeg in a mixer.
3. Now beat the egg whites in an electric mixer until it forms peaks.
4. Add this egg white foam to the egg yolk mixture.
5. Mix gently, then add brown sugar and raspberry and blend again.
6. Grease the insert of your Slow Cooker with butter.
7. Spread the raspberry batter in the cooker.
8. Put the cooker's lid on and set the cooking time to 7 hours on Low settings.
9. Slice and serve when chilled.

Nutrition Facts Per Serving:

Calories: 234, Total Fat: 6.5g, Fiber: 6g, Total Carbs: 37.51g, Protein: 6g

Pears with Grape Sauce

Prep time: 12 minutes; Cook Time: 1 hr. 30 minutes Serves: 4

Ingredients:

4 pears	4 garlic cloves
Juice and zest of 1 lemon	½ vanilla bean
26 oz. grape juice	4 peppercorns
11 oz. currant jelly	2 rosemary springs

Instructions:

1. Add grape juice, jelly, lemon juice, lemon zest, peppercorns, pears, vanilla, and rosemary in the insert of Slow Cooker.
2. Put the cooker's lid on and set the cooking time to 1.5 hours on High settings.
3. Serve when chilled.

Nutrition Facts Per Serving:

Calories: 152, Total Fat: 3g, Fiber: 5g, Total Carbs: 12g, Protein: 4g

Poppy Cream Pie

Prep time: 16 minutes; Cook Time: 6 hrs. Serves: 6

Ingredients:

5 tbsp poppy seeds	1 cup of sugar
3 egg, whisked	1 tbsp orange juice
1 cup cream cheese	1 tsp butter
1 cup flour	3 tbsp heavy cream
1 tsp baking soda	1 pinch salt

Instructions:

1. Whisk cream cheese with eggs, baking soda, and sugar in a mixer.
2. Stir in butter, heavy cream, salt, and orange juice, then mix until smooth.
3. Fold in poppy seeds and mix gently.
4. Layer the insert of Slow Cooker with a parchment sheet.
5. Spread the poppy seeds batter in the insert of the cooker.
6. Put the cooker's lid on and set the cooking time to 6 hours on Low settings.
7. Slice and serve when chilled.

Nutrition Facts Per Serving:

Calories: 395, Total Fat: 22.9g, Fiber: 2g, Total Carbs: 37.01g, Protein: 11g

Raisin-Flax meal Bars

Prep time: 15 minutes; Cook Time: 3.5 hrs. Serves: 8

Ingredients:

¼ cup raisins	1 tsp ground cinnamon
1 cup oat flour	½ tsp baking soda
1 egg, whisked	1 tbsp lemon juice
4 oz banana, mashed	1 tbsp butter
5 oz milk	1 tbsp flour
1 tbsp flax meal	

Instructions:

1. Whisk egg with mashed banana, oat flour, milk, flax meal, raising in a bowl.
2. Stir in cinnamon, lemon juice, baking soda, and flour, then knead well.
3. Grease the insert of the Slow cooker with butter.
4. Make big balls out of this raisin dough and shape them into 3-4 inches bars.
5. Place these bars in the insert of the Slow Cooker.
6. Put the cooker's lid on and set the cooking time to 3 hours on Low settings.
7. Serve when chilled.

Nutrition Facts Per Serving:
Calories: 152, Total Fat: 3.7g, Fiber: 2g, Total Carbs: 26.74g, Protein: 4g

Rice Vanilla Pudding

Prep time: 12 minutes; Cook Time: 2 hrs. Serves: 6

Ingredients:

1 tbsp butter	3 oz. sugar
7 oz. long-grain rice	1 egg
4 oz. water	1 tbsp cream
16 oz. milk	1 tsp vanilla extract

Instructions:

1. Add rice, water, egg, cream, sugar, butter, milk, and vanilla to the insert of Slow Cooker.
2. Put the cooker's lid on and set the cooking time to 2 hours on High settings.
3. Serve when chilled.

Nutrition Facts Per Serving:
Calories: 152, Total Fat: 4g, Fiber: 4g, Total Carbs: 6g, Protein: 4g

Espresso Ricotta Cream

Prep time: 2 hrs. 10 minutes; Cook Time: 1 hr., Serves: 10

Ingredients:

½ cup hot coffee	1 tsp espresso powder
2 cups ricotta cheese	1 tsp sugar
2 and ½ tsp gelatin	1 cup whipping cream
1 tsp vanilla extract	

Instructions:

1. Whisk coffee with gelatin in a bowl and leave it for 10 minutes.
2. Add espresso, ricotta, vanilla extract, sugar, cream, and coffee mixture to the insert of Slow Cooker.
3. Put the cooker's lid on and set the cooking time to 1 hour on Low settings.
4. Refrigerate this cream mixture for 2 hours.
5. Serve.

Nutrition Facts Per Serving:
Calories: 200, Total Fat: 13g, Fiber: 0g, Total Carbs: 5g, Protein: 7g

Lemony Figs

Prep time: 15 minutes; Cook Time: 6 hrs. Serves: 8

Ingredients:

3 oz. lemon	2 lb. sugar
1 lb. figs	1 tsp cinnamon
5 oz. water	½ tsp ground ginger

Instructions:

1. Add figs flesh to a bowl and mash it using a fork.
2. Transfer the flesh to the insert of Slow Cooker.
3. Stir in cinnamon, sugar, water, ginger, and lemon slices.
4. Put the cooker's lid on and set the cooking time to 2 hours on Low settings.
5. Blend cooked figs mixture using a hand mixer.
6. Put the cooker's lid on and set the cooking time to 2 hours on Low settings.
7. Serve when chilled.

Nutrition Facts Per Serving:
Calories: 586, Total Fat: 0.6g, Fiber: 6g, Total Carbs: 150.43g, Protein: 2g

Creamy Lemon Mix

Prep time: 5 minutes; Cook Time: 1 hr., Serves: 4
Ingredients:

2 cups heavy cream   2 lemons, peeled
Sugar to the taste   and roughly chopped

Instructions:

1. Whisk the cream with lemons and sugar to the insert of Slow Cooker.
2. Put the cooker's lid on and set the cooking time to 1 hour on Low settings.
3. Serve when chilled.

Nutrition Facts Per Serving:
Calories: 177, Total Fat: 0g, Fiber: 0g, Total Carbs: 6g, Protein: 1g

Tapioca Pearls Pudding

Prep time: 16 minutes; Cook Time: 1 hr., Serves: 6
Ingredients:

1 and ¼ cups of   ½ cup of water
milk   ½ cup of sugar
1/3 cup tapioca   Zest of ½ lemon
pearls, rinsed

Instructions:

1. Whisk tapioca with milk, sugar, lemon zest, and water in the insert of Slow Cooker.
2. Put the cooker's lid on and set the cooking time to 1 hour on Low settings.
3. Serve.

Nutrition Facts Per Serving:
Calories: 200, Total Fat: 4g, Fiber: 2g, Total Carbs: 37g, Protein: 3g

Banana-Melon Pudding

Prep time: 15 minutes; Cook Time: 3.5 hrs. Serves: 7
Ingredients:

1 tbsp cornstarch   1 cup cream
1 tbsp flour   ½ cup white sugar
1 lb. melon, peeled   1 tsp vanilla extract
and cubed   3 tbsp semolina
5 bananas, peel   1 tbsp butter

Instructions:

1. Add bananas, and melon to a blender jug and blend well.
2. Transfer this melon-banana puree to the insert of Slow Cooker.
3. Stir in flour, butter, semolina, sugar, vanilla extract, and cream.
4. Put the cooker's lid on and set the cooking time to 3.5 hours on Low settings.
5. Serve.

Nutrition Facts Per Serving:
Calories: 236, Total Fat: 11.5g, Fiber: 3g, Total Carbs: 32.82g, Protein: 4g

Cinnamon Hot Chocolate

Prep time: 9 minutes; Cook Time: 2 hrs. Serves: 3
Ingredients:

2 cups of milk   chips
6 oz. condensed   1 cup heavy cream,
milk   whipped
½ cup of chocolate   1 tsp cinnamon

Instructions:

1. Add milk, condensed milk, cinnamon, heavy cream, chocolate chips to the insert of Slow Cooker.
2. Put the cooker's lid on and set the cooking time to 2.5 hours on Low settings.
3. Serve.

Nutrition Facts Per Serving:
Calories: 440, Total Fat: 29.7g, Fiber: 1g, Total Carbs: 34.97g, Protein: 10g

Vanilla Crème Cups

Prep time: 27 minutes; Cook Time: 3 hrs. Serves: 4
Ingredients:

1 tbsp vanilla extract   whipped
1 cup of sugar   7 egg yolks, whisked
½ cup heavy cream,

Instructions:

1. Mix egg yolks with sugar, vanilla extract, and cream in a mixer.
2. Pour this creamy mixture into 4 ramekins.
3. Pour 1 cup water into the insert of Slow cooker.
4. Place the ramekins the cooker.
5. Put the cooker's lid on and set the cooking time to 3 hours on Low settings.
6. Serve.

Nutrition Facts Per Serving:
Calories: 254, Total Fat: 13.5g, Fiber: 0g, Total Carbs: 26.84g, Protein: 5g

Appendix 1: Measurement Conversion Chart

VOLUME EQUIVALENTS(DRY)

US STANDARD	METRIC (APPROXIMATE)
1/8 teaspoon	0.5 mL
1/4 teaspoon	1 mL
1/2 teaspoon	2 mL
3/4 teaspoon	4 mL
1 teaspoon	5 mL
1 tablespoon	15 mL
1/4 cup	59 mL
1/2 cup	118 mL
3/4 cup	177 mL
1 cup	235 mL
2 cups	475 mL
3 cups	700 mL
4 cups	1 L

VOLUME EQUIVALENTS(LIQUID)

US STANDARD	US STANDARD (OUNCES)	METRIC (APPROXIMATE)
2 tablespoons	1 fl.oz.	30 mL
1/4 cup	2 fl.oz.	60 mL
1/2 cup	4 fl.oz.	120 mL
1 cup	8 fl.oz.	240 mL
1 1/2 cup	12 fl.oz.	355 mL
2 cups or 1 pint	16 fl.oz.	475 mL
4 cups or 1 quart	32 fl.oz.	1 L
1 gallon	128 fl.oz.	4 L

TEMPERATURES EQUIVALENTS

FAHRENHEIT(F)	CELSIUS(C) (APPROXIMATE)
225 °F	107 °C
250 °F	120 °C
275 °F	135 °C
300 °F	150 °C
325 °F	160 °C
350 °F	180 °C
375 °F	190 °C
400 °F	205 °C
425 °F	220 °C
450 °F	235 °C
475 °F	245 °C
500 °F	260 °C

WEIGHT EQUIVALENTS

US STANDARD	METRIC (APPROXIMATE)
1 ounce	28 g
2 ounces	57 g
5 ounces	142 g
10 ounces	284 g
15 ounces	425 g
16 ounces (1 pound)	455 g
1.5 pounds	680 g
2 pounds	907 g

Appendix 2: Recipes Index

A

Adobo Chicken Thighs   33
African Chicken Meal   33
Allspice Beans Stew   26
Apple Chicken Bombs   34
Apple Chutney   115
Apple Cinnamon Granola   7
Apple Frittata   9
Apple Sausage Snack   101
Apple Wedges with Peanuts   104
Apricot Rice Pudding   120
Apricots Bread Pudding   8
Artichoke Pepper Frittata   7
Asian Sesame Asparagus   86
Avocado Peppermint Pudding   117

B

Bacon Cider Muffins   20
Bacon Fingerling Potatoes   113
Baked Potato   86
Balsamic-Glazed Beets   87
Balsamic-Glazed Salmon   72
Banana Almond Foster   117
Banana-Melon Pudding   127
Basic Pepper Salsa   114
Bean Pesto Dip   102
Bean Salsa Salad   103
Beans and Red Peppers   92
Beans Risotto   96
Beef Onions Mix   54
Beef Roast with Cauliflower   55
Beef Tomato Meatballs   102
Beets Salad   87
Berry Wild Rice   101
Berry-Berry Jam   11
Berry-Berry Mascarpone Cream   124
Biscuit Roll Bread   19
Biscuit Roll Bread   19
Black Eyes Peas Dip   111
Blue Cheese Parsley Dip   109
Blueberry Spinach Salad   86
Boiled Bacon Eggs   8
Bourbon Honey Chicken   34
Brisket Turnips Medley   55
Broccoli Egg Pie   29
Broccoli Filling   87
Broccoli Omelette   18
Bulgur Mushroom Chili   29
Butter Dipped Crab Legs   68
Butter Glazed Yams   91

Butter Green Beans   92
Butter Stuffed Chicken Balls   103
Butternut Squash Pudding   118
Buttery Artichokes   88
ButteryChicken Wings   34

C

Caesar Chicken Wraps   52
Candied Sweet Lemon   119
Caramel Milk Dip   103
Cardamom Lemon Pie   123
Carp Millet Soup   66
Carrot Beet Salad   88
Carrot Broccoli Fritters   101
Carrot Shallots Medley   91
Cashew Hummus Dip   103
Cashew Thai Chicken   50
Cauliflower Beef Soup   54
Cauliflower Carrot Gratin   89
Cheese Onion Dip   109
Cheese Stuffed Meat Balls   110
Cheeseburger Cream Dip   102
Cheesecake with Lime Filling   124
Cheesy Cauliflower Hash   11
Cheesy Chicken Breasts   48
Cheesy Chili Pepper Dip   104
Cheesy Egg Bake   15
Cheesy Mushroom Dip   110
Cheesy Pork Rolls   112
Cheesy Pork Wraps   57
Cheesy Potato Dip   112
Cheesy Rice   90
Chicken Broccoli Casserole   33
Chicken Burrito Bowl   8
Chicken Cabbage Medley   16
Chicken Cacciatore   46
Chicken Chickpeas   35
Chicken Curry   39
Chicken Dumplings Medley   40
Chicken Liver Stew   35
Chicken Mole   41
Chicken Mushrooms Stroganoff   39
Chicken Pepper Chili   47
Chicken Potato Casserole   37
Chicken Potato Sandwich   51
Chicken Pumpkin Stew   35
Chicken Ricotta Meatloaf   36
Chicken Sausage Stew   51
Chicken Stuffed Squid   83
Chicken Stuffed with Beans   47

Chicken Taco Nachos   114
Chicken Taco Soup   49
Chicken Tomato Salad   37
Chicken Vegetable Pot Pie   38
Chicken with Green Onion Sauce   33
Chicken with Lentils   36
Chicken with Mushroom Sauce   35
Chicken with Sweet Potato   100
Chicken with Tomatillos   37
Chicken- Pork Meatballs   9
Chickpea Hummus   111
Chili Tamarind Mackerel   67
Chinese Miso Mackerel   67
Chinese Mushroom Pork   55
Chipotle Salmon Fillets   78
Choco Liquor Crème   118
Chocolate Vanilla Toast   10
Chocolaty Chicken Mash   38
Chorizo Cashew Salad   25
Cider Dipped Clams   68
Cider Dipped Farro   96
Cider Dipped Pork Roast   64
Cinnamon Apple Butter   121
Cinnamon Apple Oatmeal   7
Cinnamon Applesauce   90
Cinnamon Banana Sandwiches   23
Cinnamon Cream Dessert   121
Cinnamon Hot Chocolate   127
Cinnamon Pear Toasts   122
Cinnamon Pumpkin Oatmeal   18
Citron Vanilla Bars   119
Citrus Glazed Chicken   38
Citrus Glazed Flounder   75
Clams- Mussels Boil   76
Coca Cola Dipped Chicken   41
Cocoa Peanut Candies   120
Cocoa Vanilla Cake   119
Coconut Meatballs Gravy   66
Coconut Vanilla Pudding   120
Cod Bacon Chowder   78
Cod with Asparagus   80
Cod with Shrimp Sauce   67
Coffee Cinnamon Roll   122
Cola Marinated Chicken   39
Continental Beef Chicken   45
Cordon Bleu Dip   104
Corn Cucumber Salad   97
Cornbread Cream Pudding   88
Cornmeal Apricot Pudding   123
Couscous Halloumi Salad   23
Crab with Oyster Sauce   85
Cranberry Almond Quinoa   10
Cream Cheese Macaroni   93
Cream White Fish   78

Creamy Asparagus Chicken   14
Creamy Bacon Chicken   41
Creamy Bacon Millet   11
Creamy Butter Parsnips   90
Creamy Caramel Dessert   118
Creamy Chicken   34
Creamy Corn Chili   23
Creamy Dark Chocolate Dessert   120
Creamy Garlic Potatoes   24
Creamy Lemon Mix   127
Creamy Mushroom Bites   114
Creamy Red Cabbage   95
Crispy Mackerel   76
Crumbly Chickpeas Snack   115
Cuban Chicken   41
Curried Chicken Strips   53

D

Dill Beef Roast   55
Dill Butter Muffins   105
Dill Crab Cutlets   70
Dill Mixed Fennel   98
Dill Shrimp Medley   67
Duck Chili   43
Duck with Potatoes   42

E

Egg Bacon Muffins   105
Eggplant Capers Salsa   105
Eggplant Mini Wraps   26
Eggplant Pate   15
Eggplant Salad   100
Eggplant Zucchini Dip   105
Eggplants with Mayo Sauce   97
Enchilada Pork Luncheon   57
Espresso Ricotta Cream   126

F

Fajita Chicken Dip   106
Farro Rice Pilaf   95
Fava Bean Onion Dip   106
Fennel Chicken   43
Fennel Lentils   25
Fish Potato Cakes   81
Flounder Cheese Casserole   72
French Vegetable Stew   24

G

Garlic Lamb Chilli   58
Garlic Mushrooms   93
Garlic Parmesan Dip   107
Garlicky Bacon Slices   107
Garlicky Black Beans   87
Ginger Chili Peppers   108
Ginger Turkey   42
Goose with Mushroom Cream   42

Greek Mushrooms Casserole   16
Greek Olive Lamb   56
Green Beans with Mushrooms   94
Green Muffins   18
Green Peas Risotto   29
Green Tea Avocado Pudding   119

H

Halibut with Peach Sauce   72
Ham Stuffed Peppers   13
Ham Stuffed Pockets   16
Harissa Dipped Cod   73
Hash Browns Casserole   19
Hasselback Potatoes   97
Hawaiian Pineapple Chicken   44
Herbed Balsamic Beets   92
Herbed Chicken Salsa   53
Herbed Cinnamon Beef   60
Herbed Eggplant Cubes   89
Herbed Lamb Fillet   61
Herbed Lamb Shanks   59
Herbed Octopus Mix   73
Herbed Pecans Snack   112
Herbed Pork Meatballs   21
Herbed Shrimps   82
Honey Carrot Gravy   24
Honey Glazed Vegetables   91
Horseradish Mixed Chicken   44
Hot Chicken Wings   49

I

Indian Fish Curry   69
Indian Harissa Pork   58
Italian Parsley Clams   69
Italian Trout Croquettes   83

J

Jalapeno Chorizo Poppers   109
Jalapeno Meal   93
Jalapeno Onion Dip   111
Jalapeno Salsa Snack   110
Jamaican Pork Shoulder   54
Japanese Cod Fillet   73
Japanese Pea Shrimp   66

L

Lamb Bacon Stew   75
Lamb Carrot Medley   61
Lamb Cashews Tagine   59
Lamb Cheese Casserole   59
Lamb Leg Mushrooms Satay   59
Lamb Leg with Sweet Potatoes   58
Lamb Potato Stew   61
Lamb Potato Stew   85
Lamb Semolina Meatballs   60
Lamb Shoulder with Artichokes   60

Lamb Vegetable Curry   81
Latin Chicken   45
Latte Vanilla Cake   121
Lemon Cream Dessert   123
Lemon Sauce Dipped Chicken   44
Lemon Spinach Orzo   28
Lemony Figs   126
Lemony Honey Beets   92
Lemony Orange Marmalade   122
Lemony Pumpkin Wedges   99
Lentil Rice Salad   25
Lime Dipped Chicken Drumsticks   40
Lobster Cheese Soup   74

M

Mac Cream Cups   89
Mackerel Stuffed Tacos   71
Mango Cream Dessert   125
Maple Chocolate Fondue   124
Maple Ginger Chicken   50
Maple Glazed Turkey Strips   108
Maple Mustard Salmon   70
Maple Rosemary Lamb   65
Marjoram Carrot Soup   23
Marsala Cheese Mushrooms   109
Mayo Sausage Rolls   20
Mediterranean Veggies   27
Mexican Avocado Rice   96
Mexican Black Beans Salad   52
Mexican Egg Bake   17
Mexican Lamb Fillet   63
Millet with Dill   99
Minestrone Zucchini Soup   27
Mix Vegetable Casserole   22
Mixed Nuts   115
Mixed Vegetable Spread   116
Mixed-Berry Marmalade   117
Morning Banana Bread   10
Moroccan Apricot Lamb   64
Moscow Bacon Chicken   45
Mozzarella Basil Tomatoes   110
Muffin Corn Pudding   90
Mushroom Chicken Casserole   16
Mushroom Pork Chop Stew   57
Mushrooms Snapper   82
Mushrooms Stuffed with Chicken   46
Mussels and Sausage Satay   71
Mussels Tomato Soup   76

N

Nut Berry Salad   93
Nutmeg Banana Oatmeal   9
Nutmeg Squash Oatmeal   13
Nutty Caramel Apples   119
Nutty Sweet Potatoes   21

O

Oats Craisins Granola   13
Octopus with Mixed Vegetable   75
Onion Chives Muffins   24
Orange Duck Fillets   46
Orange Marmalade Salmon   77
Orange Squash   88
Oregano Cheese Pie   27

P

Parmesan Chicken Fillet   47
Parmesan Rosemary Potato   56
Peachy Cinnamon Butter   12
Peanut Bombs   113
Peanut Butter Chicken   111
Pear Apple Jam   122
Pears with Grape Sauce   125
Peppercorn Chicken Thighs   49
Pepperoni Chicken   47
Pesto Pitta Pockets   113
Pink Salt Rice   100
Pinto Beans with Rice   22
Pomegranate Turkey   44
Poppy Cream Pie   125
Pork Chops Pineapple Satay   61
Pork Sirloin Salsa   60
Pork Stuffed Tamales   106
Pork Sweet Potato Stew   58
Pork Tostadas   107
Pork with Apples   62
Potato Beef Gratin   56
Potato Cups   116
Potato Onion Salsa   112
Potato Parmesan Pie   26
Poultry Stew   49
Puerto Rican Chicken   46
Pulled Maple Chicken   52
Pumpkin Bean Chili   28
Pumpkin Nutmeg Rice   91

Q

Quinoa Avocado Salad   27
Quinoa Avocado Salad   28
Quinoa Bars   17
Quinoa Black Bean Chili   30
Quinoa Cauliflower Medley   20
Quinoa Oats Bake   11

R

Rainbow Carrots   89
Raisin-Flax meal Bars   126
Ramen Noodles   98
Raspberry Nutmeg Cake   125
Raspberry Vanilla Oatmeal   12
Red Sauce Chicken Soup   48

Refried Black Beans   95
Rice Cauliflower Casserole   32
Rice Stuffed Apple Cups   30
Rice Stuffed Eggplants   30
Rice Stuffed Squid   71
Rice Stuffed Trout   82
Rice Vanilla Pudding   126
Rice with Artichokes   95
Roast with Pepperoncini   63
Romano Chicken Thighs   40

S

Saffron Chicken Thighs   48
Salmon Chickpea Fingers   79
Salmon Tofu Soup   79
Salmon with Green Sauce   80
Salmon with Lemon Relish   78
Salmon with Saffron Rice   77
Salsa Bean Pie   56
Sauce Goose   40
Saucy Beef Cheeks   54
Saucy Beef Meatloaf   12
Saucy Chicken   36
Saucy Chicken Drumsticks   42
Saucy Chicken Thighs   51
Saucy French Lamb   57
Saucy Macaroni   94
Saucy Sriracha Red Beans   21
Sausage Cream Dip   113
Sausage with Onion Jam   65
Scalloped Cheese Potatoes   97
Scrambled Spinach Eggs   17
Seabass Mushrooms Ragout   74
Seafood Bean Chili   79
Seafood Medley   84
Seasoned Beef Stew   62
Semolina Fish Balls   68
Sesame Chicken Wings   45
Short Ribs with Tapioca Sauce   64
Shri Lanka Fish Cutlet   80
Shrimp Chicken Jambalaya   70
Shrimp Clam Stew   84
Shrimp Mushroom Curry   76
Shrimp Potato Boil   80
Slow-Cooked Lemon Peel   107
Slow-Cooked White Onions   86
Smoke Infused Lamb   64
Soy Dipped Pork Ribs   65
Spaghetti Cheese Casserole   31
Spaghetti Chicken Salad   53
Spiced Baby Carrots   7
Spiced Cod with Peas   68
Spiced Peach Crisp   124
Spicy Harissa Perch   81

Spicy Mussels   115
Spinach and Artichoke Chicken   39
Spinach Cream Dip   116
Spinach Mussels Salad   108
Spinach Tomato Frittata   14
Spongy Banana Bread   117
Squash and Peppers Mix   92
Strawberry Yogurt Oatmeal   9
Stuffed Baguette   10
Summer Squash Medley   99
Sweet Mongolian Beef   65
Sweet Orange Fish   77
Sweet Pepper Boats   13
Sweet Potato Jalapeno Stew   50
Sweet Potato Tarragon Soup   30
Sweet Red Onions   99
Swiss Ham Quiche   15

T

Tamale Side Dish   98
Tangerine Cream Pie   121
Tangy Red Potatoes   98
Tapioca Pearls Pudding   127
Thai Peanut Chicken   48
Thai Salmon Cakes   74
Thai Spiced Pork   63
Thyme Chicken   52
Thyme Mixed Beets   99
Thyme Pepper Shrimp   102
Tomatillo Lamb   63
Tomato Chicken   50
Tomato Mussels Salad   108
Tomato Okra Mix   100
Tri-Bean Chili   22
Tropical Cherry Granola   18
Trout Capers Piccata   85
Tuna Mushroom Noodles   69
Tuna Noodles Casserole   69
Tuna with Chimichurri Sauce   83
Tuna with Potatoes   84
Turkey Cranberry Stew   43
Turkey Pepper Chili   51
Turmeric Buckwheat   100
Turmeric Coconut Squid   71
Turmeric Potato Strips   94

V

Vanilla Blueberry Cream   120
Vanilla Cheesecake   118
Vanilla Crème Cups   127
Vanilla Maple Oats   17
Vanilla Yogurt   14
Vegetable Almond Pilaf   53
Vegetable Bean Stew   32
Veggies Rice Pilaf   96
Vinaigrette Dipped Salmon   77

W

Warming Butternut Squash Soup   25
White Beans Luncheon   28
White Fish with Olives Sauce   70
Wild Rice Peppers   31
Wine Dipped Lamb Leg   62
Wine Dipped Pears   123

Z

Zesty Pesto Pork   62
Zesty Pumpkin Cubes   14
Zucchini Carrot Oatmeal   12
Zucchini Crackers Casserole   101
Zucchini Onion Pate   94
Zucchini Spinach Lasagne   31
Zucchini Sticks   104

Made in the USA
Coppell, TX
25 November 2020